The point o

THE PROBLEM OF TOLERANCE
AND SOCIAL EXISTENCE
IN THE WRITINGS OF
FÉLICITÉ LAMENNAIS
1809-1831

STUDIES IN THE HISTORY OF CHRISTIAN THOUGHT

EDITED BY

HEIKO A. OBERMAN, Tübingen

IN COOPERATION WITH

HENRY CHADWICK, Oxford
EDWARD A. DOWEY, Princeton, N.J.
JAROSLAV PELIKAN, New Haven, Conn.
BRIAN TIERNEY, Ithaca, N.Y.

VOLUME VII

JOHN J. OLDFIELD

THE PROBLEM OF TOLERANCE AND SOCIAL EXISTENCE IN THE WRITINGS OF FÉLICITÉ LAMENNAIS

1809-1831

LEIDEN
E. J. BRILL
1973

THE PROBLEM OF
TOLERANCE AND SOCIAL EXISTENCE
IN THE
WRITINGS OF FÉLICITÉ LAMENNAIS
1809-1831

BY

JOHN J. OLDFIELD

LEIDEN
E. J. BRILL
1973

ISBN 90 04 03650 4

TABLE OF CONTENTS

ACKNOWLEDGEMENTS

Bringing to a conclusion, with the presentation of this dissertation, four years of study at the University of Louvain, I should like to acknowledge my profound indebtedness to the professors of the Institut Supérieur de Philosophie for having, so generously and so professionally, made possible my introduction to the larger horizons of the philosophical quest.

The particular achievement of this study would have been impossible without the professional assistance and steady guidance of Professor Jacques Étienne. His availability, his patience and the lucidity of his insights and critiques have more than once saved this project from stagnation. The gratitude expressed in these phrases is but small recompense for the support and interest which he has shown and for the rewarding experience which has been mine in having had the opportunity to work in close cooperation with a man who combines so well the competence of scholarship with the qualities of gentlemanliness. In like fashion, I should like to acknowledge the advice given to me in the early stages of research by Canons A. Dondeyne and R. Aubert of the University of Louvain and by Professor Henri Gouhier of the Sorbonne. More recently, M. Louis Le Guillou of the Collège Littéraire Universitaire de Brest has most kindly shared with me his own vast erudition in mennaisian studies for which I am most grateful.

The preparation of this paper has been immensely aided by the generosity of the Frères de l'Instruction Chrétienne, spiritual sons of Ven. Jean-Marie de La Mennais, whose unforgettable hospitality during the past summer made possible a major part of the research undertaken at the mennaisian Archives maintained at Highlands, Jersey, C.I. No words of gratitude would be sufficient to acknowledge the devoted and able assistance unstintingly given by Bro. Joseph F. Libert, F.I.C., the archivist. In a similar manner, I am grateful to Bro. André Parenteau, F.I.C., whose readiness to assist in bibliographical questions has proved so helpful.

To my own superiors, former Provincial, Very Rev. Theophane Mayora, O.A.R., and the present Provincial, Very Rev. Joseph M. Santiago, O.A.R., I express my gratitude for having initiated and supported my philosophical studies at Louvain. Nor could I possibly overlook the sympathy and encouragement which I have received from my family during these many years of absence and separation.

Finally, I wish to thank my friends in Belgium who have introduced me to their homes and their culture and my fellow-priests at Louvain who have been such good companions during the past four years. I especially acknowledge the help offered by Fathers Raymond Devettere, James Hession, Joseph Kuntz, and Joseph Zenk in the preparation of the text for presentation.

INTRODUCTION

Three years ago, at the suggestion of Professor Jacques Étienne of Institut Supérieur de Philosophie, a probing mission into the problem of tolerance was undertaken which finally developed into the study which constitutes this dissertation. The problem of tolerance, philosophically and politically considered, evokes the more fundamental question of social coexistence which in turn leads to a basically metaphysical reflection upon the nature and sources of society and social being. The crucial and very contemporary character of the whole question of unity and plurality within our everyday world makes it quite evident that a constant study of the problem, its historical development, and ultimate implications, is readily justifiable and worthwhile.

In order to take a certain distance from the contemporary and to lend a character of specificity to the research, it was decided to focus upon a particular representative in the history of thought who had attempted to wrestle with the perennial problem of the one and the many as viewed within the framework of the political life of man. Our choice of Félicité Lamennais, whose pioneer contributions to the reconciliation of his co-religionists with the phenomena of secularization and modern liberties have become legendary, has proved to be an exhilarating experience. In one fashion or another, the principal philosophical questions which underlie the political phenomenon and lead, by the answers given to them, to political theory, were asked by Félicité Lamennais. Since Lamennais will be introduced more fully in Chapter One of the dissertation, our remarks in the Introduction will be limited to an explanation of the limitations imposed upon the research and to an exposition of the plan which is to be followed in the study. It might also be noted that, since a justification for our treatment of Lamennais as a philosopher is attempted in considerable detail in the main text, it need not be discussed in these introductory pages.

All imposed temporal limitations in the study of a man's thought contain something of the arbitrary. The decision to restrict our research to the writings of Félicité Lamennais which were published between the years 1809 and 1831 is, however, something more than a simple concession to the exigencies of time and the limited

1

capacities of the writer undertaking the study. This period is a unity within the whole of Lamennais's evolution as a philosopher and political thinker. These were the years in which his original authoritarian ultramontanism took root and which, quite dramatically, finally burgeoned into the philosophy of Catholic liberalism announced in "L'Avenir". Lamennais spent a lifetime of most dedicated preoccupation with the whole problem of social order and liberty, the fundamental problematic wrapped up in the notion of tolerance. But November 15, 1831, the date of the suspension of the publication of "L'Avenir", marks the close of an identifiable chapter of his life and of his thought. The alteration of his relations with the institutional Church subsequent to the tragic events of 1832-33 brought with it a re-orientation of his thought, a certain change of optic and of scope, which begins a new chapter, that of the humanitarianism of his later years. Although there is a continuity in his thought which unites both epochs of his adult life, he addresses himself to different audiences and from distinct vantage points in each period and, consequently, has left quite distinguishable legacies to history from his activities before 1831 and from those which followed this date.

Viewed from the context of the problem itself, tolerance, his treatment of this question while an active participant in the Catholic communion and a staunch defender of the Roman Church may be seen as quite other than that which he gave to the problem when no longer held by this bond. It has been considered more reasonable, by placing the thought of the early Lamennais within the framework of the history of ideas, to study the first phase since, indeed, it has been the Lamennais of "L'Avenir" who has most powerfully influenced future generations of Catholic political writers on the questions of tolerance, religious liberty, and Church-State relations.

Since both the problem and the philosopher treated in this dissertation are inextricably bound up with political, religious and cultural history, it has been considered necessary, as a means of clarifying the philosophical problem and of situating the thought of Lamennais in the proper context, to review, albeit in a summary fashion, both the history and the origin of the problem of tolerance and the history of the immediate milieu and tradition from which our philosopher drew his inspirations. The importance of seeing Lamennais against the background of the Restoration and

Romanticism will, it is hoped, become quite apparent in the unfolding of the thesis.

The Table of Contents will indicate in considerable detail the major ideational threads which are woven into the general theme of this dissertation. In our exposition, in order to show the genesis of his thought, we have chosen a basically historical approach moving, in chronological fashion, through his principal publications between 1809 and 1831. By method of textual analysis, we propose to study the major themes from these writings which form the sub-structure of the political theory of "L'Avenir" or of Catholic liberalism. We will take up such themes as tolerance, religion, society, sovereignty, law, authority, liberty and history-interrelated elements of political reality—as they appear in the course of the years which mark the transition of his thought from a form of authoritarianism to Catholic liberalism. In this study, an attempt has been made not to neglect any facet which might prove useful to a clearer understanding of Lamennais's thought, particularly, his correspondence and less well-known writings and articles.

The point of inquiry in this thesis turns about the philosopher's attempted solution of the perennial ethical problem of the rapport between liberty and authority. It is an ethical problem since it deals with man's conduct as man and his responsibility for this conduct. It was a key concern for Lamennais, who, being first preoccupied with the restoration of authority and order in the post-revolutionary French society, attempted to reconstruct the principle of authority on a broad philosophical base. Using this same philosophical groundwork, he later emerged as a champion of freedom and political liberty. How was this possible? What are the elements in his early philosophy of authority and extrinsic certitude which would allow for such an evolution? What finally is the value of Lamennais's contribution to our understanding of tolerance? We shall seek to discover the answer to some of these questions in the pages which follow.

If little is added to mennaisian studies as a consequence of this undertaking, other than a new view offered by a student from another culture and a different period of history, it reflects more the limitations of the student than the inadequacies of the brilliant innovator, Lamennais. The benefits, however, which have accrued to the writer of this thesis through a study of the whole problem of tolerance and, particularly, through a deepening acquaintance with the ardent defender of "Dieu et la liberté", have been countless.

3

CHAPTER ONE

A BIOGRAPHICAL INTRODUCTION

I. Life and Works of Félicité Lamennais

Scarcely a year passes without some addition to the already vast bibliography concerning the life, thought or influence of the priest—son of an otherwise forgotten Breton merchant whose "career", in the oft-quoted word of Harold J. Laski, "is little less than the *miroir of his age*".[1] The reasons for this enduring interest in Félicité Lamennais reflect the historical and ideological impact of a highly controversial figure whose life spanned an epoch of profound social and cultural restlessness and change. This interest is more than academic; as a most recent commentator indicates, it is "the awareness ... that Lamennais in some way epitomized the century; that in his life was the century's struggle between skepticism and faith ..."[2]

Hugues-Félicité Robert de La Mennais, about whom the above claim to historical immortality is made, was born on June 10th, 1782, at St. Malo, France,[3] to Pierre-Louis de La Mennais and Gratienne Lorin.[4] The historical and social background of Félicité's ancestors has been the subject of special study by the eminent mennaisian scholar, Christian Maréchal, in his *La famille de La Mennais sous l'Ancien Régime et la Révolution d'après les documents nouveaux et inédits* (1915). The early years of the future journalist-prophet were studied by the same author in his *La jeunesse de La Mennais: Contribution à l'étude des origines du Romantisme religieux en France aux XIXe siècle* (1915). Maréchal's painstaking and expert research filled in many of the innumerable gaps in basic historical information needed

---

[1] H. J. Laski, *Authority in the Modern State*, New Haven, 1919, p. 189.

[2] W. G. Roe, *Lamennais and England: The Reception of Lamennais's Religious Ideas in the Nineteenth Century*, Oxford, 1966, p. 194.

[3] Chr. Maréchal, *La jeunesse de La Mennais: Contribution à l'étude des origines du Romantisme religieux en France au XIXe siècle*, Paris, 1913, p. 9 (In subsequent citations, this work will be referred to simply as *La jeunesse...*).

[4] Chr. Maréchal, *La famille de La Mennais sous l'Ancien Régime et la Révolution d'après des documents nouveaux et inédits*, Paris, 1913, pp. 15-16 (In subsequent citations, this work will be referred to simply as *La famille...*).

to complete Lamennais's biography, especially concerning the early years.

Biographical research concerning Lamennais lagged for some years following his death. It was not until almost the turn of the century that a more scientific, and less polemical, approach began to dominate mennaisian studies.[5] Sainte-Beuve's character sketch in *Portraits contemporains* remained the standard source during these interim years.[6] A. Ricard's four volume attempt entitled *L'école mennaisien* (1881) lacked scientific rigor while E. Spuller's *Lamennais: étude d'histoire politique et religieuse* (1892), although interesting, remained too much on the level of controversy to be definitive. Lamennais's biography, as it has become evident, was to be the work of many. Several new contributions; Roussel, *Lamennais d'après des documents inédits* (1892, 2 vols.) and Mercier, *Lamennais d'après sa correspondance et les travaux récents* (1895), unearthed important mennaisian sources and paved the way for more serious biographical and doctrinal studies such as those of Abbé Charles Boutard, *Lamennais, sa vie et ses doctrines* (1905-13, 3 vols.) and Abbé F. Duine, *La Mennais, sa vie, ses idées, ses ouvrages d'après les sources imprimées et les documents inédits* (1922). To these must be added, of course, the already mentioned works of C. Maréchal and the countless smaller publications of correspondence, documents and particularized studies. On the level of biography, the findings of these earlier biographers and students of Lamennais have been correlated and corrected in the excellent English biography by Alec R. Vidler, *Prophecy and Papacy: a Study of Lamennais, the Church, and the Revolution* (1954).

Before briefly sketching the outline of Lamennais's life and career, insofar as it is of interest in a philosophical study, it would be helpful to clarify the variations of the family name which at times confuse readers of books concerning the subject of this thesis. The ancestral name of Félicité's forebearers was "Robert" to which had been added the title "de La Mennais".[7] The custom of thus emulating the titled nobility was fairly commonplace among the commercial upper bourgeois during the epoch of this

---

[5] A. Feugère, *Lamennais avant l'Essai sur l'indifférence: D'après des documents inédits (1782-1817)*, Paris, 1906, p. 11-12.

[6] Ibid.

[7] A. R. Vidler, *Prophecy and Papacy: A Study of Lamennais The Church and The Revolution*, The Birbeck Lectures 1952-1953, London, 1954, p. 17.

group's rising influence.[8] A patent of nobility was likely conferred on Pierre-Louis Robert de La Mennais in 1788, reportedly the last signed by Louis XVI.[9] During the earlier period of Félicité's public career, he signed his articles, letters and books under the rubric, "F. de La Mennais"; when he aligned himself with the democratic movement, he removed the aristocratic appendages and became known as "F. Lamennais".[10] In this study, he will be referred to simply as Lamennais.

In order to situate Lamennais historically, before tracing the ideological sources of his intellectual evolution, it would be useful to present a thumb-nail, chronological portrait of his life. The death of his mother in 1787[11] left Félicité a semi-orphan in the busy household of an industrious merchant and an active man of civic affairs.[12] The emotional upset caused by the mother's death and the uncertainty created by the Revolution and the ensuing Reign of Terror were, undoubtedly, unsettling factors in the early youth of Féli. An important decision was reached when the lad was near eleven years of age: his education was to be undertaken by his cultured and philosophically inclined uncle, Robert des Saudrais, brother of the elder de La Mennais.[13] The decisiveness of this step in the intellectual and spiritual formation of the future renovator of French Catholicism will be discussed more fully in the third section of this initial chapter; it will be sufficient to simply point out, in this chronological account, the importance of the years of formation under the tutelage of des Saudrais.[14]

In 1799, Félicité and his older brother, Jean-Marie, inherited, from their maternal grandfather, the country house and properties near Dinan known as La Chênaie,[15] a name which will later bear the same relationship to the French Catholic renewal as Brooks Farm was to bear to the American intellectual awakening. The two brothers retired with great frequency to this country hermitage well-separated from the road and covered by the near-by forests. Félicité, whose brief apprenticeship with the family shipping firm failed to stimulate any

---

[8] Ch. Boutard, *La renaissance de l'ultramontanisme 1782-1828* Vol. I of *Lamennais, sa vie et ses doctrines* (3 Vols.) Paris, 1905-1913, p. 5.

[9] Ibid.

[10] A. R. Vidler, *Prophecy and Papacy*, London, 1954, p. 18.

[11] Ibid., p. 17.

[12] Ibid., p. 19.

[13] Chr. Maréchal, *La jeunesse* . . . , p. 13.

[14] Ibid., p. 15.

[15] A. R. Vidler, *Prophecy and Papacy*, London, 1954, p. 31.

commercial interests, spent the greater part of his time between 1802 and 1814 in a life of withdrawal and study broken only by a brief teaching experience at a Church school in St. Malo and a long sojourn in Paris with his brother, Jean-Marie, in 1806.[16] Jean-Marie, whose influence on his younger brother becomes somewhat predominant in this period, was in the process of preparing for and beginning a priestly career which would bring him, after much personal suffering, the honors of the Church.[17]

Maréchal holds that the years between 1802-1804 were the years of Lamennais's spiritual conversion.[18] Information concerning this critical phase of his young life in which he seems to have passed from a situation of late adolescent disbelief to one of religious affirmation is meager. Lamennais himself speaks of having been "brought to Christianity through reading the philosophers".[19] The nature of these readings will be discussed in a following section of this chapter.

During this whole period, which, on the surface, seems somewhat idyllic, Félicité, in the company of his uncle and his brother, was engaged in a quest for religious certitude and meaningfulness while retired from a world in the process of rapid secularization. The drama of the epoch in which the Revolution, the Terror, the Directory and the Napoleonic Empire swiftly, and seemingly, chaotically, robbed the stage from the enlightened bourgeois who had opened the first act, had left the early actors fumbling in confusion and disillusionment. Both the senior de La Mennais and des Saudrais seem to have belonged to this category. They had supported the early revolutionary movement and had even served in official capacities.[20] They were men of their times and of their social class who had favored economic liberalism and a representation of commercial interests in government.

> M. de La Mennais and his brother were genuine liberals and, when a tyranny began to he installed under the cloak of revolutionary liberty, their enthusiasm began to cool. They had welcomed and supported the revolution because it had abolished archaic privileges, had introduced a more rational system of government, and had ushered in, as they

---

[16] A. R. Vidler, *Prophecy and Papacy*, London, 1954, p. 41.

[17] The standard biography on the Venerable Jean-Marie is *Jean-Marie de La Mennais*, A. Laveille, Paris, 1903, (2 Vols.).

[18] Chr. Maréchal, *La jeunesse* ..., Chap. III, pp. 65-87.

[19] Letter from Lamennais to Saint-Victor, La Chênaie, le 24 avril (1822) reproduced in "Lettres à Saint-Victor II" by Louis Barthou, *Revue des Deux Mondes*, Paris, 15 novembre 1923, p. 399.

[20] Chr. Maréchal, *La famille* ..., pp. 225-255.

supposed, a happier era, not least for themselves. It was the Terror, which was a brutal experience for the inhabitants of St. Malo, that shook them and led them to revise their ideas about the relation between order and liberty and about the church.[21]

The older generation, which had combined the optimism and skepticism of the century in which it had been formed with a familial, traditional piety, was forced into a reflective and questioning attitude concerning the presuppositions of their now-tarnished "Age of Reason".[22] Such certainly was the case of des Saudrais who first guided the young Féli into the realm of philosophical reflection.[23] The unedited manuscripts written during the years of semi-retirement at La Chênaie and the correspondence of the three participants unveil for the researcher both the breadth and the seriousness of the projects under consideration. Among the papers of the Ven. Jean-Marie de La Mennais to be found at the Archives des Frères de l'instruction chrétienne, Jersey, Channel Islands, are several essays and manuscripts dealing with the creation of an adequate Christian apologetic for the chaotic and unbelieving post-Revolutionary mind; a problem, which, evidently, was a core preoccupation of the three. There is no need here to enter into a lengthy discussion of these texts; they will be referred to from time to time in the main text. The problems of authorship and content have been adequately discussed by Maréchal in *La jeunesse de La Mennais* where several of these manuscripts have been partially or totally reproduced.[24]

While these early writings, prepared as much for exercise in logic and clarity of expression as for content, were intended for the very limited audience of La Chênaie, they served as the foundation for the first cooperative publication of the two brothers, *Réflexions sur l'état de l'église en France pendant le Dix-Huitième siècle, et sur sa situation actuelle*. This initial work, written in 1808 and published in 1809,[25] contains two distinct sections. The first part presents in embryo the famous mennaisian adaptation of the traditionalists' religious

---

[21] A. R. Vidler, *Prophecy and Papacy*, London, 1954, p. 29.

[22] J. Leflon, *La crise révolutionnaire 1789-1846*, Vol. 20 of *Histoire de l'Eglise*, Paris, 1951, pp. 357-366.

[23] Ch. Boutard, *Lamennais, sa vie et ses doctrines*, Vol. I, Paris, 1905, p. 10.

[24] Chr. Maréchal, *La jeunesse* . . . , Paris, 1913; see "De Dieu (Réponse aux objections des athées)", pp. 90-97; "Témoignages des philosophes modernes en faveur de la religion chrétienne", pp. 98-116; "Les philosophes modernes jugés par eux-mêmes", pp. 117-119.

[25] A. R. Vidler, *Prophecy and Papacy*, London, 1954, p. 51.

apologetic based upon the social necessity of religion.[26] The briefer second part is pastorally oriented and advances a series of proposals for internal reform and modernization of the Church which are quite remarkable for their originality and perspicacity.[27]

In 1814, a second cooperative endeavor resulted in the publication in three volumes of *Tradition de l'église sur l'institution des évêques*. *Tradition* was an erudite production written in the form of an historico-theological treatise and shows a considerable amount of research and background in Patristics and historical materials. Ideologically, this poorly received book was an initial ultramontane declaration of hostility towards the Gallican principles of the French Church on the question of Papal rights in the nomination of bishops. The problem of authorship and responsibility seems to be clarified by Félicité's admission in a letter to a friend that *Tradition* "is, in effect, my work, having prepared it in its entirety from texts which he [Jean-Marie] had collected."[28]

Lamennais's psychological and spiritual condition in the decade between his mysterious conversion and the publication of *Tradition* is best known through his ample correspondence with his brother, Jean-Marie, members of his family and a close circle of friends.[29] A psychological portrait of Lamennais has been attempted by several students of psychology[30] and is not the principal aim in this study. It should be borne in mind, however, that no grasp of Lamennais's thought can be adequate without keeping firmly in awareness the tremendous importance of the interior struggles of these anguished years.[31] The peculiar "Weltschmerz" of the romantic temperament found a most singular expression in the spiritual sufferings of Lamennais and deeply branded the whole of his literary and philosophical production.[32]

[26] Lamennais, *Réflexions sur l'Etat de l'Eglise en France pendant le Dix-Huitième Siècle, et sur sa Situation Actuelle*, Paris, ed. 1819, p. 75.
[27] Ch. Boutard, *Lamennais, sa vie et ses doctrines*, Vol. I, Paris, 1905, p. 55.
[28] Letter from Lamennais to Simon Bruté, Londres, le 25 avril 1815, reproduced in A. Blaize, *Œuvres inédites de F. Lamennais*, (2 Vols.) Paris, 1866, T. I, p. 206.
[29] For a chronological ordering of Lamennais's correspondence see A. Feugère, *Lamennais avant l'Essai sur l'indifférence*, Paris, 1906.
[30] The most important psychological studies are: J. C. Verluys, *Essai sur le caractère de Lamennais*, Amsterdam-Paris, 1929; and R. Bovard, *Drame de conscience: le caractère et l'évolution religieuse de Lamennais*, Paris, 1961.
[31] L. Le Guillou, *L'évolution de la pensée religieuse de Félicité Lamennais*, Paris, 1966, pp. 5-16.
[32] H. G. Schenk, "Lamennais 1782-1854 I.", *The Month*, London, March 1954 p. 155.

After a self-imposed exile in England during the Hundred Days of Napoleon's attempted return to power,[33] Lamennais was ordained priest at Vannes, March 9th, 1816. Ordination had been a long delayed commitment, which, when finally taken, not only did not assuage his constant depression and sadness,[34] but seemed to add to his presentiments of personal and public disaster.[35] Under the steady pressure of his spiritual director, Abbé Carron, and his Sulpician advisor, Abbé Teysseyre, Lamennais completed a project originally conceived by the Sulpician as a new Christian apologetic.[36] The result appeared as the first volume of *L'Essai sur l'indifférence en matière de religion* in early December 1817. The new apologetic for an ancient religion was an immediate and brilliant success. The highly controversial second volume (1820) met with less success and considerable opposition.[37] A *Défense de l'Essai sur l'indifférence en matière de religion* (1821) is the author's response to the critics of the epistemology of "sens commun" proposed in Volume II. The third and fourth volumes were published in 1823. A planned fifth volume never advanced beyond the stage of a rough schematization.[38] The *Essai sur l'indifférence* is the foundation piece of the mennaisian structure; its philosophical content will be discussed in the main part of this thesis.

The resounding success of the 1817 publication of the first volume of the *Essai* projected the Breton curé into the forefront in the ideological conflicts of the Restoration; for the young Christian elite, he became "the greatest thinker that the French clergy had produced since Boussuet."[39] Except for occasional prolonged sojourns in Paris and an important trip through Switzerland and Italy in 1824,[40] Félicité retired with greater frequency to the seclusion of La Chênaie. His vast correspondence from these years outlines the progression of his thought and reveals the concerns which tormented his solitude. These were not restful years. His near fatal illness in the summer of 1826

[33] W. G. Roe, *Lamennais and England*, Oxford, 1966, pp. 60-70.

[34] R. Bovard, *Drame de conscience*, Paris, 1961, pp. 31-33.

[35] Ch. Boutard, *Lamennais, sa vie et ses doctrines*, Vol. I, Paris, 1905, p. 124.

[36] Chr. Maréchal, *La jeunesse* ..., pp. 598-633.

[37] Chr. Maréchal, *La Mennais; La Dispute de l'Essai sur l'indifférence*, Paris, 1925, pp. V-VI. (In subsequent citations, this work will be referred to simply as *La dispute* ...).

[38] A. Blaize, *Œuvres inédites*, Paris, 1866, T. II, pp. 287-294.

[39] J.-R. Derré, *Lamennais, ses amis et le mouvement des idées à l'époque romantique (1824-1834)*, Paris, 1962, p. 227.

[40] P. Dudon, "Lamennais en Italie", *Etudes*, Paris, 20 février 1935, pp. 422-442.

weakened him considerably and forced him to take an extended rest in the Pyrenees with his friend the Abbé Salinis.[41] During the years preceding and following the completion of the *Essai sur l'indifférence*, he made frequent contributions of articles to various royalist and conservative journals and newspapers which were collected and published as the *Mélanges religieux et philosophiques* (1819) and the *Nouveaux Mélanges* (1826).

De la religion considérée dans ses rapports avec l'ordre politique et civil (1826), released in two parts, is a critical signpost in Lamennais's rapidly evolving socio-political thought in this decade. The strident anti-Gallican position taken by the now famous priest-writer won for him governmental opposition and a mild fine imposed by the civil court for having incited citizens to disobey the law of the realm, in this case, for having opposed the required teaching of the Declaration of 1682.

The six years between the publication of *De la religion considérée...* and the closing of "L'Avenir" in November of 1831, were years of an almost feverish creativity. He dreamed of writing a three volume general theory of society[42] of which only an outline remains.[43] The ideas, however, which were to furnish the superstructure of this study in depth of the social nature of man, are to be found in various edited and unedited works dating from the same period. *Des Progrès de la Revolution et de la guerre contre l'Eglise* (1829), containing his famous analysis of liberalism and Gallicanism, which was at the base of his new concept of an alliance of the Church with the struggle for modern liberties, was followed by the doctrinally important *Première* (March, 1829) and *Seconde Lettre à Monseigneur l'Archevêque de Paris* (April, 1829). It was also in the latter part of 1828 that Lamennais's disciples and followers organized themselves into the Congregation of St. Peter, a new religious community designed to meet the needs of the modern world and a changing historical situation.[44]

The long searched-for lessons which were supposedly given by

---

[41] Letter from abbé Gerbet to Count de Senfft, Paris, 19 août 1826, reproduced in E. D. Forgues, *Œuvres Posthumes de F. Lamennais: Correspondence*, (2 Vols.), Paris, 1859, T. I, p. 191.

[42] Letters from Lamennais to Countess de Senfft, Paris, 21 mai 1826; and to Count de Senfft, Paris, 14 juin 1826; to same, Versailles, 27 juin 1826; reproduced in E. D. Forgues, *Œuvres Posthumes*, Paris, 1859, T. I, pp. 180; 182; 183.

[43] A. Blaize, *Œuvres inédites*, Paris, 1866, T. II, pp. 295-310.

[44] A. R. Vidler, *Prophecy and Papacy*, London, 1954, p. 145.

Lamennais to ecclesiastical and lay students at the college of Juilly in 1830-31 were first reconstructed by Maréchal from the notes of former students under the title *Essai d'un système de Philosophie Catholique* (1906). It was not until 1954 that a second *Essai d'un système de Philosophie catholique par M. l'abbé F. de La Mennais* was published by Yves Le Hir on the basis of unedited papers attributed to Lamennais and uncovered at the University of Rennes.[45] The importance of this as yet insufficiently studied work has been pointedly underlined by Maréchal.[46]

The articles proclaiming the alliance of "Dieu et Liberté" which form the core of inspiration for "L'Avenir", the epoch-making newspaper published by Lamennais and his friends between August, 1830, and November, 1831, have been published in various collections. The above works along with his extensive correspondence will provide the basic raw material for this study which will attempt to trace the evolution of his philosophical approach to the particular problems of tolerance and social coexistence from the time of his first writings until the conclusions attained in "L'Avenir".

Subsequent to the ill-fated pilgrimage to Rome undertaken by Lamennais, Montalembert, and Lacordaire, Félicité returned to the semi-obscurity of La Chênaie under the shadow of the Papal condemnation of the political program of "L'Avenir" announced in the encyclical "Mirari vos". It is beyond the intent of this work to enter into the details of this crisis or into the innumerable facets of the ensuing eventful years. The dates of subsequent publications indicate the new tendencies dominating his thoughts after his bold declaration for democracy in *Paroles d'un croyant* (1834) which was denounced in the strongly worded "Singulari nos" of Gregory XVI. *Affaires de Rome* (1836-37) gives voice to his disillusionment with the hierarchical Church while his writings after this, *Livre du Peuple* (1838), *De l'esclavage moderne* (1839) and *Le pays et le gouvernement* (1840) proclaim his new republican committment. *Esquisse d'une philosophie* (T. I, II, III 1840 and T. IV 1846) represents his final effort to attain a unified philosophical synthesis but, by this time, removed from the religious affiliations of the past.

---

[45] For a discussion of the history of this manuscript, see Y. Le Hir, *Essai d'un système de philosophie catholique par M. l'abbé F. de La Mennais*, Rennes, 1954, Introduction, pp. VII-XIV.

[46] Chr. Maréchal, "Note Critique sur les Conférences de philosophie catholique de l'abbé de La Mennais", *Revue d'Histoire Littéraire de la France*, Paris, 1939, pp. 175-178.

These were years of hardship and bitter oppositions. He lived not in the solitude of his beloved Breton countryside but in the obscurity of different Paris residences. For his brochure, *Le pays et le gouvernement*, he was sentenced to one year in the prison of Saint-Pélagie where he continued working on his *Esquisse, Du passé et de l'avenir du peuple* (1841) and *Discussions critiques et pensées diverses sur la religion et la philosophie* (1841).

His friends of these years after his break with Roman Catholicism were the artists, writers and activists of the republican left. He headed causes and aided with his habitual generosity the poor and the persecuted. After the Revolution of 1848, Lamennais was elected to the National Assembly as a deputy for one of the districts in Paris. Re-elected in 1849 to a Constituent Assembly, he remained to see his struggles for sweeping constitutional reform frustrated by the accession of Louis Bonaparte to power in 1851. With the return of a regime with monarchical pretensions, Lamennais, by now weak and aging, retired from public life to complete his translations of the New Testament (1851) and of La Divine Comédie de Dante Alighieri which was published after his death in 1855.

On February 27th, 1854, Félicité Lamennais died after a brief illness having refused the ministrations of the Church and surrounded by his friends of his later years.[47] He was buried without ceremony in a common grave at Père Lachaise. Lamennais has been alternately condemned and beatified by succeeding generations. Whatever position might be taken in reference to this enigmatic figure dominating the religious history of the nineteenth century, it might be at least agreed upon that he lived a life true to the ideal which he proposed for himself in a letter to Victor Hugo written in 1825. "Let men think of it what they will, I will sacrifice neither truth nor my conscience to them and, if there is a voice from the grave, you will hear coming from mine the same words."[48]

II. LAMENNAIS AS A PHILOSOPHER

In what measure is it possible to speak of Félicité Lamennais as a

---

[47] For a discussion concerning the controversy over the death of Lamennais, see A. Blaize, *Œuvres inédites*, Paris, 1866, T. II, pp. 351-384; also, Ch. Boutard, *Lamennais, sa vie et ses doctrines*, Paris, 1913, Vol. III, Chap. XVII, pp. 447-475.

[48] Letter from Lamennais to Victor Hugo, without date (1825), quoted in A. Feugère, *Lamennais avant l'Essai sur l'indifférence*, Paris, 1906, p. 306.

philosopher? Is a study of his treatment of the problem of tolerance or social co-existence a justifiable investigation for a doctoral dissertation in philosophy? Without venturing into an extended inquiry into the definition of and the nature of philosophy, an attempt will be made in the following pages to show that F. Lamennais occupies a place in the history of philosophy and that his works may be fruitfully subjected to a philosophical scrutiny. To do this, three questions are proposed to be answered. What is the place which others, historians and philosophers, have assigned to Lamennais in the history of ideas? What description did Lamennais himself ascribe to his multiple efforts? And, finally, given the possibility of attaining an acceptable definition of philosophy, may the writings of the "solitaire de la Chênaie" fit under this definition?

It would be pointless to deny that Lamennais does occupy a place in the history of ideas. No history of the nineteenth century would be complete without referring to him and to his doctrines. Lamennais "in the religious domain, Karl Marx in the social, are the two great visionaries of the 19th century. One can refuse their ideas but cannot deny their clairvoyance: the future has obeyed their prophecies."[49] Certainly, his influence on the social and political history of modern French Catholicism has been clearly established.[50] But prophets and social reformers are not necessarily philosophers. It is precisely on account of this multiplicity of roles assumed by Lamennais that commentators speak of him in contradictory terms and a valid question is raised concerning the authenticity of his claim to a place in the history of philosophy.

Some seek to avoid the difficulty by reducing the heterogeneous literary output of Lamennais to a single categorical designation. The unity of his thought and the singularity of his vision "was that of a sociologue".[51] For others, his apologetical preoccupations and polemical spirit so narrowed his philosophical endeavors as to render his doctrine sterile.[52] This attitude is even retained by some modern commentators who tend to stress the minimal importance of Lamennais as a philosopher or as a theologian; his ideas are merely

---

[49] A. Dansette, "La Mennais contre son temps", *Revue de Paris*, Paris, novembre 1947, p. 115.

[50] J.-B. Duroselle, *Les débuts du catholicisme social en France (1822-1870)*, Paris, 1951, pp. 36-40.

[51] C. Carcopino, *Les doctrines sociales de Lamennais*, Paris, 1942, p. 68.

[52] P. Dudon, "La Bibliothèque de Lamennais", *Études*, Paris, 20 avril 1912, pp. 234-237.

"the symptoms of a sad situation in the theological and philosophical studies of his times."[53] And, again for others, notably Emile Bréhier, such ideological systems as those integrating in some fashion the religious claims of a supernatural revelation, which is the case of the traditionalist reconstruction, are eliminated a priori from consideration philosophically.[54]

With few exceptions a more critical and objective attitude towards the philosophical and social implications of mennaisianism was not really adopted until the beginning of this century after the already mentioned phase of more scientific biographical investigation.[55] Nonetheless, the mordant character of Lamennais's attack against philosophy, especially the entrenched Cartesianism and positivism, as well as his unsparing treatment of the "philosophes", brought about a similarly strong reaction from various University and Gallican circles.[56] Opposition within the French Church grew more implacable as Lamennais's influence and prestige grew among the young clergy and the Catholic intellectual elite.[57] While it is not necessary to accept totally Maréchal's portrayal of Lamennais as the victim of plots and machinations,[58] it is prudent to be aware of the large degree of prejudice concerning him which remained in the academic and religious circles in the years following his death. The more serious, scientific works based upon wider research, greater knowledge of the period, and availability of previously unknown sources by such authors as Maréchal, Feugère, Poisson, Derré, Le Guillou, and Jürgensen render greater justice to the philosophical and ideological importance of the writings of F. Lamennais. Such studies would seem to justify this comment of Fonck in his excellent article on mennaisianism:

> By the doctrines of Lamennais, I understand not so much the political directives of *De la religion considérée...* or of "L'Avenir", as this background of philosophical and religious ideas which were his and

[53] W. Gurian, "Lamennais", *The Review of Politics*, Notre Dame, Indiana, April 1947, p. 206.
[54] E. Bréhier, "Y a-t-il une philosophie chrétienne?" published in *Études de Philosophie Moderne*, Paris, 1965, pp. 18-39.
[55] A. Feugère, *Lamennais avant l'Essai sur l'indifférence*, Paris, 1906, p. 13.
[56] M. Deschamps, Souvenirs Universitaires: "L'Université et Lamennais", *Mémoires de l'Académie des Sciences, Inscriptions et Belles-Letttres de Toulouse*, Tome V, Toulouse, 1893, pp. 36-51.
[57] Ch. Denis, "Les contradicteurs de Lamennais", *Annales de Philosophie chrétienne*, avril-septembre, 1900. Paris, pp. 221-231; also L. Le Guillou, *L'évolution de la pensée religieuse de Félicité Lamennais*, Paris, 1966, pp. 199-222.
[58] L. Le Guillou, ibid., p. 2.

which constituted that which might be called his mental structure or intellectual encasement and which may be considered as philosophy, properly speaking, and as philosophy of religion.[59]

He was virtually alone, in the opinion of P. Janet, among the French philosophers of the nineteenth century to attempt a general philosophical synthesis.[60]

Part of the problem concerning Lamennais the philosopher arises particularly from his own seeming repudiation of philosophy. The philosophical spirit, as he saw it, was "the incurable imbecility of mankind".[61] Philosophy was another name for "materialism";[62] it was, as he indicated in an early article, "Que le Christianisme rapproche l'homme de Dieu et que la Philosophie l'en sépare", the root of atheism.[63] Philosophy is "even more impotent than presumptuous, it hoodwinks or degrades all of our faculties."[64] Such comments are to be found in abundance, particularly in the early articles and in the *Essai sur l'indifférence*, and could be properly understood only if one bears in mind the historical context of the post-Enlightenment. Philosophy had become, popularly, the patrimony of the "philosophes".[65]

A more serious objection, which can only be considered summarily here, is Lamennais's rejection of reason, at least as it was taken in the Cartesian tradition, which is very evident in Volumes I and II of the *Essai sur l'indifférence.* His theory of universal consent as the basis of certitude represents for some "the mark, in itself, of a spirit destitute of philosophical Sense".[66] Such a criticism, however, is far from universal.[67] And even if Lamennais's skepticism or fideism were as anti-rational as supposed by some, and this is to be questioned, his criticism of reason and human knowledge would still be a legitimate

---

[59] A. Fonck, "Lamennais (Félicité de)", *Dictionnaire de Théologie Catholique*, Tome XVIII, 2ième Partie, Paris, 1925, col. 2513.

[60] P. Janet, La philosophie de Lamennais, Paris, 1890, p. 102.

[61] Lamennais, "L'influence des doctrines philosophiques sur la Société", (1815), Œuvres Complètes, Paris, (1836-1837), T. VI, p. 119.

[62] Ibid., p. 124.

[63] Ibid., T. VIII, pp. 66-68.

[64] *Lamennais, Essai sur l'indifférence en matière de religion*, Œuvres Complètes, Paris, 1836-1837, T. I, p. 250. (In subsequent citations this work will be referred to simply as *Essai sur l'indifférence . . .*).

[65] For the intellectual crisis among Catholics on the eve of the French Revolution, consult J. Leflon, *La crise révolutionnaire*, Paris, 1951, pp. 23-31.

[66] E. Faguet, *Politiques et Moralistes du XIXe siècle*, (3 vols.) Paris, 1898, T. II, p. 103.

[67] Chr. Maréchal, "La vraie doctrine philosophique de La Mennais. Le retour à la raison", *Revue philosophique*, Paris, 1949, Tome CXXXIX, pp. 319-330.

object of a study employing the philosophical tools and criteria just as much as a Pascal or a Rousseau or skepticism itself offers ample area for philosophical investigation.

It would seem that Lamennais gives two meanings to the word "philosophy". He definitely excoriates that philosophy opposed to Christianity "which appears under two forms: skepticism as long as it follows rigorously a rational method; pantheism insofar as, tired of doubt, it affirms that which it logically has no right to affirm".[68] But he refers to his own efforts in the *Essai sur l'indifférence* as "philosophical doctrine".[69] He speaks of Volume II of this work as "a new system of philosophy for which the highest dogmas of religion are the base".[70] Writing to Joseph de Maistre, he defends, while respecting the validity of traditional scholastic methods, his new methodology which he deems necessary for the religious crisis of the period.[71] As Lamennais progressed beyond the initial critical stage of the *Essai sur l'indifférence*, he became more and more concerned with the creation of a universal system of philosophy which would incorporate the whole of human experience. "Today, it is necessary", he wrote to his Roman friend, Father Ventura, in 1827, "... to consider all of the great questions of philosophy under a more scientific, a more elevated and more general point of view".[72] Especially in the years immediately preceding Juilly and "L'Avenir", Lamennais, in close cooperation with Gerbet, was singularly dedicated to the formation of a Catholic philosophical synthesis.[73]

Finally, the problem of accepting Lamennais as a philosopher will depend upon the vexing question of the relationship between theology and philosophy. It would be well beyond the scope of this paper to review and discuss in detail this lively polemic which has been renewed in recent decades.[74] Nevertheless, it will be necessary to touch

[68] Lamennais, *Des Progrès de la Révolution et de la Guerre contre l'Église*, Œuvres Complètes, Paris, 1836-1837, T. IX, p. 190.
[69] Letter from Lamennais to Grandi, La Chênaie, août 1821, reproduced in A. Blaize, *Œuvres inédites*, Paris, 1866, T. I, p. 405.
[70] Letter from Lamennais to his brother, Jean-Marie, 8 mai 1818, reproduced in ibid., p. 356.
[71] Letter from Lamennais to Joseph de Maistre, 2 janvier 1821, reproduced in A. Feugère, *Lamennais avant l'Essai sur l'indifférence*, Paris, 1906, p. 288.
[72] Letter from Lamennais to Ventura, La Chênaie, le 28 novembre (1827) reproduced in P. Dudon, "Lettres inédites de Lamennais à Ventura (1827-1829)", *Études*, Paris, 20 avril 1910, p. 246.
[73] J.-R. Derré, *Lamennais, ses amis et le mouvement des idées à l'époque romantique*, Paris, 1962, p. 104.
[74] For a summary discussion of the controversy concerning the possibility of a

briefly upon the problem in light of its specific bearing upon the character of Lamennais's so-named Catholic Philosophy.[75] Indeed, it will be encountered again in the main text of this dissertation, particularly, in Chapter Three, II, 2, "A Social Theory of Certitude", where Lamennais's early theory of the relationship between faith and reason will be treated, and, again, in Chapter Four where his later refinements on the nature of this relationship will enter into consideration. Our purpose here is simply to show that an a priori exclusion of Lamennais from the history of philosophy would be tendentious and unjustified.

If all thinkers, who, in one fashion or another, received inspiration from the theological teachings of Judaism and Christianity, were to be eliminated from the ranks of those recognized as philosophers, the history of Western philosophical thought would be quite slim or almost non-existent. "The Bible and biblical tradition form one of the bases of our philosophy", notes Karl Jaspers, since ". . . philosophical research in the West—admit it or not—is always done with the Bible, even while combatting it".[76] Although this may be generally granted, a question might be raised concerning the manner in which revelation is employed and the value given to it; the resolution of this question would establish, in the view of the philosopher treating the question, the distinction between theology and philosophy. As history attests, the answers have not been uniform, thus, admitting of a certain fluidity in the use of the terms "philosophy" and "theology" which allows them to spill-over from the categorical containers into which they have been placed.

If one allows for the shifting standards upon which the respective roles of philosophy and theology are decided, a minimal notion of philosophy as a total reflection on or total confrontation with reality by man using his human resources in such an effort,[77] it would not be difficult to recognize in the traditionalist current of thought the makings of a philosophical vocation. Reacting to the exclusivism of the rationalism of the 18th century, which made little allowance for

Christian Philosophy, consult, M. Nedoncelle, *Existe-t-il une Philosophie Chrétienne?*, Paris, 1956.

[75] Such was the name given to Lamennais' philosophical endeavors by L. de Potter in a letter to Lamennais, 15 mars 1835, reproduced in L. Le Guillou, *L'évolution de la pensée religieuse de Félicité Lamennais*, Paris, 1966, p. 287.

[76] Quoted from Karl Jaspers, *La foi philosophique*, in M. Nedoncelle, *Existe-t-il une Philosophie Chrétienne?*, Paris, 1956, p. 7.

[77] Ibid., p. 89.

revelation and the phenomenon of faith, Lamennais and his contemporaries were bent upon a re-definition of the respective domains of faith and reason in such a fashion as to give the religious fact its due. Although the act of faith assumes the principal and sustaining role and reason a secondary one in their conceptualization of the act of knowledge, reason was not, by that, to be annihilated. One may question the success of the undertaking but not the right of its progenitors to a place in the history of philosophy.[78]

It will be somewhat more evident if it can be shown that Lamennais's idea-system — and here we limit our inquiry to his efforts before 1831 — can be adequately described under the various acceptations and standard definitions of the word "philosophy". For our purposes, it will be sufficient to employ, in this very brief demonstration, the meanings A, B, and C given in *Vocabulaire Technique et Critique de la Philosophie* under the word "Philosophie".[79]

The first sense of the word "philosophy" is that it means a rational knowledge or science, that is, the reliance upon reason to reflect upon experience and to abstract or dis-engage from it the elements of a proposition. Was Lamennais concerned with such a rational science? Anthropologically, he defines man as a creature created to know.[80] What sort of knowledge does man possess? In Volume II of the *Essai sur l'indifférence* and in *Sommaire d'un système des connoissances humaines*, a work prepared by Gerbet but incorporated by Lamennais as an appendix to *Des Progrès de la Révolution...*, he erected a theory of knowledge proposing the limitations, capacities and possibilities of human reason. This propaedeutic included a severe critique of the individual reason as then understood among the followers of Cartesianism and the scholastic methods.

> If we insist upon the feebleness of particular reason, it is in order to establish the general reason, in proving that the primitive truths, which are its foundation, have an infinite certitude, and that the

---

[78] M. Nedoncelle, *Existe-t-il une Philosophie Chrétienne?*; Paris, 1956, p. 61.

[79] *Vocabulaire Technique et Critique de la Philosophie*, (ed. A. Lalande) Neuvième Edition, Paris, 1962, pp. 774-777: The following acceptations of philosophy are given as the most common: A. "Savoir rationnel, science, au sens le plus général du mot". B. "Tout ensemble d'études ou de considérations présentant un haut degré de généralité, et tendant à ramener soit un ordre de connaissances, soit tout le savoir humain, à un petit nombre de principes directeurs". C. "Ensemble des études qui concernent l'esprit, en tant qu'il se distingue de ses objects, qu'il est mis en antithèse avec la nature".

[80] Lamennais, L'Essai sur l'indifférence... T. II, p. 227.

secondary truths which reason deduces from it are equally certain: from which it follows that individual reason itself has, consequently, a sure standard upon which to judge its own thoughts... Thus, far from destroying reason, we place it, on the contrary, upon an unassailable base...".[81]

It can be noted, and will become more evident in the course of the following chapters, that Lamennais does not exclude the work of reason nor the validity of a rational knowledge; but he attempts to show that reason cannot be isolated from faith. Philosophy, as a consequence, joins theology in a higher synthesis in which the order of faith serves as the ground and the guide for the order of conceptualization.[82]

It would seem that the second meaning of philosophy, Sense B, is even more clearly applicable to the mennaisian idea structure. While it would be necessary to push our investigation to an analysis of the whole of Lamennais's literary output in order to see the final result of a lifetime effort of ideological synthesis, the trend towards a total view of reality is evident even at the earlier stages. His *Essai d'un système de philosophie catholique* is the first flowering of his attempt to achieve a metaphysic or an ultimate reduction of the whole of human experience and knowledge to the unity of essential, elementary principles. From his earliest writings, he manifested a highly-motivated ambition to restore to man and to society a living unity based upon a common participation in truth.

> ... return all things to unity, to find a singular and great truth of theology, morality and physics, which would command the obligatory adhesion of all reasonable men. For when faith would have married science and science itself would be penetrated by faith, what fool would then dare to place himself beyond that truth which includes all and which would provide, insofar as possible, the reason of all?
>
> Such had been the goal sought by Lamennais both before and after his condemnation; it was the goal of the *Essai*, that of "L'Avenir", and still that of *Discussions critiques*, in 1841.[83]

A cursory reading of his various writings on politics, law and society would be sufficient to show that he was concerned with a reflective

[81] Lamennais, *L'Essai sur l'indifférence* ..., T. II, pp. LXVI-LXVII.
[82] Lamennais, *Sommaire d'un système des connoissances humaines*, Œuvres Complètes, Paris, 1836-1837, T. IX, pp. 303-305.
[83] L. Le Guillou, *L'évolution de la pensée religieuse de Félicité Lamennais*, Paris, 1966, p. 289.

inquiry into the causes and principles beyond the facticity which rules the empirical sciences. Such an attitude would seem to be in conformity with Sense C, in that Lamennais's reflections upon the realities of the natural and the social worlds were "studies of the spirit" which envisioned wider and higher generalities than those of the particular sciences. The dual characteristics of the philosophical intention, the search for truth and the explicitation of what is seen in this search through a coherent discourse, do not seem to be lacking in Félicité Lamennais.[84]

This brief justification for the study of Lamennais's thought as philosophical may not be considered as definitive. There is room for more ample discussion; but, even if the hypothesis were advanced that Lamennais is more properly a theologian or a literary figure than a philosopher, a philosophical investigation of his world-view on the sole basis of its historical importance would be nonetheless more than justifiable. The discovery of the directing principles underlying the point of view from which Lamennais elaborated his vision, regardless of the form of expression which he employed, would in itself be a contribution to understanding the history of ideas in modern times.

III. The Philosophical Education of Lamennais

If Lamennais's career as a writer-philosopher had ceased with the publication of the last volumes of the *Essai sur l'indifférence* in 1823, he could possibly be considered as simply a more eloquent version of the dry and theoretical progenitor of traditionalism, Louis de Bonald. His subsequent intellectual evolution, however, with its seemingly revolutionary leaps from authoritarianism, to Catholic liberalism, to radical republicanism, has raised for all students of Lamennais the problem of sources and the problem of reconstructing the genesis of his originality. Given the seriousness of his philosophical efforts, it is necessary to ask about the philosophical influences which entered into his particular and articulated intuitions. What education did he receive? What philosophers did he read and what ideas form a part of his cultural milieu? The historical and ideological frame of references within which Lamennais fashioned his peculiar "world-view" will be

[84] For a discussion of the philosophical intention, see H. Gouhier, *Les Grandes Avenues de la Pensée Philosophique en France depuis Descartes*, Louvain-Paris, 1966, pp. 30-43.

treated more extensively in Chapter Two. In this brief section of Chapter One we will be concerned simply with the known components of his philosophical preparation without judging which current dominates or evaluating rigorously, at this point, the relative importance of each element.

Books alone do not form a philosopher; but knowing which books a philosopher has read makes it much easier for one to decode the content of his message. Reading was particularly important in the case of Lamennais since he represents an unusual figure in modern philosophy, the case of a self-educated metaphysician. Obviously, such a personal history of secluded study and random reading might be seen as either the cause of his originality or the source of his incoherencies.

Of course, self-education is never accomplished in isolation. When the term "autodidacte" is applied to Lamennais, it means essentially that he was not subjected to University formation nor to the methodological training of the seminaries of the epoch. He cannot be placed with the same facility with which his University-trained contemporaries may be placed within an intellectual tradition or school. This problem is endemic to the whole traditionalist movement for which a definitive study remains to be accomplished.[85] But Félicité did have his mentors, chiefly, the beloved "Tonton", his paternal uncle, Robert des Saudrais. Chr. Maréchal maintains that Lamennais was educated according to the method proposed by Rousseau in his pedagogical masterpiece, *Emile*.[86] He was allowed, as a youngster, to develop his interests freely in his uncle's well-stocked library.

The manuscripts of themes written during this peaceful philosophical incubation, which were referred to earlier,[87] establish quite clearly the matter studied by Félicité under the guidance of his uncle and his brother, Jean-Marie. For Maréchal, the early introduction to Rousseau was definitive. "It was always as a disciple of Rousseau that he played, worked and relaxed".[88] But his readings extended far beyond Rousseau. Along with the Latin poets, he read and discussed the "philosophes" of the 18th century, as evidenced by

[85] E. Hocedez, *Histoire de la théologie au XIXe siècle*, (3 vols.), Paris, 1947-1952, T. I, p. 104.
[86] Chr. Maréchal, *La jeunesse* . . . , p. 16.
[87] See Chapter One, I, footnote 24.
[88] Chr. Maréchal, *La jeunesse* . . . , p. 17.

his contribution to his uncle's essay, "Les Philosophes",[89] and his own "Les philosophes modernes jugés par eux-mêmes".[90] Chateaubriand's *Le Génie du Christianisme*, read shortly after its resounding appearance, awakened an early interest in Pascal whose presence pervades the *Essai sur l'indifférence*.[91] Both the example and the writings of the converted savant, La Harpe, seem to have had a considerable impact upon the impressionable youth in search of religious meaning.[92] Maréchal gives considerable importance to the critically timed reading of Nicole's *Traité de la Morale* and of the Church Fathers, particularly, Tertullian, in the period of Lamennais's conversion.[93]

Des Saudrais's philosophical letter of 1806 shows the mutual interest of uncle and nephew in the "spiritual philosophy" of Malebranche.[94] Félicité early acquired a passion for the writings of his older contemporary, Louis de Bonald, which was not at all shared by his uncle.[95] The trip to Paris in 1806 for reasons of health provided the occasion for Féli's introduction to the world of Saint-Sulpice and the intellectual traditions of 17th century French Catholicism, particularly, Bossuet.[96] He long maintained an acute interest in Fénélon.[97]

The years of research and investigation which were shared with Jean-Marie in preparing *Tradition de l'Église sur l'institution des évêques* oriented his readings towards the Church Fathers and ecclesiastical history. In later years, he will defend his method as being in conformity with "the method of the Church Fathers, perhaps a bit too neglected in the schools".[98] Indeed, the "quod ubique, quod semper, quod ab omnibus creditum est" of the Vincentis Lirinensis

---

[89] A. Feugère, *Lamennais avant l'Essai sur l'indifférence*,Paris, 1906, p. 41.

[90] Chr. Maréchal, *La jeunesse* ... , p. 117.

[91] F. Duine, "La Mennais et Pascal", *Annales de Bretagne*, Tome XXXV, 1923, Rennes-Paris, pp. 569-576.

[92] F. Duine, "Influence de La Harpe sur La Mennais", *Annales de Bretagne*, Tome XXVIII, janvier 1913, Rennes-Paris, pp. 198-202.

[93] Chr. Maréchal, *La jeunesse...*, pp. 65-69.

[94] Letter from des Saudrais to Lamennais, 1806, reproduced in A. Blaize, *Œuvres inédites*, Paris, 1866, T. I, pp. 25-26.

[95] Letter from des Saudrais to Félicité, 1807, quoted in A. Blaize, T. I, ibid., pp. 37-38.

[96] Chr. Maréchal, *La jeunesse* ... , pp. 121-157.

[97] Letter from Lamennais to Baroness Cottu, La Chênaie, le 24 mars 1822, reproduced in d'Haussonville, *Lettres inédites de Lamennais à la baronne Cottu 1818-1854*, Paris, 1910, p. 125.

[98] Letter from Lamennais to Grandi, La Chênaie, août 1821, reproduced in A. Blaize, *Œuvres inédites*, Paris, 1866, T. I, p. 405.

Commonitorium will remain a permanent ingredient in his theory of universal consent.[99] The same letter of self-explanation indicates that he was not unfamiliar with St. Thomas of Aquinas.[100]

Part of the schooling according to the free methods of des Saudrais was the study of languages. Félicité not only studied the traditional classical languages, Latin and Greek, but undertook Hebrew as well and indicated a considerable interest in Biblical criticism and orientology.[101] In the same epoch, he acquired a certain mastery of German[102] and became familiar with the writings of F. Schlegel,[103] whom, in later years, he will evoke in his own defense "as probably the most distinguished writer in Germany".[104] It is likely that he acquired a certain fluency in English while living in England[105] and references to numerous English sources, especially in the *Essai sur l'indifférence*, support this belief.

Lamennais's trip to Italy in 1824 apparently sparked a keen interest in the nation where he found "this religion which is found everywhere, which under every form and at every moment is in contact with the people".[106] Within a few years, he could write about his extensive readings in Italian literature.[107] Dante begins to gain an ascendency in his imagination in the very years in which Catholic liberalism was born and it was Dante who preoccupied him in his final years. "As Dante, M. de La Mennais had started by being a Guelph before being a Ghibelline".[108]

Lamennais did not limit his reading of contemporary works to those of Bonald whom he so much admired in these early years.[109] Not only did he express his profound admiration for the writings of Joseph de

[99] A. Blaize, *Essai Biographique sur M. F. de La Mennais*, Paris, 1858, p. 53.

[100] Letter from Lamennais to Grandi, La Chênaie, août 1821, reproduced in A. Blaize, *Œuvres inédites*, Paris, 1866, T. I, p. 405.

[101] Letter from Lamennais to his brother, Jean-Marie, 2 septembre 1809, ibid., pp. 63-64.

[102] Letter from Lamennais to his brother, Jean-Marie, 1809, ibid., p. 60.

[103] Letter from Lamennais to his brother, Jean-Marie, 4 septembre 1809, ibid., p. 54.

[104] Lamennais, "Seconde Lettre à Monseigneur l'Archévêque de Paris", *Œuvres complètes*, Paris, 1836-1837, T. IX, p. 396.

[105] W. G. Roe, *Lamennais and England*, Oxford, 1966, pp. 60-70.

[106] Letter from Lamennais to his brother, Jean-Marie, Gênes, 8 juin 1824, reproduced in A. Blaize, *Œuvres inédites*, Paris, 1866, T. II, p. 11.

[107] Letter from Lamennais to Countess de Senfft, 19 décembre 1827, reproduced in E. D. Forgues, *Œuvres Posthumes*, Paris, 1859, T. I, p. 319.

[108] A. Blaize, *Essai biographique sur M. F. de La Mennais*, Paris, 1858, p. 141.

[109] Lamennais, *L'Essai sur l'indifférence* ..., T. I, p. 220.

Maistre in his correspondence with the Savoyan diplomat.[110] But he also, in a remarkable letter to his friend, the Countess de Senfft, written many years after Maistre's death, acknowledged the continuity of the influence of the author of *Du Pape* and *Soirées de Saint-Petersbourg*.[111] Lamennais absorbed from the ideological atmosphere of the epoch all that he could find there to be of value. He was quick to seize upon the preliminary insights of Auguste Comte published in "Le Producteur".[112] The similarity of purpose and the common indebtedness of both Comte and Lamennais to Maistre have been underlined elsewhere.[113]

This short summary of a widely varied series of influences does little to reveal any clear pattern of sources at the base of the mennaisian superstructure. If a study of Lamennais's extraordinary library of some 7900 titles, which was sold at public auction in 1837 and for which his publishers prepared a complete catalogue,[114] were undertaken, it would only confirm the eclectic character of his tastes in languages, history, philosophy, politics, law and spirituality. Nonetheless, the judgement drawn by Dudon that the owner of this library was "neither a humanist, nor an erudite, nor a theologian, nor a philosopher, but an apologist, a polemicist, a publicist",[115] seems far too narrow. It was the library of a man guided by his sensibility, "always subject to the influence of others"[116] yet remarkably true to himself.[117]

There are many influences in the life and in the thought of Lamennais and only a very careful study of his writings and his correspondence will allow us to understand just how he took these multiple historical threads to weave his own philosophical design. It is impossible to categorize him as a disciple of Rousseau, or of Malebranche, or of anyone else. They were all present but what is

---

[110] The correspondence between Lamennais and Maistre is reproduced in A. Feugère, *Lamennais avant l'Essai sur l'indifférence*.Paris, 1906, p. 228, and in Rodolphe De Maistre, *Lettres et Opuscules inédits du comte J. De Maistre*, Paris, 1869, T. II, pages 116, 117, 120-122.

[111] Letter from Lamennais to Countess de Senfft, 8 octobre 1834, reproduced in E. D. Forgues, *Œuvres Posthumes*, Paris, 1859, T. II, p. 399.

[112] C. Calippe, "Les relations d'auguste Comte et de Lamennais", *Revue du clergé français*, 1ᵉʳ octobre 1918, Tome XCVI, Paris, p. 19.

[113] J. Poisson, *Le romantisme social de Lamennais: Essai sur la métaphysique des deux sociétés*, Paris, 1931, p, 45.

[114] "Catalogue de la Bibliothèque de M. F. de La Mennais", Daubrée, Paris, 1836.

[115] P. Dudon, "La Bibliothèque de Lamennais", *Études*, Paris, 20 avril 1912, p. 233.

[116] P. Lavedan, "La Mennais et Jean-Jacques Rousseau", *Mercure de France*, Paris, 16 mars 1914, p. 314.

[117] C. Carcopino, *Les doctrines sociales de Lamennais*, Paris, 1942, p. 14.

really present here is a man with a problem who uses his material as he finds it to find a base for his own religious belief and a principle upon which to unite men in society. "We come nearest to understanding the mystery [of Lamennais] when we realize that he saw everything in terms of religious faith".[118]

[118] W. G. Rce, *Lamennais and England*, Oxford, 966 p. 27.

CHAPTER TWO

HISTORICAL BACKGROUND

I. A Precision on the State of the Question

No one would question the inadequacy of the word tolerance or toleration, etymologically considered, for the task that has been historically assigned to it. It has a definite ring of negativity, a sense of "supporting" or of "putting up with" another who believes or acts distinctly. While such a meaning, establishing the idea of sustaining something foreign or painful as central, fits admirably with the usage of the word in physics, it fails to convey the more fully positive sense which has been connected with the term in modern ethics. The notion that "tolerance is essentially and basically a moral virtue, that is, a project and a dynamic quality of our will in regard to the 'humanizing' of our being with others"[1] has replaced the more traditional conceptualization which viewed tolerance as "that impossibility of prohibiting every evil".[2] The mutation which has taken place concerning the notion of tolerance, the transformation of a philosophical and theological justification for a legal permissiveness into "an ethical task of justice",[3] reflects the metamorphosis obtained in the social and political order with the passing of medieval unity and the coming of modernity and pluralism.

Although some would prefer to substitute "sympathy" or "respect"[4] to express those personal attitudes of acceptance of the dissenting other and of moderate behaviour in the face of heterodoxy implied in a positive definition of tolerance, such a change of nomenclature would be also a change of meaning. "Sympathy" and "respect" describe postures taken within the area of interpersonal

---

[1] A. Dondeyne, *Faith and the World*, (Translation of *Geloof en Wereld*), Pittsburgh, 1963, p. 284.

[2] Interpretation of St. Thomas of Aquinas' notion of tolerance found in L. Janssens, *Liberté de conscience et liberté religieuse*, Paris, 1964, Footnote 1, pp. 146-147.

[3] A. Dondeyne, *Faith and the World*, Pittsburgh, 1963, p. 284.

[4] For a discussion concerning the confusion surrounding the use of the word "tolerance", see *Vocabulaire Technique et Critique de la Philosophie*, (ed. A. Lalande) Neuvième Édition, Paris, 1962, pp. 1133-1137.

28

relations, the obligations emanating from the "I-Thou" encounter, qualities of human conduct on a level not necessarily including legal or juridical relationships. Certainly, if tolerance is to be considered as a virtue, "an imperative of common life in society, and even more deeply, an exigency which imposes itself [on men] as an obligation of conscience",[5] it pertains without doubt to the zone of ethics and personal morality.

But tolerance refers as well and, essentially, to the "we" of the social order; it is a problem of the "polis". By this, it should be understood that tolerance, as a question concerning responsible human actions and as a definition of relationships within the structure of human political society, touches and, in turn, is defined by both ethics and politics. The existential source of the problem is the same, that is, the fact of diversity in human beliefs, religious, philosophical, moral, and, consequently, diversity and even conflict of acts within the same political and social unity. The fact of co-existence evident on the primitive level of consciousness of other[6] gives rise to the consideration of tolerance as an expression of "living-together-with-our-fellow-men".[7] Among certain authors, there is a tendency to describe the willingness to allow for this diversity, even when contradictory, as a requirement of love on the level of inter-subjective relationships.[8] Such a position may indeed describe tolerance when considered as a virtue within the structure of personal morality but this usage only underlines the endemnic weakness of the word when removed from the realm of politics.

It is rather because the word "tolerance" pertains to politics, that is, to the study of the constitution of the body-politic,[9] that its meaningfulness and use are maintained. Without going into the vast and complex problem of the distinction between ethics and politics,[10] it is necessary to point out, in order to clarify the treat-

---

[5] A. Hartmann, S.J., *Vraie et Fausse Tolérance*, (Translation of *Toleranz und Christlicher Glaube*), Paris, 1958, p. 129.

[6] For a discussion of intersubjectivity in modern philosophy see W. Luijpen, O.S.A., *Existential Phenomenology*, Pittsburgh, 1960, Chapter Three, "Phenomenology of Intersubjectivity", pp. 176-260.

[7] A. Dondeyne, *Faith and the World*, Pittsburgh, 1963, p. 281.

[8] L. Janssens, *Liberté de conscience et liberté religieuse*, Paris, 1964, p. 131.

[9] Aristotle, *Politics*, (Trs. B. Jowett), Modern Library, New York, 1943, Book III, IV, pp. 125-208.

[10] For a provocative, modern discussion of the question confer E. Weil, *Philosophie Politique*, Paris, 1956, pp. 12; 27-57.

ment given to the problem in this paper, that tolerance must be seen bi-focally, that is, as implying reasonable human actions which are both moral and political.[11] If morality speaks of the "ought" of human decisions, politics, while sharing this ethical dimension, is concerned with organization and structure in reference to the totality of social acts and the juridical significance of these acts.

> ... although it is true that morality and law have a common basis, in that both express a deontological requirement ..., it is also true that each has a logical structure of its own with its own special characteristics, and for this reason, attempts at interpenetration on mutual absorption, whether in the direction of a *legalization of morality* or of a *moralization of law*, cannot but prove fallacious.[12]

To be sure, there is an analogy between the ethics of the individual and the ethics of the state,[13] but, whereas, at least in the Aristotelian conceptualization, individual ethics point to "the good life in the mean; in the ethics of the state, he [Aristotle] saw it in an equilibrium between power and liberty, between authority and its checks".[14] Tolerance, within the context of this study, must be considered less as an attitude taken on the level of inter-personal relations, which may prescind, at times, from such political considerations as social unity and the common good, and more as a problem posed within the sphere of politics, namely, the rapport between the individual and authority, or, multiplicity and unity in the body-politic.

As a political problem, tolerance is a history-laden term. Indeed, since it might be agreed that history is political and politics is historical,[15] it would be both valuable and necessary for our study of Lamennais's treatment of the problems posed by the historical phenomena grouped around the word "tolerance" to trace briefly the historical appearance and subsequent evolution of both the term and the problem.

---

[11] E. Weil, *Philosophie Politique*, Paris, 1956, pp. 11-12; E. Weil see both ethics and politics as "action raisonnable et universelle" but this action in politics is aimed "sur le genre humain" while the action of ethics is "de l'individu, considéré comme représentant de tous les individus, sur lui-même en vue de l'accord raisonnable avec lui-même". On the level of experience, "... une action politique est compréhensible sans référence à la réflexion morale et sans qu'elle soit positivement morale".

[12] G. Del Vecchio, *Justice*, (Translation of *La giustizia*), Edinburgh, 1952, p. 26.

[13] Aristotle, *Politics*, (Trs. B. Jowett), New York, 1943, No. 1333b 37, p. 310.

[14] *Ibid.*, Introduction by M. Lerner, pp. 22-23.

[15] E. Weil, *Philosophie Politique*, Paris, 1956, pp. 14-15.

II. Tolerance: A Modern Problem

Sociological and anthropological data render explicit the primordial human experience of co-existence.[16] The political union as the existential representation of community purpose reflects a specific type of rationality which is autonomous, that is, irreducible to the domestic and the economic, and which becomes,for that reason, the material object of political philosophy.[17] The most sophisticated expression of the political purpose of a community is the state. Such a sense of purpose or consensus might be defined as "an ensemble of substantive truths, a structure of basic knowledge, an order of elementary affirmations that reflect realities inherent in the order of existence".[18] Granted then, the necessity of adhesion to the community consensus for the very survival of the political union, what is to be the lot of those who, although sharing the same geo-political space, refuse to accept the community purpose? Thus, the whole question of tolerance, politically as allowance for dissent or as designation of the limits of elasticity within the socio-political union, touches the most fundamental political interest of the city, namely, its unity and preservation.

Historically, social integration and not diversity seems to be prior in the order of human experience.[19] It might be ventured that the manifestation of the human personality through a deeper self-consciousness and an awareness of its proper autonomy is at the source of the process of disintegration. Speaking of the well-known case of Socrates, Canon Leclercq has drawn the perceptive conclusion that, at least in the conscience of the West, "the human personality manifests itself by non-integrated attitudes".[20] This does not, however, lessen the necessity of social integration as the very basis of the possibility of a life which is properly human and, therefore, personal.[21]

The various ways in which diversity within the integrated social whole has been thematized on the theoretical level and treated on the practical are indicative of the shifting historical sub-soils underlying

---

[16] W. Luijpen, *Existential Phenomenology*, Pittsburgh, 1960, pp. 191-195.

[17] P. Ricœur, *Histoire et Vérité*, Paris, 1955, (2nd Edition), p. 249.

[18] J. C. Murray, S.J., *We Hold These Truths, Catholic Reflections on the American Proposition*, New York, 1960, p. 9.

[19] J. Leclercq, *La liberté d'opinion et les Catholiques*, Paris, 1963, pp. 27-29.

[20] Ibid., pp. 32-33.

[21] Ibid., pp. 33-35.

31

the discussion. If, for example, the discussion passes from the scholastically framed disputes concerning the rights of an erroneous conscience to modern theorizing on liberty of conscience and personal autonomy, it is evident that there has been a concomitant change in the very statement of the problem and in the philosophical intuitions leading to its statement. It has been justly noted that, in comparison with the medieval theories of society based upon the pre-eminence of a metaphysically based objective order and a theologically inspired religious commonwealth, the problem of tolerance, with its emphasis of subjective and anthropocentric elements, is a uniquely modern problem.[22]

Tolerance, considered as a measure of the limits to diversity within the body-politic, may refer to any sort of threat to the political bond, but the term has become, and with great historical justification, more especially connected with the phenomenon of a plurality of religious beliefs within the city or nation-state. It would be much beyond the scope of this paper to enter into the entire history of the relationship between religion and political society. Nonetheless, the nature of the link connecting the organization of political life, with its implications of community purpose and power of coercion, and man's theorizing about ultimate realities will be a central concern. Lamennais and the traditionalist philosophers were so keenly aware of the political function of theology that they have been quite correctly designated as "theocrats".[23] A study of the history of political theories would clearly substantiate the designation of traditional and classical theorizing about the organization of the "polis" as civil theology.[24]

The high degree of social, religious and political unity present throughout the historical period known as the Middle Ages has often been remarked. The German philosopher, Ernst Cassirer, gives the following account of the political thought which sustained this structure.

> The medieval theory of the state was a coherent system based upon two postulates: the contents of Christian revelation and the Stoic conception of the natural equality of men ... The medieval thinkers could quite well

[22] B. Olivier, O.P., "Le Problème de la Conscience errante" in *Tolérance et communauté humaine*, Tournai, 1952, p. 163.

[23] D. Bagge, *Les idées politiques en France sous la Restauration*, Paris, 1952. See Deuxième Partie: "L'École Théocratique et Contre-Révolutionnaire", pp. 187-330.

[24] A most interesting analysis of civil theology is given in E. Voegelin, *The New Science of Politics*, Chicago, 1952, particularly, Chapter III, "The Struggle for Representation in the Roman Empire", pp. 76-108.

accept the Stoic doctrine that there is one great republic—the same for God and men. They were convinced, too, that the spiritual and the secular order, notwithstanding their differences, form an organic unity ... More and more the *corpus Christianum* was conceived as an unbroken whole. The *corpus morale et politicum* was at the same time a *corpus mysticum*.[25]

The Renaissance with its humanistic orientation marks the beginning of the erosion of this unity: " ... the Renaissance was the moment, par excellence, of the becoming aware of the pluridimensional character of truth".[26] It was more the Protestant Reform, however, than the Italian Renaissance which became the more immediate occasion for the radical reshaping of the fundamental institutions of the West. The effects of this religious trauma were not immediate in the political sphere. "From 1520 to 1560, the traditional rule prevailed one faith, one law, one king".[27] With the growth of powerful Protestant minorities in the kingdoms of Western Europe, the civil theology of the Holy Roman Empire was threatened by the necessity of dealing with the disintegrating factor of religious plurality. The "tolerandi" of St. Thomas Aquinas[28] became a substantive[29] and, with this change, there was a shift of emphasis but not yet a qualitative mutation of meaning in the use of the word. It was the banner-word of a positive agitation for liberty of sect, but, with few exceptions, tolerance was not used in a positive sense, that is, as a desirable moral virtue.

> In the sense of a permission, a concession touching religious liberty, the word "tolerance" appears in the second half of the 16th century, in Germany (Toleranz) and the Low-Countries (Tolerantie), somewhat belatedly, without doubt, in France.[30]

Although Luther's revolt in the name of conscience was considered by the writers and theorists of the Enlightenment as the source of the positive notion of tolerance or liberty of conscience, it is difficult to find in his writings on conscience any passages which could be

---

[25] E. Cassirer, *The Myth of the State*, New Haven, 1963, pp. 106-107.

[26] P. Ricœur, *Histoire et Vérité*, Paris, 1955, p. 165.

[27] J. Lecler, *Histoire de la Tolérance au siècle de la Réforme*, 2 vols., Paris, 1955, T. II, p. 5.

[28] For a discussion of the use made of "tolerandi" in the Summa Theologica of Aquinas (2.2, q.10, a. 11) by the Reformers see ibid., T. I, pp. 9-10.

[29] Ibid., p. 9.

[30] Ibid., the subsequent development of the word "tolerance" in the century following the Reformation has been magnificently traced in the two volumes of J. Lecler.

interpreted "in the sense of a religiously autonomous conscience".[31] The voices demanding toleration during the century and a half following the stand of Luther against Pope and Emperor were numerous as were the reasons given for the advocacy of peaceful co-existence among a plurality of religious groups. The Christian humanists, the spiritualists and the Ana-baptist currents define various religiously motivated advocates of religious liberty while the "Politiques", notably in France, proposed toleration in the interests of the State.[32] A man of politics, such as the publicist, Jean Bodin, concluded that "the state should not perish for the sake of religious conscience".[33] Such a position was a fore-shadowing of a new secular world-view in the making, but, in this period under consideration, it had not yet been fully evoked.

An important element linking the cause of tolerance in the 16th century with the ideology of tolerance which took roots in the latter part of the 17th was the appeal to conscience. "The Reformers were not so very sensitive to this sort of argument: ... But after the mid-point of the century, with the extension of religious wars, the requests for 'liberty of conscience' sum up the demands of oppressed minorities".[34] The generic sense of the word "tolerance", however, remained intact throughout this epoch of change. It "supposes then a certitude in him who tolerates, but supposes as well, for whatever motive, the judgement that he ought not to impose his way of seeing things".[35]

The growth of the positive, moral sense of the word, which came to describe the very stuff of the 18th century "world-view", was the result of the rapid and extraordinary development of the secular and scientific mind towards the end of the 17th century.[36] Briefly stated, the philosophical genesis of "tolerantismus" begins with the epochal and revolutionary introduction of Descartes' famous methodological doubt, the cornerstone of modern philosophy, into the mainstream of

---

[31] A. Hartmann, *Vraie et Fausse Tolérance*, Paris, 1958, p. 11.

[32] For a discussion of the various positions see J. Lecler, *Histoire de la Tolérance au siècle de la Réforme*, Paris, 1955, T. II, pp. 411-421.

[33] H. J. Laski, *The Rise of European Liberalism*, London, 1962, p. 33.

[34] J. Lecler, *Histoire de la Tolérance au siècle de la Réforme*, Paris, 1955, T. II, pp. 434-435.

[35] J. Leclercq, *La liberté d'opinion et les Catholiques*, Paris, 1963, p. 223.

[36] For a discussion of the revolutionary changes in European culture in this epoch, consult Paul Hazard, *The European Mind 1680-1715*, (Translation of *La Crise de la conscience européenne*), Paperback Edition, London, 1964.

Western thought. There will be occasion to return to a discussion of the social and political implications of Cartesianism but, for the sake of continuity in the present resumé, it will be simply noted with Émile Bréhier that, whereas before Descartes "human understanding was situated ... in function of universal order, it is now universal order which will be defined in function of the understanding".[37] Although initiated in the name of orthodox religious beliefs, Cartesianism, by reliance upon the method of systematic doubt and the authority of reason alone, contained the germs of the ideological rationalism of the following century.[38]

Descartes took great care to place the truths of faith and morality beyond the reach of his universal doubt,[39] but there was no assurance that those who would follow would respect the caution of their great predecessor. The "great onslaught on the Church in the name of Cartesian philosophy",[40] foreseen by Bossuet, was not long in materializing.

> For Descartes, it was sufficient to set aside the truths of faith and the principles of the political order in order to avoid any scruple ... He had no doubt, however, that once his method was adopted it ought not be applied to every problem. Bayle used it for the benefit of scepticism. Voltaire applied it to religion, Montesquieu, Rousseau and the whole eighteenth century to the political and social order.[41]

This "great onslaught" might be identified, admitting, of course, the limitations of such categorizations, to the triumph of the secular ideal. To Descartes' methodological split between liberty and authority must be added the conscious and unconscious workings of the entire West in all realms of human activity. This "emergence of secularism" resulted as much from the breakdown of the old theology, or "Roman outlook", as from the rise of capitalism, the impact of the discovery of new worlds, the rebirth of antiquity, and a whole series of never sufficiently identified ingredients which are distinguished

[37] É. Bréhier, "L'esprit cartésien", published in *Études de Philosophie Moderne*, Paris, 1965, p. 50.

[38] P. Hazard, *The European Mind 1680-1715*, London, 1964, pp. 157-161.

[39] R. Descartes, *Meditationes de Prima Philosophia*, Paris, 1963, "Abrégé des six méditations suivantes", in which Descartes remarks, "Et que je n'entends point y parler des choses qui appartiennent à la foi, ou à la conduite de la vie, mais seulement de celles qui regardent les vérités spéculatives, et connues par l'aide de la seule lumière naturelle". p. 17.

[40] Letter from Bossuet to Huet, 18 May 1689, quoted in P. Hazard, *The European Mind 1680-1715*, London, 1964, p. 249.

[41] P. Janet, *La philosophie de Lamennais*, Paris, 1890, p. 27.

from the whole only when beheld by a viewer distant in time.[42]

More particularly, in the region of philosophy, the idea of toleration was to win out in the 18th century in proportion to the breakdown of the old civil theology. Pierre Bayle continued the disrupting task of dismantling the older order by his attacks against the presumptions of the revealed religions and through the employment of his important distinction between morality and religion. "He is essentially a master of relativism and even a master of irreligion ... According to him, morality is independent of theoretical principles. On his relativism, he builds his apology of tolerance".[43] Nonetheless, the irreligion of Bayle was not fundamentally anti-religious; he directed his brilliant efforts of criticism towards a re-orientation of the study and discussion of religious subjects in such a fashion that prejudice, superstition, and fixed positions would not hamper the efforts of reason to throw light on the content of faith. True to Descartes' method, if not to his caution, Bayle extended the honorable use of doubt to the previously privileged area of dogma. E. Cassirer has perceptively noted that the new generation which inaugurated the work of the Enlightenment regarded "religious certitude" as "no longer the gift of a supernatural power or divine grace; it is for man alone to raise himself to this certitude".[44] In the name of philosophy, Bayle upheld religious liberty and tolerance as universal values. "He denounced constraint as absurd and intolerable in a purely ethical sense, that is, in function of the criteria of moral reason".[45]

John Locke, on the other hand, proposed in one of his writings on tolerance, that toleration is a "duty"[46] which is "agreeable to the gospel of Jesus Christ, and to the genuine reason of mankind".[47] His apology for the toleration of diverse religious communities in the England in which the idea of constitutional, representative government had recently won victory over the "divine right" theory, was based upon a new conception of Church-State relations which, in turn,was deeply influenced by the idea of a natural religion. Locke viewed the Church

---

[42] For a discussion of the rise of secularism consult H. J. Laski, *The Rise of European Liberalism*, London, 1962, pp. 11-58.

[43] J. Wahl, *Tableau de la philosophie française*, Nouvelle Edition, Paris, 1962, p. 44.

[44] E. Cassirer, *La philosophie des lumières*, (Translation of *Die Philosophie der Aufklärung*), Paris, 1966, p. 179.

[45] Ibid., p. 181.

[46] J. Locke, "The Spirit of Toleration", published in *Locke Selections* (ed. S. P. Lamprecht), New York, 1928, p, 45.

[47] Ibid., p. 43.

as basically and essentially a voluntary society whose aim is strictly spiritual and whose power is strictly limited in exercise and in jurisdiction to those who accept membership in this association. The political or secular order, on the other hand, as viewed in his contract theory, is rational in origin and devoid of any theocratic presuppositions.[48] The idea of a natural religion or a religion of reason stands in the background of his ecclesiology. Locke was swept along by the same current of ideas as those which were directing the efforts of the English Deists to discover the natural or rational core of dogma and religious beliefs which lies beyond the particularities of cult and culture.[49] Locke did not in any way propose an anti-religious political order. Quite to the contrary, he established certain limits to toleration as being necessary for the common good. He excludes from participation in the affairs of the commonwealth those who arrogate to their sect a special religious authority over the civil authority or over others who are not members of that sect; those who are, by their religion, affiliated with a foreign prince; and those who deny the existence of God.[50] In brief, the common truths of the natural religion should be recognized by most men and should form the basis of social unity; but the acquisition of personal religious experience and faith requires the toleration of diversity.

Bayle's relativism and Locke's liberal political philosophy both entered into the heated atmosphere of the ideological disputes of the 18th century. In their century, the 17th, reason, in the domains of science and philosophy, had "emancipated itself from the guardianship of theological thought".[51] The problem of the 18th was to achieve, in the area of the human sciences, for ethics and politics, the independence won by the natural or pure sciences. Could the *Mathesis universalis* be extended into the thickets and the under-brush of that sector of life watered by passions and emotions?[52] The theoretical attempt had been made by Grotius, Hobbes, Locke, Leibniz, Spinoza and others,[53] but the experimental and pragmatic application of these efforts to "geometrize" politics took place in the

---

[48] H. J. Laski, *Political Thought in England from Locke to Bentham*, Tenth Printing, London, 1961, pp. 38-40.

[49] A. Hartmann, *Vraie et Fausse Tolérance*, Paris, 1958, pp. 27-28.

[50] J. Locke, "The Spirit of Toleration", published in *Locke Selections* (ed. S. P. Lamprecht), New York, 1928, pp. 49-50.

[51] E. Cassirer, *The Myth of the State*, New Haven, 1963, p. 167.

[52] Ibid., p. 164.

[53] Ibid., pp. 163-175.

century of the Enlightenment, during which, political philosophy became "the very focus of all intellectual activities".[54]

By the close of the 17th century, "the secular state had established itself"[55] after a period of growing self-awareness and self-sufficiency.[56] Laski sees in this process the victory of the liberal philosophy,[57] of which, "toleration has been the parent".[58] Even if toleration won out over the demands of religious unity and truth largely through the pragmatic requirements of the new economic structures,[59] this useful solution did not by any means end the theoretical difficulties which tolerance poses for theology and metaphysics. No doubt, the commercial spirit, which pre-empted other factors and dominated the scene in England and Holland, was supported by a common agreement within the community on the limits of dissent. Such societies, while officially Protestant, extended the requirements for admission to the commonwealth beyond adhesion to certain dogmas of a positive religion to a general consensus which, while nominally Christian, approached that sort of natural religion which was hinted at by Locke. In nations such as France, where a dogmatic and positive religion retaining official status and the medieval concept of Church-State harmony was still in a position of power, the arguments concerning tolerance went more to the metaphysical marrow of the issue.

Set off by the revocation of the Edict of Nantes, which was theoretically in unison with Bossuet's famous sermon, "Compelle intrare",[60] the debate became singularly bitter. There could no longer be any broadly-based union of disparate religious groups through the acceptance of certain commonly recognized dogmas of Christian revelation such as hoped for by Leibniz.[61] This ill-fated attempt to safe-guard medieval social integrity and to revive European unity on a religious base was doomed by the very fact that the historical situation itself could no longer support the civil theology of the ancient order. Not only was there a multiplicity of Christian sects but there was also the unrelenting advance of Deism among the

---

[54] E. Cassirer, *The Myth of the State*, New Haven, 1963, p. 176.
[55] H. J. Laski, *The Rise of European Liberalism*, London, 1962, p. 57.
[56] Ibid., p. 101.
[57] Ibid.
[58] H. J. Laski, *Authority in the Modern State*, New Haven, 1919, p. 187.
[59] H. J. Laski, *The Rise of European Liberalism*, London, 1962, pp. 43-44; 87.
[60] P. Hazard, *The European Mind 1680-1715*, London, 1964, p. 262.
[61] Ibid., p. 263.

intellectuals. Tired of religious conflicts and bent upon the reconstruction of society in harmony with science, reason, and the new liberal anthropology, the "philosophes" sought to uproot the very notion of revealed religion and, consequently, its claims to authority over the individual conscience.

The positions taken by the thinkers of the Enlightenment, although commonly inspired by Locke's empiricism,[62] were multiple and even contradictory.

> There is only one point, it seems, on which they found themselves in agreement; this is the negation of psychological liberty and the affirmation of liberty and tolerance as values.[63]

Following more the relativism of Bayle than the more nuanced and less skeptical liberalism of Locke, the "philosophes" would readily agree upon Voltaire's definition of tolerance as the "lot of humanity" for "we are all full of weakness and errors; let us pardon one another our stupidities, this is the first law of nature".[64] The disruption of the old notion of social unity was completed and there was need for tolerance as a "law of nature" because skepticism had undermined the claims of revealed religion and metaphysics to speak in the name of truth. The old distinction between civil and theological tolerance, an adjustment which would still allow for the demands of positive religion for belief in dogma while taking into account the multiplicity of religious sects, was rejected by the most deeply religious spirit of the Enlightenment, Rousseau.[65] At bottom, the new creed of tolerance was founded upon "a relativism of religious faith",[66] which distinguishes it from the older juridical and political concept of toleration.

Conceived by Voltaire as the "common ground of humanity",[67] it became known to Lamennais as "dogmatic" or "philosophic" tolerance[68] devised "to favor the progress of a philosophy of which doubt is the essence".[69]

[62] P. Hazard, *The European Mind 1680-1715*, London, 1964, pp. 277-290.

[63] J. Wahl, *Tableau de la philosophie française*, Paris, 1962, pp. 60-61.

[64] Voltaire, *Dictionnaire philosophique*, édition Garnier-Flammarion, Paris, 1964, article "Tolérance", pp. 362-363.

[65] J. J. Rousseau, *Émile ou de l'éducation*, édition Garnier, Paris, 1964, p. 382; *Du Contrat Social ou Principes du droit politique*, édition Garnier, Paris, 1962, p. 335.

[66] A. Hartmann, *Vraie et Fausse Tolérance*, Paris, 1958, p. 16.

[67] Voltaire, *Dictionnaire philosophique*, Introduction by René Pomeau, Paris, 1964, p. 12.

[68] Lamennais, "De la Tolérance", Œuvres Complètes, Paris, 1836-1837, T. VIII, p. 334.

[69] Ibid., p. 337.

III. Tolerance in the Restoration

The over-riding dogma of the 18th century rationalists and empirists implying

> ... that the conditions, a product of faith, time and custom, in which they and their forefathers had been living, were unnatural and had all to be replaced by deliberately planned uniform patterns, which would be natural and rational ...[70]

both inspired and was tested by the French Revolution. The erosion of the old structures was now surpassed by a violent sweeping away through a traumatic social and political experience which came to form both the backdrop of and the point of departure for European political thought following its dramatic bursting upon the West. The necessity of providing a new basis for social adhesion and political unity after the elimination of the monarchy gave ample occasion for experimentation and for implementation of various theories concerning political sovereignty and liberty which had been the normal intellectual fare for a generation of readers of the *Encyclopedie.*

With the Constituent Assembly, there was a solemn consecration of the liberal principles of the 18th century thinkers in the Declaration of the Rights of Man. The principle of tolerance, however, was institutionalized in a limited fashion. "No man can be disturbed for his religious opinions nor troubled in the exercise of worship".[71] This measure, joined by those concerning the secularization of Church property and the restrictions upon the independence of the hierarchy and the clergy, manifested the new attitude towards religion, especially, towards the ancient Gallican Church. Both ecclesiastical privilege and religious autonomy were suppressed and religion became a function of the State.[72]

Liberal ideas, so closely attached to the principle of private property, were victorious in the first phase of the Revolution. The State lost its sacred character; indeed, for Helvetius, property "makes possible the unity of the state".[73] The contractual, associationist political society was supported by the new secular moral codes for which the ultimate

---

[70] J. L. Talmon, *The Origins of Totalitarian Democracy*, London, 1962, p. 3.

[71] Quoted from "La déclaration des droits de l'homme", in J. Leflon, *La crise révolutionnaire 1789-1846*, Paris, 1951, p. 53.

[72] Ibid., p. 56.

[73] Quoted in H. J. Laski, *The Rise of European Liberalism*, London, 1962, p. 142.

norm was self-interest. It was, however, a conditioned liberalism, limited to the propertied middle-class. Despite their precautions, they had awakened forces which they would have rather ignored. The masses became aware of liberal slogans and new secular messianic religions came to replace the void left by the banishment of the old civil theology. Terror triumphed over reasonableness; the bourgeoisie had been chastened by their first experience of political power.

> Extreme individualism thus came full circle in a collectivist pattern of coercion before the eighteenth century was out. All the elements and patterns of totalitarian democracy emerged or were outlined before the turn of the century.[74]

The idea of tolerance for different cults, which attained prominence in the Declaration of the Rights of Man, became a weapon of intolerance and persecution against the Catholic Church under the rule of the Convention. There could be no tolerating of superstition and fanaticism in the new civic religion which was to replace the old Roman Church.[75] In the natural society inspired by Rousseau, it should be recalled, religions proclaiming dogmatic intolerance were among the excluded cults.[76] The influence of Rousseau among the later revolutionaries was enormous.[77] We shall have occasion to return to a discussion of Rousseau's notion of natural religion in the subsequent chapters.

Although Napoleon sought to restore the French State through a policy of force and of compromise on the religious question, there was no return to the principles underlying the ancien régime. The failure to discover a substitute for the doctrine of legitimacy, which supported the claims to sovereignty of the ancient monarchy, caused the nation to return to a most primitive, nonetheless, effective, guarantee of order and unity in military despotism, the triumph of physical force over systems of law and rights. In religious matters, the new government followed a policy of opportunism, grounded in political realism, which, while seeking to legitimize Church-State relations through Concordats,[78] was not for that less secular in its inspiration and

---

[74] J. L. Talmon, *The Origins of Totalitarian Democracy*, London, 1962, p. 252.

[75] J. Leflon, *La crise révolutionnaire 1789-1846*, Paris, 1951, pp. 123-124.

[76] J.-J. Rousseau, *Du Contrat social*, Paris, 1962, p. 335.

[77] For a discussion of the influence of the religious ideas of the Enlightenment among the later revolutionaries, particularly, Robespierre, consult, J. L. Talmon, *The Origins of Totalitarian Democracy*, London, 1962, pp. 21-24; 147-148.

[78] J. Leflon, *La crise révolutionnaire 1789-1846*, Paris, 1951, pp. 235-273.

execution. The idea of departmentalizing religion under government administration was but one of the secular doctrines born of liberalism which became permanently institutionalized in the Napoleonic administrative reforms. It might be said that liberalism required the administrative genius of a Napoleon to attain the legal consistency which it had lacked in the earlier phases of the Revolution. "The code ... lays down with a clarity that is almost startling the effective principles of that French liberalism which triumphed in 1789".[79]

The Revolution and the Napoleonic Empire, two colossal events in the experience of the French nation, were certain to produce a spirit of reaction once they had outrun their original dynamisms. "In religion as in politics, revolutions fulfill themselves and retrogress. They go to their conclusions; then order is re-established or death overcomes".[80] Lamennais, in this comment written in 1819, sums up the general sentiment which was spread throughout the France of the Restoration. Such is the aptly descriptive designation for the fifteen years of French history following the final defeat of Napoleon. The return of the Bourbon monarchy was not so much the result of popular demand as of sheer necessity born of fatigue with experimentation, sentiment for order and religion, the pressure of the Allies and the able efforts of Louis XVIII and his advisers.[81] It was an adroitly managed truce of fifteen years, "a cross-roads of two worlds"[82] at which irreconcilable ideologies coexisted,[83] and through which the experience of the old order and of the Revolution passed into the modern world.

Rarely have there been such pauses for serious debates on the fundamental questions of political philosophy. Lamennais expressed the consternation of a society with the time to ask itself the grand questions; "... all is in doubt. What is power? Who may command? What is law?"[84] If politics is considered as "the great dialogue between the individual and the State ... it is in the face of this that the two

---

[79] H. J. Laski, *The Rise of European Liberalism*, London, 1962, p. 147.

[80] Lamennais, "Sur un ouvrage intitulé *Exposition de la doctrine de Leibnitz sur la religion, suivie de Pensées extraites des ouvrages du même auteur*; par M. Emery, ancien supérieur-général de Saint-Sulpice", Œuvres Complètes, Paris, 1836-1837, T. VI, p. 399.

[81] G. de Bertier de Sauvigny, *La Restauration*, Nouvelle Edition, Paris, 1963, pp. 16-41.

[82] D. Bagge, *Les idées politiques en France sous la Restauration*, Paris, 1952, p. 7.

[83] Ibid., p. 14.

[84] Lamennais, "De la réunion des différentes communions chrétiennes", Œuvres Complètes Paris, 1836-1837, T. VIII, p. 44.

currents of thought, which still divide the world, separate".[85] In this proposition, Dominique Bagge, a modern commentator on the political ideas of the Restoration, recognizes, as primordial to the political discussions of the era, the core problem which Lamennais pointed out to his friend, Senfft, that is, "... to know how the alliance of Power and Liberty operates, the necessary condition of social existence."[86] It is certainly within this frame of references that the problem of tolerance must be discussed since it was the restored nation's primary concern to know what kind of unity is necessary for order and, indeed, for the very survival of a society and what would be the conditions of adherence to and acceptance by that society. Sovereignty, rights, power, liberty, all of these will become the currency of the Restoration debates in which the revival of the old, the defense of the newly acquired, and an inventive theorizing for the future will conspire to give the epoch its historical coloration.

1. *Revival of the Old*

The political restoration of the Bourbon monarchy in France coincided with an englobing spiritual movement which swept Europe under the title of Romanticism. It was a complex, humanist reaction to the previous rationalist currents which had been foreshadowed by the pietism of the 18th century[87] and by the writings of Rousseau, forerunner of the new apologetics of religious sentiment.[88] Too broad to be restricted to a specific definition, Romanticism is probably best described as a constant of the human spirit which somehow bypasses the limitations of reason and which, periodically, bursts upon the historical scene:

> ... an eternal element of the human soul which never ceases to search out its way between the "I will" of the Titan and the "I obey" of the believer, either in the Promethean manner of the free, conscious will, or through respectful adhesion to the law of order and by submission to powers which surpass and guide us.[89]

[85] D. Bagge, *Les idées politiques en France sous la Restauration*, Paris, 1952, p. 22.
[86] Letter from Lamennais to Count Senfft, le 17 avril 1829, reproduced in E. D. Forgues, *Oeuvres Posthumes de F. Lamennais*, Paris, 1859, T. II, p. 40.
[87] H. Lichtenberger, "Qu'est-ce que le Romantisme?", Cahiers du Sud, mai-juin 1937, Marseille, p. 352.
[88] J. Leflon, *La crise révolutionnaire 1789-1846*, Paris, 1951, p. 358.
[89] H. Lichtenberger, "Qu'est-ce que le Romanticisme?", Cahiers du Sud, mai-juin 1937, Marseille, p. 358.

It will be important to retain in mind this dual character of the romantic soul, emphatic defense of all that is human in the name of sentiment mixed with loyalty to the past.

More than in any other way, Romanticism revealed itself in the new attitude taken towards the past, a discovery of the historical dimension in a way never visualized by the historians of Europe's ages of Classicism and Enlightenment. It was the epoch of "the birth of the modern historical conscience".[90] A passion for a sympathetic historical reconstruction of the past led to a greater willingness among the intellectuals to accept those facets of religious experience which had been condemned as mere aberrations by the encyclopedists. A new period of religious search and artistic creativeness flowered after long years, during which, as Lamartine remarked, "only the geometers had the word".[91]

Romanticism was the outer sphere, descriptive of several lesser spheres sharing the same élan but, often, contradictory among themselves. Born in Germany and England but international in its expression, it entered into the various manifestations of the human spirit and even into such intellectual disciplines as philosophy. Traditionalism is the name ascribed to a particular philo-sophico-theological expression of the new spirit born in France "of a reflection on the Revolution of 1789".[92] A soul-searching caused by the destruction of ancient institutions and the reversal of traditional value systems began shortly after the anarchical effects and chilling excesses of the revolutionary Terror became known to the contemporaries of the events.

All of Europe suffered from the shock. Edmund Burke, "great watershed of English political philosophy",[93] stigmatized the French Revolution in the name of tradition in his *Reflections on the French Revolution* published in 1790. An obscure French thinker, Saint-Martin, is held to have originated the notion that the French Revolution was a punishment of Divine Providence brought against a society which had separated itself from the laws of religion and morality.[94] Joseph de Maistre, an exiled Savoyan nobleman, known to

[90] G. de Bertier de Sauvigny, *La Restauration*, Paris, 1963, p. 337.

[91] Quoted in G. de Bertier de Sauvigny, *La Restauration*, Paris, 1963, p. 327.

[92] J. Droz, *Restaurations et Révolutions (1815-1871)*, Vol. 1 of *L'Epoque Contemporaine*, Paris, 1953, p. 1.

[93] H. J. Laski, *The Rise of European Liberalism*, London, 1962, p. 128.

[94] J. Droz, *Restaurations et Révolutions (1815-1871)*, Paris, 1953, p. 6.

have associated with the group directed by Saint-Martin[95] and a reader of Burke's analysis of revolutionary theory,[96] published, in 1796, the first tract of the French movement of reaction, *Considérations sur la France.* In the same year, working separately but under similar conditions of exile, Louis-Gabriel-Ambroise de Bonald, another member of the dispersed French nobility, wrote *Théorie du pouvoir politique et religieux dans la société civile.* These writings initiated the ideological counter-revolution and form the basis of the intellectual antithesis to the then triumphant rationalism and materialism of the revolutionaries. It was not, however, until "around 1815 that these works began to bear fruit".[97] To these, of course, must be added the vastly popular aesthetic and sentimental defense of the ancient Christian faith, *Génie du Christianisme,* written by Chateaubriand in 1802.

Out of the agony of exile and loss, a new philosophical and religious movement came to life of which "de Maistre was the precursor, Bonald the father, and Lamennais the herald".[98] In the name of religion, tradition and society, they inaugurated a

> ... fight without mercy against an individualism, which, failing to recognize the most necessary and natural solidarities, refuses to accept between the human person and the State, and, a fortiori, alongside and above the same, any element apt to provide an effective counter-weight to its power, and, if such should be the case, to the tyranny of governments.[99]

The political theories of the traditionalists have been admirably studied elsewhere.[100] The object of the present review is simply to enunciate the major themes of the traditionalist writers which will enter into consideration in the study of Lamennais's treatment of the problem of tolerance. Of primary importance is the very impact of the events of the revolutionary rule on French institutions and on the lives of those who had previously accepted the traditional order as inviolable. If the architects of revolutionary thought had deemed it necessary to re-construct the whole of society, the traditionalists were quick to seize upon the very violence of the Revolution and the

---

[95] D. Bagge, *Les idées politiques en France sous la Restauration*, Paris, 1952, p. 193.
[96] Ibid., p. 197.
[97] J. Droz, *Restaurations et Révolutions (1815-1871)*, Paris, 1953, p. 1.
[98] E. Hocedez, *Histoire de la Théologie au XIXᵉ siècle*, Paris, 1947-1952, T. I, p. 105.
[99] J. Poisson, *Le romantisme social de Lamennais*, Paris, 1931, p. 32.
[100] A complete contemporary analysis is to be found in the already cited work of D. Bagge, *Les idées politiques en France sous la Restauration*, Paris, 1952.

chaotic events which followed as proof of the folly of the task and of the error of the rationalists' methodology. The Cartesian image of the subsistent, thinking-self impregnated the minds of the European representatives of enlightened thought to such a degree that they had begun to believe in the invincibility of unshackled, individual thought. But these thoughts contemplated in the order and safety of an absolutist Europe gave disastrous results when used as weapons by the revolutionary activists. To get at the root of the disaster it was necessary to attack the theoretical presuppositions of the revolutionary creed.

For Maistre, the abstractionist, deductive method of the rationalist, when applied to the human sciences and the art of government, was absurd. "History is experimental politics".[101] Following Burke and, to some degree, Montesquieu, the Savoyan condemned all such systems for failing to take into account the larger picture, the history of man and of nations.[102] Contrary to 18th century thought which had attributed a "fictive origin to all of the most important facts of human nature: society, language and religion",[103] Maistre preferred to have recourse to the lessons of history which alone would reveal the general laws of society. When these laws, sanctioned by history and religion, are abandoned, the result is social and political calamity, punishment of a Divine Providence.[104]

The capital question concerns the nature of sovereignty; "the organization of power" became the central issue.[105] Whom must man obey? What is the source of the right to command and the duty to obey in the social order? The theocratic thesis that religion was the basis of all social order, the common ideological ground for Maistre, Bonald, Chateaubriand and Lamennais, was the key to the solutions which they would offer to the problem of sovereignty.[106] But religion is historical, a revelation, not an abstract construct of the human mind. Not Nature as proposed by Rousseau, but history would make known to man the contents of the general laws governing his existence as a

---

[101] Quoted in D. Bagge, Les idées politiques en France sous la Restauration, Paris, 1952, p. 246.

[102] D. Bagge, *Les idées politiques en France sous la Restauration*, Paris, 1952, p. 246.

[103] P. Janet, *La philosophie de Lamennais*, Paris, 1890, p. 18.

[104] D. Bagge, *Les idées politiques en France sous la Restauration*, Paris, 1952, pp. 264-268.

[105] J. Poisson, *Le romantisme et la souveraineté*, Paris, 1932, p. 7.

[106] A. Feugère, *Lamennais avant l'Essai sur l'indifférence*, Paris, 1906, p. 81.

social being.[107] Nonetheless, as will be evident in subsequent chapters of this study, Rousseau was to wield a powerful influence over the traditionalist movement.

Divine Revelation, as contained in the books of Sacred Scripture, had been subjected to a severe rational, ethical, and historical criticism by the philosophers of the Enlightenment.

> The *content* of revelation was thereby substantially reduced while the idea of revelation still remained intact; but revelation should have no other role than that of confirming and sanctioning precisely the truths which are evident and fully in accord with reason.[108]

This supreme confidence in reason, however, was severely undermined even before the century of Enlightenment had run its course. Not only the critiques of Hume and Rousseau but also the return of the irrational in the cloak of revolutionary violence drove men to search for the origin of religion in more primitive sources. Using the very results of the empiricists' analysis of the origin of language, Bonald succeeded, through the development of a theory of language which will be discussed later, in not only returning revelation to a central position in intellectual life but also in making reason itself dependent upon revelation for its very functioning.

Due to a Divine Revelation, which, for the traditionalists, is at the origin of human history, events have meaning. If there is violence, terror, and anarchy, it is a sign that man has betrayed his nature "for the nature of a being is to exist as the Creator has willed it. And this will is made perfectly plain by the facts".[109] Something is out of place when

> ... there is nothing but violence in the world; for we are tainted by modern philosophy which has taught us that *all is good*, whereas evil has polluted everything and in a very real sense *all is evil*, since nothing is in its place.[110]

Reversing the fictive devises of the political philosophers who followed Hobbes, Maistre maintained that man is social by nature; society is prior to the individual.[111] But there is no people, no society,

---

[107] J. de Maistre, *The Works of Joseph de Maistre*, (Translation and Selections by J. Lively) London, 1965, from Introduction by J. Lively, p. 39.

[108] E. Cassirer, *La philosophie des lumières*, Paris, 1966, p. 189.

[109] J. de Maistre, *Study on Sovereignty* published in The Works of Joseph de Maistre, (ed. Lively), London, 1965, p. 95.

[110] Ibid., *Considerations on France*, p. 65.

[111] J. de Maistre, *Study on Sovereignty*, pp. 94-98.

without sovereignty.[112] Such sovereignty, the common center of social adhesion and source of order, derives from God and, as such, is absolute and inviolable.[113] The extremely rich critique of individualism and of basic libertarian notions made by Maistre was not entirely negative. He sought the key to historical understanding by proposing, as a ground for his interpretations of events, the historical universality of Christianity, a doctrine which will reverberate in the writings of Lamennais. For Maistre, Christianity antedates its Founder, in fact, "it was born on the day that days were born".[114] Something of this idea was present among the English Deists for whom the truths of Christianity were simply the truths of reason; Tindal published a work of this tenor in 1730 with the revealing title, *Christianity as old as the Creation.*[115] Voltaire, on the other hand, had used this argument concerning the universal rational content of certain Christian dogmas as evidence against the uniqueness of the Christian claim to a special spiritual authority. In the opinion of E. Faguet, Maistre and, later, Lamennais turned this argument against Voltaire and the Deists by upholding that these universal truths, known through faith and not reason, are the results of a common revelation and, consequently, a single religion of which Christianity is the historical continuation.[116] Again, this will be treated in greater detail in Chapter Three of the present dissertation.

There is also a messianic quality in the writings of Maistre, particularly in his prognostications concerning the renewal of religion and a new revelation of the Holy Spirit,[117] which did not escape the notice of such perceptive younger intellectuals as Lamennais[118] and Auguste Comte.[119] While Maistre admitted liberty of thought, there could be no question of a doctrinaire tolerance for a man

---

[112] J. de Maistre, *Study on Sovereignty*, p. 99.

[113] Ibid., pp. 112-129.

[114] J. de Maistre, *Considérations on France* published in *The Works of Joseph de Maistre*, (ed. Lively), London, 1965, p. 74. For a discussion of the influence of this idea upon Lamennais consult F. Brousse, *Lamennais et le christianisme universel*, Paris, 1963, pp. 19-23; also E. Faguet, *Politiques et Moralistes au XIXe siècle*, Paris, 1898, T. II, pp. 100-102.

[115] A. Hartmann, *Vraie et Fausse Tolerance*, Paris, 1958, p. 27.

[116] E. Faguet, *Politiques et Moralistes du XIXe siècle*, Paris, 1898, T. II, pp. 101-102.

[117] L. Le Guillou, *L'évolution de la pensée religieuse de Félicité Lamennais*, Paris, 1966, p. 50.

[118] Y. Le Hir, "Eschatologie et Messianisme", Introduction to *Les paroles d'un croyant de Lamennais*, Paris, 1949, p. 36.

[119] C. Calippe, *L'attitude sociale des catholiques français au XIXe siècle*, 3 vols., Paris, 1911, T. I, pp. 40-60.

who considered religion to be "the true nerve of the States. . ."[120]

Maistre supported his principle of authority on religion, history and a pessimistic anthropology while Bonald's approach and methodology were more abstract and deductive.[121] More theoretical than the other traditionalists, Bonald grounded his unified, authoritarian system in Sacred Scripture, Romans XXII, 1, "Non est potestas nisi a deo".[122] This absolute character of a unique divine Revelation is the true foundation of all power. Such a position, of course, had not been unfamiliar to the medieval theorists or to Bossuet. The originality of Bonald is to be found more in the theory of language which he uses to demonstrate the necessity of both Revelation and society.

Language achieves a central position in the synthesis developed by Bonald and most completely expressed in his *La législation primitive considérée dans les derniers temps par les seules lumières de la raison* (1802). Bonald united the contemporary discussions on the origins of language to the Christian belief in a Divine Revelation. "The Creator", in the thinking of Bonald, "did not communicate reason directly to the first man but, indirectly, through the intermediary of the spoken word which becomes the expression of reason".[123] Thus, man depends upon language for thought. Reason is not the possession of the autonomous individual but the truth inherent in the nature of man received in and through language. The psychology of Bonald is that of the 18th century empiricists insofar as it insists upon the passive character of the human knowing process.[124] Not only does the fact of language demonstrate the necessity of a Divine Revelation but it also manifests the eminent sociability of man. Thus a theory of language and the traditionalist thesis that the true philosophy is revelation are joined at the base of a social and political theory that is the anti-thesis of that emanating from the contractual and associative notions of the Enlightenment.[125]

It is an organic vision of a society which is founded upon the Divine Will in which man's liberty consists in acceptance of that Will and the order ordained by it. Power is one and independent of those who are

---

[120] D. Bagge, *Les idées politiques en France sous la Restauration*, Paris, 1952, p. 192.

[121] C. Calippe, *L'attitude sociale des catholiques français an XIXᵉ siècle*, Paris, 1911, T. I, pp. 73-74.

[122] H. J. Laski, *Authority in the Modern State*, New Haven, 1919, p. 136.

[123] L. Foucher, *La philosophie catholique en France au XIXᵉ siècle*, Paris, 1955, p. 23.

[124] Ibid., pp. 23-24.

[125] Ibid., p. 26.

subject to it.[126] It supports the political order and such an order is of necessity intolerant for "unless we have a religious and political unity, man cannot discover truth, nor can society hope for salvation".[127] Bonald was more concerned about the restoration of a certain social and political order and less about the religious problem than Maistre or Lamennais and this will be a cause for a separation between Lamennais and Bonald in later years.[128]

The ideas of both Maistre and Bonald will re-appear with great frequency, especially in the early works of Lamennais. To one enthusiastic follower, they will be known as the new "Holy Fathers",[129] "a triumvirate of catholic philosophy whose members never or scarcely see one another but whose declarations and acts are in nearly perfect accord".[130] But the two generations of romantics will separate and both the drama and content of this separation, particularly on the problem of sovereignty, will be shown in the discussion of the transitional role of Lamennais in the chapters following.

2. Defense of the New

As much as Bonald might have sought to re-impose the political theology of the 17th century or Lamennais the hierarchical order of the Middle Ages, there could be no simple return to the ancient socio-religious unity; the idea of national unity was no longer dependent upon religious unity. The Charter granted by Louis XVIII in 1814 was a clear confession of the necessity of compromising with the 18th century. It was the effort of realistic statesmen "to express in simple and practical political principles that which remained of the best of political thought of the 18th century after it had passed through the crucible of experience".[131] Among the principles considered fundamental was the idea of toleration, implemented in article 5 of the Charter, an idea, which "if it had been bent by the

[126] D. Bagge, Les idées politiques en France sous la Restauration, Paris, 1952, pp. 297-299.

[127] Quoted in H. J. Laski, Authority in the Modern State, New Haven, 1919, p. 143.

[128] J.-R. Derré, Lamennais, ses amis et le mouvement des idées à l'époque romantique, Paris, 1962, p. 66.

[129] Letter from Ventura to Lamennais (1825) reproduced in G. Goyau, Le portefeuille de Lamennais (1818-1836), Paris, 1930, p. 39.

[130] E. Faguet, Politiques et Moralistes du XIXᵉ siècle, Paris, 1898, T. II, p. 93.

[131] G. de Berthier de Sauvigny, La Restauration, Paris, 1963, p. 73.

oppression of Napoleon and the unclean craftiness of Fouché, was far from broken".[132]

The Doctrinaires,[133] directed by Royer-Collard and Guizot, erected a theoretical super-structure enshrining the notions of balance and compromise. Through Royer-Collard, the "common sense" philosophy of Thomas Reid entered into the University circles; it was quite in keeping with the cautious attitude of the advocates of constitutionalism in politics and eclecticism in philosophy.[134]

For the Doctrinaires, there was no contradiction between a broad toleration of religious beliefs, as in article 5, and the recognition of Roman Catholicism as the State religion in article 6. Society, for them, is organic and necessary[135] but government is the work of finding a balance of interests.[136] Rejecting both the authoritarian view of the theocrats and the libertarian view of the extreme liberals, they sought "to harness liberty and necessity to the same chariot".[137] On the crucial problem of the nature of sovereignty, Royer-Collard sought to show that such is a false problem by denying the very existence of a unique sovereignty or of any absolute power. "His insistence that sovereignty is no more than a peculiar synthesis of power is immensely valuable".[138] It is "an affirmation of political pluralism".[139] As such, politics is a constant effort to balance the claims of the person and the requirements of the social order through the parliamentary forum.

Royer-Collard and his followers stood mid-way between the unitary conservatism of the traditionalists for whom toleration was a sign of a diseased society and the liberal heirs of Voltaire who could admit no sovereignty beyond that of the individual. It is impossible here to enter into the various shades of liberal thought in this period when the liberal was so powerful but it would be helpful, in order to understand the general context in which Lamennais elaborated his liberal

---

[132] H. J. Laski, *Authority in the Modern State*, New Haven, 1919, p. 282.
[133] For a discussion of the political thought of the Doctrinaires consult, D. Bagge, *Les idées politiques en France sous la Restauration*, Paris, 1952, particularly, Chapitre II, "Les doctrinaires", pp. 93-143.
[134] G. de Berthier de Sauvigny, *La Restauration*, Paris, 1963, p. 347.
[135] D. Bagge, *Les idées politiques en France sous la Restauration*, Paris, 1952, p. 142.
[136] H. J. Laski, *Authority in the Modern State*, New Haven, 1919, p. 289.
[137] D. Bagge, *Les idées politiques en France sous la Restauration*, Paris, 1952, p. 143.
[138] H. J. Laski, *Authority in the Modern State*, New Haven, 1919, p. 303.
[139] Ibid., p. 308.

Catholicism, to simply point out two of the major tendencies within liberalism.

Although reaction to the 18th century and fear engendered by recollections of the Convention and the Terror dominated both politics and letters, the spirit of the Enlightenment with its dogmas of faith in reason, science, and progress and of tolerance was far from being underground. If there was a lack of originality among the most rigid followers of the "ideologues", the numerous re-editions of the works of Voltaire and Rousseau in this period clearly indicate that they were not forgotten.[140] If the first evaluations of the French Revolution, those of the traditionalists, were negative, it was not long before serious historical apologists of the Revolution, such as A. Thiers and F. Mignet, began to be heard.[141] More than any other event, the Revolution was seen as the beginning of the triumph of the liberal idea.

While the various self-identified liberals shared the same characteristic belief in individualism, they were not unaffected totally by the intrusion of Romanticism. The most important liberal thinkers of the Restoration era were Mme. de Staël and Benjamin Constant, both of whom participated in, and indeed, aided the growth of the romantic revolt. They adhered to a negative definition of liberty, that is, more as an inherent power of the subject to resist authority than as a definition of relationships.[142] Like the more mitigated liberals of the Doctrinaire group, they rejected the notion of popular sovereignty out of fear of succumbing to a despotism of the masses.[143]

The originality of both Mme. de Staël and Constant is more evident, however, in their attitude towards religion. Mme. de Staël rejected any authority over the individual in religious matters but she did not fall into the harsh anti-religious attitudes of her predecessors. But Benjamin Constant is particularly representative of the new type of liberal thinker who rejects the strident rationalism of a Voltaire and sees the essentials of the liberal creed as being compatible with religious dogma.[144] A tolerant Christianity with a liberal spirit began to make inroads among the intellectuals.

[140] G. de Berthier de Sauvigny, *La Restauration*, Paris, 1963, p. 343.
[141] H. Barnes, *A History of Historical Writing*, (Second Revised Edition) New York, 1962, p. 215.
[142] D. Bagge, *Les idées politiques en France sous la Restauration*, Paris, 1952, p. 159.
[143] J. Poisson, *Le romantisme et la souveraineté*, Paris, 1932, p. 65.
[144] J.-R. Derré, *Lamennais, ses amis et le mouvement des idées à l'époque romantique*, Paris, 1962, pp. 68-69.

For Voltaire, tolerance is the principal virtue of the religion of reason, the redeeming humanitarian quality of reasonable men unblemished by the exclusivism or the fanaticism which Voltaire saw as inseparable from positive religions such as those in existence in his own era. This attitude represented "a violent reproach directed against the Christian beliefs".[145] Rousseau, however, was much more influential in the religious thinking of the Romanticists than Voltaire. On the theoretical level, to recapitulate briefly, Rousseau recognizes two species of religion, a religion of interiority, "the pure and simple religion of the Gospel", and a civil religion such as those of ancient Greece and Rome.[146] There is also a third species of religion which has supranational pretensions, "the religion of the priests".[147] All men of good will are bound by sentiment to follow the first pure religion which is an expression of their natural relations with Providence; but, such a religion is devoid of political meaning; its interests lie beyond human and national ambitions. A public cult is therefore necessary which will include all citizens and give a sense of purpose to the common goals of the community, in brief, a source of patriotism and solidarity. All religions, such as Roman Catholicism, which divide the unique sovereignty of the State are to be forbidden as enemies of the common good.[148]

It would require a much more complete study to present, in amplitude, the religious thought of Rousseau such as it is developed in *Contrat Social* and the *Profession de foi du Vicaire Savoyard.* Although some have seen a clash between the positions assumed by Rousseau in the two works, it would seem to be more apparent than real. In the *Contrat Social*, he is treating of the religion of society, its political and social importance; but he does not in any way deny the importance of the interior religious experience which is so richly expressed in *Profession de foi du Vicaire Savoyard.*[149] To Rousseau, the particularity of the civic cult does not detract from the universality of the interior religious sentiment.

The Romanticists did not accept integrally the program of *Contrat Social*, but the lessons taught by Rousseau concerning the social necessity of religion and the sublime character of a pure Christianity

[145] A. Hartmann, *Vraie et Fausse Tolérance*, Paris, 1958, p. 29.
[146] J.-J. Rousseau, *Du Contrat Social*, Paris, 1962, p. 331.
[147] Ibid.
[148] Ibid., pp. 332-335.
[149] J. L. Talmon, *The Origins of Totalitarian Democracy*, London, 1962, p. 24.

of moral sentiment were not overlooked by them. Interestingly, Rousseau had defended at one and the same time both tolerance and a unique civic religion. The tolerance advocated by Rousseau is not the product of doubt but a moral imperative stemming from ethical truths or that "religion without fanaticism" which Rousseau places above the particularities of dogma.[150] The "bon curé", a literary figure idealized by Rousseau and discovered by the Romantics, is the model of those who are at once believing men and practitioners of tolerance.[151]

No less, and perhaps more, than the "bon curé", the literary creations of Lessing, the German critic and philosopher, were unquestionably of great influence among the German, and somewhat later, the French Romanticists. The hero of Lessing's early works is Nathan the Jew, a persecuted man of reason, who, in the course of his travels, finds among men of other religious traditions similarly enlightened souls who, in spite of traditional differences, go beyond the limitations of dogma to discover their common religion of humanity and reason.[152] Lessing did much more than weave moralizing tales. Profoundly influenced by Spinoza in his ideas of a universal Nature and pure immanence, Lessing fashioned a new way of conceiving the unity in diversity of religious experience.

> The only true, "absolute" religion is that which envelopes in itself the totality of the phenomenal forms of the religious. Nothing individual is absolutely lost to it; no vision, no matter how particular, not even error ... From this fundamental thought is born Lessing's *Education of Humanity* ... in conceiving religion as a divine plan of education, Lessing elaborates a theodicy of history, that is, a system of justification which values religion not in function of a stable being given at the beginning of time but in function of its becoming and of the finality of this becoming.[153]

This vision making of "historical, revealed religions ... the pedagogical instruments of mankind"[154] entered vigorously into the evolutionary currents which began to sweep the romantic world. Every religion contributes to the achievement of the true religion of reason

[150] J.-J. Rousseau, *Émile ou de l'éducation*, Paris, 1964, pp. 382; 480-481.
[151] J.-J. Rousseau, *Profession de foi du Vicaire Savoyard*, (Critical edition by P.-M. Masson), Paris, 1914, pp. 427-428.
[152] A. Hartmann, *Vraie et Fausse Tolérance*, Paris, 1958, pp. 29-36.
[153] E. Cassirer, *La philosophie des lumières*, Paris, 1966, p. 202.
[154] A. Hartmann, *Vraie et Fausse Tolérance*, Paris, 1958, p. 33.

which is a long-term, final goal of humanity. Thus, each religion must be respected as the bearer of some truth; but, it should also be kept in mind that this truth is historical, that is, opaque and partial. Although there is a certain similarity to Voltaire and the English Deists in this fundamental rationalism, Lessing takes greater care to defend all religious sentiment and the positive character of historical religions.

J. Derré has contended, in his excellent study on the movement of ideas in the first quarter of the 19th century in France and Germany, that the reception of Lessing's ideas into France through Mme. de Staël and B. Constant was crucial to the revision of attitudes taken towards religion by the first post-revolutionary generation of Romanticists.[155] He goes so far as to hold that by 1830 the ideas of Lessing had become the common fare of liberal Christians in France.[156] L. Le Guillou, on the contrary, takes a more guarded position regarding the degree of influence exercised by Lessing before the appearance of the first translation into French of *Education of Humanity* in 1832.[157]

Be that what it may, there was definitely something in the air, a mutual sharing of common ideas flowing from the last years of the Enlightenment concerning historical religions and their value as educators of humanity in its forward progression. Constant well represents this transposition of religious values which took place between the declining generation of the Enlightenment and the first generation of Romanticists. A believer in the rationalist traditions of his forebearers and spiritually converted to Protestant pietism during his long sojourns in Germany, Constant tried to mold into an acceptable harmony a broad tolerance and genuine religious sentiment. *De la religion considérée dans sa source, ses formes, et ses développements*, (1824) is the fruit of his long investigations and spiritual experiences. Incorporating the German ideas on the progressive nature of dogma and rejecting fixed religious postures, the eloquent spokesman of liberalism wrote essentially a defense of the basic religiosity of man and of the nobility of a simple Christianity.

---

[155] For an interesting discussion of the role of Lessing in the romantic current of ideas consult J.-R. Derré, *Lamennais, ses amis et le mouvement des idées à l'époque romantique*, Paris, 1962, particularly, pp. 32-53.

[156] Ibid., p. 39.

[157] L. Le Guillou, *L'évolution de la pensée religieuse de Félicité Lamennais*, Paris, 1966, p. 21.

Unlike the traditionalists, who were also rediscovering the value of religion for humanity, Constant took a more personal and less social view of the religious experience. At bottom, Constant's approach was not unlike that of the liberal Protestantism which was then emerging in Germany.[158]

The phenomenon of a layman, scion of a liberal and rationalist heritage, writing a treatise on the value of religion, is representative of the fusion of ideas which was taking place. With the aid of German pietism, Constant succeeded in conciliating for himself the exigencies of a religious stance with the ideal of liberty inherited from the Enlightenment. Tolerance became for him the ideal Christian virtue; he rejected the tolerantismus of his predecessors as atheistic intolerance.[159]

A dynamic interpretation of religion, much in keeping with the newly-acquired historical awareness of the Romanticists, proved much more acceptable to the liberal mind than the uncompromising "ne varietur" approach of a Bossuet. The adjustments of liberalism, under the influence of the romantic spirit, to history and to religion were not without great importance to Lamennais at the hour of his crucial re-assessment of political liberalism. Could not the adjustment of religion to the quest for liberty so manifest among the peoples result from a philosophy of religion made flexible by a common awareness of the temporal character of religious forms and, finally, even of dogmatic expression?

3. Theorizing for the Future

The fall of Napoleon brought with it an unusual sense of intellectual liberation.[160] The military Empire with its new industries, its engineering spirit, and the concurrent censorship of religious and philosophical discussions had materialized the intellectual and spiritual atmosphere of France.[161] The Restoration, on the other hand, provided a release for thought and for imagination as witnessed in the vast increase of literary publications and newspapers, the foundation of learned societies, and the readiness to receive with sympathy all that

---

[158] J.-R. Derré, *Lamennais, ses amis et le mouvement des idées à l'époque romantique*, Paris, 1962, Chapitre II "Benjamin Constant, théoricien du sentiment religieux", pp. 67-114.

[159] Ibid., p. 88.

[160] G. de Berthier de Sauvigny, *La Restauration*, Paris, 1963, p. 328.

[161] Chr. Maréchal, *La Dispute* . . . , p. 6.

was foreign as well as that which was old.[162] Discussions filled the air and the printed pages and the peaceful combat allowed the belligerents ample opportunity to change side with great facility resulting in an immense complexity of ideologies. Ready-made categorizations are quite inadequate as containers for the romantic mind. For the romantic, the separation between philosophy and literature, as between philosophy and theology, was by no means considered absolute.

Out of an age of fusion of opposites and cross-pollination of contraries, new movements and ideologies would arise from obscure origins to capture the future. Romanticism was the breeding ground for such diverse messianic creeds as the democratic mystique, Saint-Simonianism, Fourierism, and Communism. It would be impossible to trace the genesis of these movements in this limited thesis but it is important to realize that such currents were in the making at the time of the "L'Avenir".[163] All seemed to realize that the Restoration was transitional; it was necessary to search for a new basis for the society of the future. Of necessity, the great problems of sovereignty and of the nature of political society would be seen in a new context. Political, social and economic factors would soon render sterile the erudite debates which dominated the early days of the Chamber of Deputies.[164]

Once a new generation of romantics broke with the conservative and traditionalist inclinations of the older generation,[165] a new alliance, that of liberalism and the romantic spirit occasioned by the Greek War for Independence, became possible.[166] With such shifting terrains, the discussions concerning liberty, tolerance, and sovereignty would also be seen in a new light. Lamennais shared in the work of both generations of romantics. His own conceptualizations of religion and of the political and social order will reflect this metamorphosis in the intellectual evolution which carried him from the hardy traditionalism of the *Essai sur l'Indifférence en matière de la religion* to the reconciliation between religious faith and liberty which he boldly proclaimed for the future in "De l'Avenir de la Société". While, in the

---

[162] G. de Berthier de Sauvigny, *La Restauration*, Paris, 1963, pp. 328-330.

[163] For an excellent bibliographical study of the various ideological movements in the romantic period in France, consult J. Poisson, *Le romantisme et le souveraineté*, Paris, 1932.

[164] Ibid., pp. 15-16.

[165] G. de Berthier de Sauvigny, *La Restauration*, Paris, 1963, p. 353.

[166] Ibid., p. 357.

chapters which follow, an attempt will be made to show the unity and continuity of his thought, in spite of apparently contradictory conclusions, it will be important to remember that he was a thinker very much in dialogue with his epoch.

CHAPTER THREE

LAMENNAIS AND THE RESTORATION
OF AUTHORITY

I. Traces of Traditionalist Philosophy
in his early writings

1. *Metaphysical options of Réflexions sur l'état de l'église en France
pendant le dix-huitième siècle, et sur sa situation actuelle*

As was pointed out earlier,[1] *Réflexions sur l'état de l'église en France
pendant le dix-huitième siècle, et sur sa situation actuelle* was the joint
publication of the two Lamennais brothers. It was, however,
considered important enough by Félicité to include it among his
various collected works published long after the initial appearance of
Réflexions sur l'état... in 1809. There are several preliminary
philosophical orientations or preferences found in this work which
can be seen as previsions of the basic principles of his philosophical
and theological thought which will endure throughout the multiple
variations which mark his ideological evolution. Such initial intuitions,
outgrowths of the prolonged study and variegated readings at La
Chênaie, plus, of course, the personal factor of an interior spiritual
struggle, form the ribs of an intellectual scaffolding which will remain
remarkably stable in spite of the apparently radical transformations in
the conclusions which he fashioned.

As indicated in the title, the 18th century stands before the author
as the object of consideration; but, more profoundly, it is the religious
dimension of man, "l'état de l'église", which is the point of focus
through which is to be seen the whole of science and history. A
religious concern or a spiritualistic orientation manifested in his first
writings will remain unchanged during all of the eventful and
tumultuous years between the publications of *Réflexions sur l'état...*
and *Esquisse d'une philosophie*, his final attempt at a philosophical
synthesis. The present task, in this section, is expository; the criticism
of these options and the derived conclusions and applications will be
the burden of the final chapter of the dissertation.

[1] See Chapter One, 1. "Life and Works of Félicité Lamennais".

The first half of the *Réflexions sur l'état...*, the part most explicitly attributed to Félicité,[2] has been quite justly called "a first rough draft of the *Essai sur l'indifférence...*".[3] In this section Lamennais reveals his profound and passionate concern for uniting reason and revelation and for ending the conflict of the 18th century between scientific thought and authority. The crux of the argumentation will be to show the absolute necessity of religion, and, thus, authority, for both individual man[4] and for society.[5] His demonstrations of this position are merely schematized in *Réflexions sur l'état...*, but the very elements of a wider and more coherent development, that of the *Essai sur l'indifférence...*, were embryonically in life eight years before that major endeavor.

At the base of the mennaisian structure is to be found a metaphysics, which, as "the science of general truths, is the foundation of all other sciences since they borrow from it their principles and their certitude".[6] What is the source of this metaphysics? What does it contain?

> ... it is good to teach our students ... that all of the sciences of which they are so vain only live and grow, so to speak, under the protection of the moral sciences and that the progress of both is equally due to Christianity which has opened to man the route to all truths by raising him to a knowledge of God, supreme truth, and which, by freeing the spirit from the senses, has introduced that severe metaphysics, those rigorous methods of reasoning of which mathematical analysis is but a particular application...[7]

Important notions are postulated in this text: the primacy of the moral over the physical and the union of both in a Divinity from which they derive. Christianity provides the means to the higher science in which all truths are united.

In choosing his principles, Lamennais chooses his philosophers as well. For him, Malebranche is like the "explorer who traces the length of the stream in order to discover its unknown source... raising himself to the very breast of God to search therein the beginning of

---

[2] A. Feugère, *Lamennais avant l'Essai sur l'indifférence*, Paris, 1906, p. 76.

[3] A. R. Vidler, *Prophecy and Papacy*, London, 1954, p. 46.

[4] Lamennais, *Réflexions sur l'état de l'église en France pendant le dix-huitième siècle, et sur sa situation actuelle*, Paris, ed. 1819, pp. 7-8 (In subsequent citations, this work will be referred to simply as *Réflexions sur l'état...*).

[5] Ibid., pp. 97, 130.

[6] Ibid., p. 103.

[7] Ibid., pp. 102-103.

thought".[8] It has been quite sagely pointed out that this early predilection of Félicité for the philosophical theories of Malebranche is crucial to an understanding of his future thought.[9]

This election of Malebranche is particularly illustrated by the long discussion in *Réflexions sur l'état*. . . concerning the philosophical dispute on the origin of ideas. Before discussing the reason for the consideration of this epistemological problem in the context of *Réflexions sur l'état*. . ., it will be useful to show here the impact of the Oratorian on Lamennais's evolving philosophical views. Briefly, Lamennais sees the problem of the origin of ideas as a critical issue in the ideological developments of the previous century. "All metaphysicians before Locke and Condillac believed it necessary to return to God in order to explain human thought".[10] For Descartes, ideas were made innate by an act of creation while, for Leibnitz, these same ideas, although not innate in man after the fashion of Descartes, were pre-existent but formless in the soul of man.[11]

Such solutions were inadequate for Malebranche, who "searching in very depths of Christianity"[12] found an acceptable explanation.

> He states that since men understand one another they must have similar ideas and similar ideas suppose a common model, archetypical ideas both immutable and eternal which can only be found in the eternal and immutable, that is, in God. God then, or thought, the Word of God, is the light which illuminates the intellect.[13]

Lamennais further elucidates, faithfully following Malebranche, the consequences of the famous illuminist theory of knowledge. The knowing subject does not intuit ideas in himself but sees them in God for it is only in God that the human knower can see whether or not certain ideas exist necessarily or whether or not these ideas are seen by other intellects as they are seen by the subject himself.[14] It is important to note that Lamennais sees in God not only the source of ideas but also, in a way not clearly explicitated in this book, the source of their certitude. Chr. Maréchal accurately ascribes to Malebranche the inspiration for the mennaisian notion of a universal reason which

---

[8] *Réflexions sur l'état* . . . , p. 16.
[9] J. Poisson, *Le romantisme social de Lamennais*, Paris, 1931, p. 156.
[10] *Réflexions sur l'état*. . ., p. 52.
[11] Ibid.
[12] Ibid.
[13] Ibid., pp. 52-53.
[14] Ibid., p. 53.

will be expounded in Vol. II of the *Essai sur l'indifférence*.[15] It is significant as well to be aware of the importance of the phrase "since men understand one another". The notion of communicability is scarcely developed in *Réflexions sur l'état*. . . but one can readily agree with J. Poisson that "the metaphysical principle of communication was always recognized by Lamennais as the true basis of all society".[16]

Although this whole discussion may seem to be an erudite aside in a general work written ostensibly on the situation of the Church in the 18th century, it is indicative of the seriousness with which Lamennais began his public dispute with the ideological currents of the Enlightenment. In order to understand the events which shook France in the Revolution of 1789, it is necessary to reach back to the ideological sources of revolt and disorder. Social bodies resist deterioration longer than individuals.[17] Chaos and great changes in the State can only be explained by the destructive influence of ideas which undermine the foundations upon which the social structure rests.[18] For Lamennais, events are ideas incarnate.

This intimate relation between metaphysics and history or between ideas and events, not unsimilar to that held by other traditionalist thinkers, is a pivotal concept in mennaisian thought. If metaphysics is identified with the "vast system of Christianity",[19] history becomes essentially the history of religion. Lamennais does not yet, in this work, identify completely the primitive revelation or religion with Catholicism as he does in the *Essai sur l'indifférence*. . .; but the idea is present in germ. His remarks in this book are simply reflections written "while awaiting a writer who wishes or is capable of embracing it [the history of the Church] in the whole of its extent".[20] He describes, however, the position which must be assumed by the Christian philosopher before the chaotic events of the revolutionary period just brought to a close.

> An interesting work would be that in which one would show, insofar as it is permissible for a man to do so, what had been the ends of Providence in the persecutions against the faith.[21]

[15] Chr. Marcéchal, *La Dispute*. . ., p. 226.
[16] J. Poisson, *Le Romantisme social de Lamennais*, Paris, 1931, p. 254.
[17] *Réflexions sur l'état*. . ., p. 38.
[18] Ibid.
[19] Ibid., p. 97
[20] Ibid., p. 6.
[21] Ibid., p. 4.

Again, in speaking of the apparent illogicality of the official encouragement of the unbelieving "philosophes" by the absolutist regimes during the 18th century, he proposes that "history will reach the cause of this prodigious blindness only by interrogating Providence and by meditating upon its profound designs".[22]

This bold proposal "to interrogate Providence" by a self-styled "feeble historian of the sufferings of the Church"[23] is remarkably illustrative of Lamennais' unchanging and constant desire to view the whole of reality and to grasp it in its totality. Although he admits that it is not possible for man "to imagine the why and the because" of the truths contained in the infinite domain of the Supreme Being, "he can, at least, and this is sufficient for him, conceive the necessity of them".[24] This necessity of which man should be aware is not the necessity of the unintelligible nor is it to be seen as a fatalistic recognition of a sort of overwhelming destiny, for Lamennais clarifies his position in the same context by stating that "I do not fear to advance that there is not one mystery in the Christian religion which cannot be thus demonstrated by reason".[25] It is revealing to note that the theme of utility—religion is necessary because it is essential to the social order—dominates the interest of Lamennais in the various apologetical notes and writings before the publication of the *Essai sur l'indifférence*.[26]

[22] *Réflexions sur l'état . . .*, p. 31.

[23] Ibid., p. 71.

[24] Ibid., p. 99.

[25] Ibid., p. 99 (A most interesting and previously unedited rough draft of a chapter on "Miracles" prepared for the *Essai sur l'indifférence* ... by Lamennais has been published by L. Le Guillou, *L'évolution de la pensée religieuse de Félicité Lamennais*, Paris, 1966, Appendix 14, pp. 437-439. This text is an excellent example of Lamennais's employment of the argument that the necessity of an action, once admitted, is evidence of its natural and, thus, reasonable character. Miracles are necessary to accredit a divine revelation; therefore, miracles can be shown to be reasonable or, at least, compatible with a natural order which itself is inconceivable without revelation. It is interesting to note here a certain similarity, admitting, of course, the wide differences in approach and basic points of departure, between the mennaisian apologetic and the semi-rationalism of Georges Hermes and his followers in Germany. The apologetic of Hermes was inspired by the aim of showing that Christian faith imposes itself upon the human spirit with "eine absolute Notwendigkeit", see R. Aubert, *Le problème de l'acte de foi*, Louvain, 1958, Chap. III, Article III, "Au XIXᵉ siècle—Rationalisme et fidéisme", pp. 102-112. The spirit of the Enlightenment, although violently rejected by Lamennais, was not entirely absent in his apologetic any more than it was missing from the efforts of his contemporaries in German-speaking nations, Hermes and Günther.)

[26] P. Lavedan, "La Mennais et Jean-Jacques Rousseau", *Mercure de France*, Paris, 16 mars 1914, p. 314.

In these various assumptions the outlines of a philosophy that is at once intellectualist and pragmatic begin to take form. There is an ultimate reasonableness underlying human affairs which is presupposed and which is to be found only with the aid of the authority of religion. He is an intellectualist insofar as he holds firmly to the possibility of being able to discern the pattern of Providence, the source of all truths and history, and pragmatic insofar as he will rely heavily upon the social results of ideas as the measure of their truthfulness.

Looking back upon the Revolution, quite obviously, for Lamennais at this moment, a social catastrophe, he sought to show how erroneous ideas necessarily result in such vast and desolating disruptions.

> There is in man a rectitude of spirit, a natural logic, which does not permit him to separate himself even partially from the truth: it is necessary that he continue the route once he has started on it; and error is really so dangerous because, sooner or later, all of the consequences are necesarily derived from it.[27]

The most clear historical example of this maxim is to be found in the historical evolution of the principle of private interpretation of the Sacred Scriptures inaugurated by the Protestant Reform. This is the root-error through which the Protestant Reformers "established anarchy in principle in the Church and in the State".[28] The doctrine of popular sovereignty is seen as inextricably related to the Protestant notion of private judgement.[29] Philosophy, considering the individual reason to be the final arbiter of truth, joins the Reformers in a common rejection of authority.[30] Lamennais considers the advance from Protestantism to rational philosophy to skepticism to be a perfectly logical development in the history of an error.[31] The French Revolution is the "final consequence and necessary result of their maxims".[32]

What is extremely pertinent in this concern about the origin and growth of error is Lamennais's essentially optimistic view of the whole, based upon his unlimited confidence in a beneficent and, finally, logical Providence. The Protestant Reformation did not require a

[27] *Réflexions sur l'état...*, pp. 51-52.
[28] Ibid., p. 7.
[29] Ibid., p. 47.
[30] Ibid., p. 44.
[31] A. Feugère, *Lamennais avant l'Essai sur l'indifférence*, Paris, 1906, p. 83.
[32] *Réflexions sur l'état...*, p. 7.

Luther; it had had a deeper cause and had been prepared for long in advance.[33] Like all persecutions, it served a divine purpose. From a providential optic, "one would see that each error produces the development of a truth, each crime gives birth to a virtue".[34] There is an almost mechanical balance of forces in the universe, a self-correcting moral order directing all of history. The history of the Church must be seen in the light of the controversies and heresies which have the divinely given role of forcing the Church to explicitate the truth contained in revelation but previously formless or hidden.[35] Similarly to the past persecutions, one certain effect of the most recent, the Revolution, will be to open new possibilities for the growth of doctrine.[36] This remarkable fixation upon the notion of the rapport between history and doctrinal development situates Lamennais in a position of openness to the evolutionary concepts of history so current among the Romantics. Much more will be said concerning the mennaisian philosophy of history and concerning the "apocalyptic moment"[37] or the function of evil in the universe in subsequent chapters.

Réflexions sur l'état... is primarily a book in which Félicité and Jean-Marie summarize the results of their readings. Félicité is very much under the influence of Bonald who, for him, has prepared "a new route open to the defenders of Christianity".[38] This influence is seen most clearly in the emphasis which Lamennais places upon the relation between religion and the political order.[39]

> ... I cannot resist bringing to the attention of the reader the constant rapport of religious and political principles during the course of the French Revolution. In 1791, presbyterianism in the Church concurred with democracy in the State; in 1793, the destruction of all cult with the abolition of all government; in 1795, a government without unity and without consistency with a vague and ˙feeble religion, or Theophilanthrophy; finally, in 1800, the Catholic religion and the unity of power are together re-born, and the authority of the head of the

[33] *Réflexions sur l'état...*, p. 9.
[34] Ibid., p. 4.
[35] Ibid., p. 6.
[36] Ibid., pp. 98-100.
[37] The notion of the "apocalyptic moment" as the "Funktion des Bösen in der Weltgeschichte" was developped by W. Gurian in "Lamennais", Perspektiven, Heft 3, Mai 1953, and is treated in K. Jürgensen, *Lamennais und die Gestaltung des Belgischen Staates*, Wiesbaden, 1963, pp. 20-21.
[38] *Réflexions sur l'état...*, p. 99.
[39] Chr. Maréchal, *La jeunesse...*, p. 237.

Church, like that of the head of the State, acquires, in a corresponding proportion, a new degree of force necessary to the re-establishment of religious and political order.[40]

Lamennais's initial retreat from this position of Bonald on the rigid parallelism of the religious and political will be discussed in the section immediately following. In 1809, he accepted it integrally. In a similar manner, he ascribes to the bonaldien thesis on the nature of power. "... *All power comes from God* and there alone is found the reason of power and of obedience without which society cannot exist".[41] Lamennais will never disavow this notion but its application will be profoundly modified. The newest spokesman of the traditionalist reaction is also beholden to Maistre for his reliance upon the idea of a transcendent Providence working in history.[42]

A more original thought, although not entirely so, is his recognition of indifference in religious matters as a type of persecution against religious truth and as an effect of the Revolution and revolutionary ideology.[43] There is no detailed analysis of religious indifference such as he will undertake in the *Essai sur l'indifférence...*, but he warns against the "modern politicians who see in religious disputes only quarrels over words because they only see in religion itself but a name".[44] These advocates of tolerance equate truth and opinion and, in so doing, actually persecute the truth.[45] Have they not seen the evil social effects of theological errors? Had not Jean-Jacques Rousseau's rejection of original sin produced the final subversion of society?[46] Men of government, in this instance, the Emperor Napoleon, should realize that "the unity of spirit, of views and efforts" required for society and the State "can be achieved only by a religious body".[47] With this as a basic principle, "the author, with a clairvoyance sharpened by all of the antipathy that he feels already for the spirits of moderation, analyzes ... tolerance whose evil effects he demonstrates".[48]

[40] *Réflexions sur l'état...*, p. 93.
[41] Ibid., pp. 84-85.
[42] A. Feugère, *Lamennais avant l'Essai sur l'indifférence*, Paris, 1906, p. 82.
[43] *Réflexions sur l'état...*, p. 99.
[44] Ibid., p. 49.
[45] Ibid.
[46] Ibid., pp. 50-51.
[47] Ibid., p. 75.
[48] A. Feugère, *Lamennais avant l'Essai sur l'indifférence*, Paris, 1906, p. 84.

This attack against any weakening of the religious bond—at this period he believed in the possibility of a harmonious union of Church and State[49] —is typical of the polemical side of Lamennais's character. He wrote with immediate purposes in mind. This quality, however, does not necessarily detract from the theoretical concerns of the author but it does explain some of the harshness and the sense of immediacy which appear in these pages. As early as 1809, certain definite characteristics of approach and certain theoretical committments make their shadowy appearance. Methodologically, he reveals a certain preference for the principle of non-contradiction, an unusual ability to reduce conflicting thoughts to mutually exclusive opposites thereby forcing an obvious either/or proposition to the fore. Although a certain dualism appears in his analytic procedures arising from this abrasive use of logic and, perhaps, from a certain "spiritualistic dualism"[50] in his own religious psychology, such does not lessen the unitary, synthetic nature of the metaphysics which he takes as his point of departure and as the end to be attained in his philosophical efforts. Another methodological characteristic is his reliance upon and use of history. His approach is not entirely positive but it is a shift from the traditional, non-historical method dominant in the seminaries and philosophy manuals of the period. The relationship between the mennaisian methodology and doctrine will be treated more extensively in subsequent chapters, particularly, Chapter Five; our treatment here is simply to show the elements of continuity in his thought.

In résumé, Lamennais may be seen, from the date of his earliest publications, as theoretically committed to a sort of ontologism styled on the philosophy of Malebranche and to the social theories of Bonald. These preferences are not purely theoretical for they arise from a religious preoccupation which is constantly in the foreground of his concerns. Reverse the secular trend, restore religious and social authority, return man to God, these are the goals of the co-author of the *Réflexions sur l'état...* Parallel themes and similar methods, sharply but unsystematically present at this stage, will be reasserted and employed with vigor in his later works.

---

[49] *Réflexions sur l'état...*, pp. 130-132.
[50] W. Gurian, "Lamennais", *The Review of Politics*, Notre Dame, Indiana, April, 1947, p. 212.

2. An early discussion of the nature of Spiritual Sovereignty

The co-authored *Tradition de l'Église sur l'institution des évêques* referred to earlier[51] has never figured prominently in the studies on the genesis and evolution of mennaisian thought largely because of the fact that Lamennais himself seemed to disassociate himself from this ambitious work of pre-ordination days. It was never included in his collected works as was the jointly written *Réflexions sur l'état...* Aside from this difficulty, the very nature of this three volume inquiry into the canonical and historical question of Papal rights in the nomination of bishops seems to separate it from the mainstream of Lamennais's posterior endeavors. It is a work of historical erudition on a technical point of ecclesiology and is not as directly philosophical and social as are the later writings of Félicité. *Tradition...*, however, does have very definite ideological overtones which are of interest in our study. These are to be found particularly in the Introduction where he establishes the principles of the research undertaken and the aims to be attained.

Several factors had intervened between the publication of *Réflexions sur l'état...*, 1809, with its more benign attitude towards the Empire[52] and the appearance of *Tradition...* in 1814. The rude treatment of Pope Pius VII by the Emperor and the imperial government's administrative coercion of the Church awakened in the Lamennais brothers a lively reaction.[53] Félicité even complains bitterly of government censorship in his correspondence with Jean-Marie during this epoch.[54] In the crucible of historical events, as will be the case in the future, a new horizon opened for Félicité which he was not loathe to accept.

The ostensible aim of *Tradition...* was to combat the claims of the Gallican theories concerning the limits of Papal authority. It would be useful here to elucidate, briefly, the characteristics of this theory to which Lamennais was to show such unrelenting antipathy. A very useful distinction between theological and political Gallicanism has been advanced which clarifies considerably the study of this tendency.[55] Theological Gallicanism arose out of the conflicts

---

[51] See Chapter One, I, "Life and Works of Félicité Lamennais".

[52] *Réflexions sur l'état...*, pp. 93-93; 97.

[53] A. R. Vidler, *Prophecy and Papacy*, London, 1954, p. 54.

[54] Letter from Lamennais to his brother, Jean-Marie, 7 juillet 1814, reproduced in A. Blaize, *Œuvres inédites de F. Lamennais*, Paris, 1866, T. I, p. 149.

[55] C. Butler, *The Vatican Council 1869-1870*, Westminster, Maryland, 1962, p. 27.

concerning Papal authority during the Council of Constance (1414-17). It is essentially a theory of ecclesiology proposing the theory of conciliar supremacy in ecclesiastical matters. The theory survived, particularly in France, thus the name "Gallican", and received its classical exposition in Bossuet's *Defensio Declarationis Conventus Cleri Gallicani.*[56] The ecclesial organization for the Gallicans was not simply monarchical in the sense of an absolute monarchy in the spiritual realm but a monarchy limited by the episcopate which also claimed direct succession from the Apostles. For this reason, the Gallicans conceded the Papal nomination of bishops as a privilege and not as a right.[57]

Lamennais in *Tradition...* will deal directly with this question, privilege or right, concerning Papal installation of bishops; but he is more deeply concerned with the ramifications of political Gallicanism. This particular tendency emerged out of the innumerable conflicts between temporal princes and the Papacy over the extent and the limits of the spiritual authority of the Church in the temporal order. The victory of Philip the Fair of France over Pope Boniface VIII was a triumph for the principle of the independence of the secular authority in the temporal sphere. The theory is quite similar to theological Gallicanism since it is directed as well towards the limitation of Papal authority. In choosing to combat both forms of Gallicanism, Lamennais set himself in opposition to a powerful tradition within the French Church on the crucial question of the relations between Church and State.[58]

To treat of this problem, the author of *Tradition...* directs himself specifically to the nature of the Church and her spiritual authority. Although there is an a priori position to defend, that of ultramontanism, "the method is positive and historical".[59] He is determined to settle the long-discussed problem of Papal rights in episcopal nominations in favor of the Papacy and against the claims of the Gallican canonists. Although it is best "to consider the government of the Church in itself, in its primitive institution and successive developments, such as history has made them known to

[56] C. Butler, *The Vatican Council 1869-1870*, Westminster, Maryland, 1962, p. 31.

[57] M. Dubruel, "Gallicanisme", *Dictionnaire de Théologie Catholique*, T. VI, Paris, 1925, col. 1098-1099.

[58] P. Janet, *La Philosophie de Lamennais*, Paris, 1890, pp. 38-41.

[59] E. Hocedez, *Histoire de la Théologie au XIXe siècle*, Paris, 1948, T. I, p. 101.

us",[60] he had no illusions concerning the possibility of a purely historical approach.[61] Historical facts can be manipulated: the final proof will be determined by meditating the "invariable principles of the government of the Church".[62]

Lamennais's reflections upon the Church are of importance in this study since they will help to shed light upon his understanding of the Church-State relationship. In view of his religiously-based social philosophy of a later period, these earlier definitions of spiritual sovereignty may be looked upon as source elements. In face of a society that had lost its cohesion and unity, Lamennais saw in the Church the model of social perfection and unity. The Christian religion alone had solved the problem of constituting a society which embraces all men, epochs and civilizations. It has united the nomad and the farmer, the ignorant and the sage. The Church has brought about an ordering of the erratic and destructive in human tendencies through a social control linked to its expiatory functions.[63]

How has this unity been achieved? "First, and before all else, through the effects of the promises and the assistance of its Divine Founder; but also through the very force of its constitution".[64] This marvelous constitution is monarchical but not in the same fashion as temporal monarchies because of the difference between the mode of selecting a Pope and the hereditary principle of secular monarchies and, more importantly, because of the difference in jurisdictions. In the kingdoms of the world, the ruler is not the judge; but in the spiritual realm the Pope is ruler and judge.[65] The basis of this spiritual monarchy of the Church is to be found in John XVII, 11, "Ut unum sint. . ."[66] The Church exists that men may be spiritually united and its monarchical constitution is such as to fulfill this end, "without a center, no unity; without graduated sub-ordination, no center; no subordination without a head. . ."[67] Religion means unity; the Catholic

---

[60] *Tradition de l'Église sur l'Institution des Évêques*, (3 Tomes) Liège, 1814, T. I, p. IX (This first edition of *Tradition*... appeared without the names of the authors, probably, due to the political situation at the time of publication. Subsequent citations will be simply under the title *Tradition*...).

[61] Ibid., p. XVIII.

[62] Ibid., p. XXI.

[63] Ibid., T. I, p. VIII.

[64] Ibid.

[65] Ibid., p. IX.

[66] Ibid., p. X.

[67] Ibid.

Church, as seen in *Tradition. . .*, is the vibrant, living manifestation of this primary mennaisian principle.

> . . . the purpose of religion is none other than to tend towards a most perfect unity. The cooperation of the human will with Divine action. . . has thus for its final goal *perfect unity: "ut sint unum"*. On this question, as on many others, Lamennais did not evolve as much as one might believe.[68]

The power of the Church, emanating from its divine mission, the source of its sovereignty or claim to jurisdiction, is absolute in the sense that it is independent of men; but such power is not arbitrary since it is limited by divine law and its own juridical structure.[69] The emphasis here, in opposition to the Gallicanism of the French State and, to a wide extent, the French clergy and hierarchy, is upon the liberty of the Church to conduct its own affairs without intervention from the temporal authorities. The Church is "totally independent of temporal powers"[70] in his estimation; but he feels that his theory will go unheeded. Governments have already ceased to believe; power is no longer a matter of legitimate rights for it has become merely the exercise of force by particular interests.[71] Although the Empire has disappeared, the same tendencies favoring a temporal subjugation of the spiritual are dominant in political circles.[72] Lamennais does not advocate any radical separation between the two jurisdictions; on the contrary, Princes should realize that any weakening of the spiritual sovereignty of the Roman Pontiff is a weakening of their own temporal jurisdiction.[73] The Popes have no direct nor indirect power over temporal rulers in temporal affairs; they cannot free subjects from their bonds of loyalty and obedience to their rulers.[74] It can readily be seen that such notions were not revolutionary in any way as stated in *Tradition. . .*; these same ideas, however, when subjected to future consideration within the context of Lamennais's evolving notion of a spiritual society, will undergo considerable change.

To Lamennais, the error of Gallicanism, a refusal to admit the absolute and independent character of spiritual authority, which Lamennais locates in the Papacy, is the theological counterpart of the

---

[68] J. Poisson, *Le romantisme social de Lamennais*, Paris, 1931, p. 175.
[69] *Tradition. . .*, T. I, p. LXVI.
[70] Ibid., p. XCII.
[71] Ibid.
[72] Ibid., p. LXXVI.
[73] Ibid., T. I, p. XCIII.
[74] Ibid., p. LXXII.

political aberration contained in the doctrine of popular sovereignty. Thus, he recognizes in Rousseau's theory of social contract or government by the consent of the governed a necessary and logical consequence of the conciliar theories.[75] Is it not possible to derive the propositions of the *Contrat Social* from the revolutionary theology of Gerson and Richer?[76] Developed by the Protestant Reformers and adapted by Rousseau, the conciliar theory upon which Gallicanism is founded is at the origin of the social chaos and the tyranny of the masses experienced in the Revolution.[77] Legitimate authority and the just exercise of power can only be restored by a return to the "simple, pure and eminently social Catholic doctrine" which teaches political society to revere a power which proceeds from and is responsible to God alone.[78]

On the face of it, the notions of ecclesial rights are within a certain traditional frame and, in themselves, without reference to future developments, could scarcely be seen as harbingers of a future liberalism. Nonetheless, *Tradition...* prepared the way for that "ultramontanism of spiritual opposition"[79] which distinguishes Lamennais from the other traditionalists, such as Bonald. Seen in the context of the historical situation which arose with the experience of the Empire and its final collapse, *Tradition...* offers a rather radical departure from the ecclesial theories dominant in the French seminaries and among the professors of Saint-Sulpice. The phenomenon of a purely secular state in the form of the Napoleonic Empire had presented a new danger to organized religion which Lamennais had seen, perhaps, with greater perception than most.

> In effect, the Concordat had underlined a great change. A certain equilibrium which should have been established between the Papacy and the monarchy was no longer possible... Temporal power was no longer Christian. Confronted with a structurally non-Christian society, the Church regrouped her forces.[80]

While invoking the political theory of power taught by Bossuet and Bonald, the Lamennais brothers begin to separate themselves notably

---

[75] *Tradition...*, pp. XCXV-XCXVI.
[76] Ibid., p. CVI.
[77] Ibid., p. XCXV.
[78] Ibid., p. CXV.
[79] Chr. Maréchal, *La Dispute* ..., p. 78.
[80] J. Audinet, "L'enseignement *De Ecclesia* à Saint-Sulpice sous le Premier Empire et les débuts du gallicanisme modéré", published in *L'ecclésiologie au XIXᵉ siècle*, Paris, 1960, p. 123.

from monarchical absolutism defended in this theory and implicit in the moderate Gallicanism of the chief disciples of Bossuet, the school of Saint-Sulpice.[81] The rigid parallelism between the natural constitution of the ancient monarchy and the traditional constitution of the Church upon which Bonald elaborates his political theory in *Théorie du Pouvoir* is finally rejected by Lamennais as an inadequate if not erroneous understanding of the nature of the relationship between the civil order and the spiritual realm. Ultramontanism or the conferral, in principle and in fact, of the unique spiritual sovereignty to the Papacy is the only correct manner, in the eyes of the two brothers, of understanding the independent and original character of the Church. The Church can no longer be considered as dependent upon a particular political order but is capable of standing apart no matter how unnatural or chaotic the civil order becomes. If the Church and the State are viewed as parallel structures, there is a tendency to see them as mutually dependent, and, to some extent, equal partners in the global religio-political reality. Assuming equality of rights in the partnership, the Gallican Church had conceived it justifiable to reserve for itself certain liberties which, in effect, for Lamennais, were not liberties but restrictions upon the spiritual freedom of the universal Church. Without, as yet, ceasing to be a monarchist, Lamennais displays a marked hostility towards an ecclesial theory which would seem to bind the fortunes of the Church too closely to those of the royalty and monarchical institutions. It would not be pretentious to see in this ultramontane attitude the origins of a more flexible approach to Church-State relations than had been previously advanced. The liberty of the Church and not the restoration of the Bourbons is paramount. If the return of the ancient monarchy would simply result in the re-establishment of the old Gallican restrictions, what would the Church have gained by its support of the monarchy or what would have civil government learned from the experience of revolution and despotism?

With this in mind, it is possible to see germinating in Lamennais's thought the identification between the spiritual independence of the Church and religious liberty which he will make at a later date. The very statement of the problem of the spiritual liberty of the Church in reference to the civil order resembles more the liberal approach to the whole question of sovereignty than that of the classically

[81] Chr. Maréchal, *La jeunesse,* ... p. 415.

conservative political theorists. Like the liberals, he shows a marked suspicion of temporal political authority. Bossuet, who inspired Bonald on his notions of power,[82] considered the Church to be an authority which teaches men to respect all laws and authority while, for Lamennais, the Church becomes "an authority limiting another."[83] What E. Faguet means by this descriptive phrase is not that Lamennais had found himself in accord with Montesquieu on the notion of the separation of powers but that he had, through theoretically establishing the independence and superiority of the spiritual order, namely, the Church, established limits to the pretentions of secular powers. In fact, within the framework of his theologically inspired principle of the unique spiritual sovereignty, the secular exercise of temporal power is seen more as a function within a morally united whole than as an independent entity. *Tradition...* does not provide any satisfactory answers to the particular questions of just how the accord between the two orders is to be harmoniously achieved; but the principles upon which the accord is to be fashioned are such that the liberty of the spiritual will be insured and, with it, a just ordering of the whole attained. The authority and the leadership of the Church are spiritual in character and need not be feared by temporal authorities for if the Church is free to exercise her mission men will be taught to willingly obey just rulers and the imposition of violence will become unnecessary.

> ... an empire is not founded upon the point of a sword. Even for despotism another basis is necessary and this basis is the duty to submit imposed upon the passions by conscience. If one departs from this, only violence remains which is another sort of weakness, the most dangerous of all...[84]

Tradition... leaves many questions unanswered for those who seek a fully formed philosophy of liberty or fully developed political solutions for, indeed, neither is present. Nonetheless, with *Tradition* ..., an affirmative step towards the doctrine of liberty espoused in "L'Avenir" was firmly taken. Just as the liberals restrict the authority of the State in the name of individual liberty, Lamennais places boundaries upon the temporal in the name of the higher spiritual order. Who will establish limits on the interference of the Church in the temporal order? Lamennais does not propose to answer this

[82] H. Laski, *Authority in the Modern State*, New Haven, 1919, p. 142.
[83] E. Faguet, *Politiques et Moralistes du XIX° siècle*, Paris, 1898, T. II, p. 109.
[84] *Tradition...*, p. XCXIV.

question. In the ideal order, the Church would limit her activities to the purely spiritual, which is not clearly defined by Lamennais; and, in the practical order, it was not the Church but the State which had to be feared. Lamennais might well be accused of a lack of realism but his intention in *Tradition*. . . is highly theoretical; subsequent writings will alone show the practical impact of the ultramontanism of this early work. Quite similar in some aspects to the position which Maistre will take some years later, the ultramontanism of *Tradition*. . . was sufficiently radical and new as to open the way to those important advances in Lamennais's thought which will be discussed in subsequent chapters.

II. THE FIRST MENNAISIAN SYNTHESIS:
ESSAI SUR L'INDIFFÉRENCE EN MATIÈRE DE RELIGION

1. *Philosophy of Religion: A Social Apologetic*

a) *Tolerance and Indifference*

While in Paris in the company of his spiritual director, following his return from London, Lamennais, although suffering torments of doubt and spiritual abandonment, considered writing a major work in defense of revealed religion which he fancied calling *Esprit du Christianisme* in imitation of Chateaubriand's enormously successful *Génie du Christianisme*.[85] Plunged into a spiritual darkness following his ordination to the priesthood,[86] Lamennais became the object of special concern to Abbé Teysseyre of Saint-Sulpice. Both Carron and Teysseyre were cognizant of the great talent of the newly ordained cleric and they sought to free him from his doldrums by engaging him in apologetical writing.[87] Teysseyre was pressing him as early as 1815 to finish his projected *Esprit*. . .,[88] but, by 1817, Felicité

[85] See the note concerning the mention of *Esprit du Christianisme* in Lamennais's correspondence, A. Feugère, *Lamennais avant l'Essai sur l'indifférence*, Paris, 1906, p. 226; for the influence of Chateaubriand on Lamennais confer A. Viatte, *Les interprétations du catholicisme chez les romantiques*, Paris, 192, pp. 97-136; also, L. Le Guillou, *L'évolution de la pensée religieuse de Félicité Lamennais*, Paris, 1966, pp. 51-57.

[86] A. R. Vidler, *Prophecy and Papacy*, London, 1954, pp. 64-67.

[87] Concerning the role of Abbé Teysseyre of Saint-Sulpice during this period, confer Chr. Maréchal, *La jeunesse*. ., pp. 595-598.

[88] Letter from Lamennais to his brother, Jean-Marie, Paris 31 décembre 1815, reproduced in A. Blaize, *Œuvres inédites de F. Lamennais*, Paris, 1866, T. I, p. 248.

announced to his brother the coming publication of the *Essai sur l'indifférence...*[89]

Apparently more modest in dimension than his dreamed of *Esprit*, the *Essai sur l'indifférence...* became nonetheless a work of capital importance in the literature of religious apologetics. The book is important not only because it was the first public recognition of a figure who did, in fact, dominate by acceptation or by rejection the geography of French Catholicism for a quarter of a century; but also, and more interestingly from the point of view of this study, because the *Essai sur l'indifférence...* is the point of departure of the mennaisian philosophical synthesis containing the basic principles of his social and political philosophies, a positive philosophy of religion, his theory of certitude and the foreshadowings of a philosophy of history. Even his harshest critics make note of the importance of this work. "It is there that we can draw out the content of his thought".[90] On the basis of this work, his reputation was established.

The very title of this four volume undertaking is somewhat peculiar to the modern reader and does require a certain clarification. In selecting the word "indifference", Lamennais joined himself to a certain tradition of apologetical writing which reaches back to Pascal and the problem which he raised in *Pensées* concerning those morally indifferent individuals who live without knowing God- and without searching for Him.[91] Pascal did not limit his concern to the lazy or to the sensuous, but, more directly, he turned his attention to those who, by conviction, profess neutrality in religious matters.

> There is an open war between men in which each one must take part and necessarily ally himself either with dogmatism or with Pyrrhonism. Indeed, whoever considers remaining neutral will be a pyrrhonian par excellence. This neutrality is the essence of the cabal.[92]

The word "indifference", however, has a longer history dating to the Stoic notion of αδιάφορον, referred to as "indifferens" by Cicero, and

---

[89] Letter from Lamennais to his brother, Jean-Marie, Paris 22 avril 1817, reproduced A. Blaize, *Oeuvres inédites*, Paris, 1866, T. I, p. 278.

[90] J.-M. Querard, *Notice Bibliographique des ouvrages de M. de La Mennais de leur réfutations, de leurs apologies et des biographies*, Paris, 1849, p. 17.

[91] For an interesting discussion of this apologetical development confer A. Monod, *De Pascal à Chateaubriand: les défenseurs français du christianisme de 1670 à 1802*, Paris, 1916.

[92] B. Pascal, *Œuvres Complètes*, Paris, 1963, p. 515.

meaning that which belongs neither to vice nor to virtue.[93] In the scholastic tradition, following St. Augustine's distinction between "libertas" and "liberum arbitrium", the terms "libertas indifferentiae" or "liberum arbitrium indifferentiae" were employed to describe the latter, which, according to Augustine, identified the human psychological possibility of choosing between good and evil.[94] The general acceptance of the term "liberty of indifference" is "the power of acting without any other cause than the very existence of this power, that is, without any reason relative to the content of the act accomplished".[95] This particular psychological description of liberty or free will aroused considerable philosophical discussion during the 17th century which cannot be entered into here.[96] What is worth noting, however, is that this liberty of indifference, described by Descartes as "this indifference which I feel when I am not drawn towards one side rather than towards another by the weight of some reason" and as "the lowest form of liberty",[97] became associated with the notion of religious liberty, that is, the freedom of the person to accept or reject religious beliefs.

To the defenders of religion and of tradition, the demands for tolerance in matters of religious belief as advanced by such thinkers as Bayle and Voltaire were based upon skepticism which made of religious dogmas the objects of an indifferent choice. Commenting on Bayle's *Commentaire philosophique*, L. Le Guillou has the following perceptive remark.

> . . . in preaching tolerance, in the very name of the inaptitude of man to attain with certitude religious truth, Bayle removes from Catholicism or any other religion the right to affirm itself as the only and unique truth.[98]

Tolerance thus becomes the solution of the epistemological problem posed by the claims of religion and it is this problematic

---

[93] See article, "Indiferencia", *Diccionario de Filosofía*, (ed. José Ferrater Mora), Buenos Aires, 1965, T. I, p. 929.

[94] See article, "Albedrio (libre)", ibid., pp. 61-62.

[95] See article, "Liberté", Sens F., *Vocabulaire Technique et Critique de la Philosophie*, (ed. A. Lalande), Paris, 1962, p. 563.

[96] For a discussion of "libertas indifferentiae", confer R.-M. Mossé-Bastide, *La liberté*, Paris, 1966, particularly, Chapitre III, "La liberté d'indifférence", pp. 35-49; also Chapitre V, "Les degrés de la liberté", pp. 58-66.

[97] R. Descartes, *Meditationes de Prima Philosophia*, Paris, 1963, Meditatio IV, pp. 57-58.

[98] L. Le Guillou, *L'évolution de la pensée religieuse*, Paris, 1966, p. 20.

which was taken up by a series of religious apologists during the century and a half preceding the appearance of the *Essai sur l'indifférence*... In the language of the theological schools, "indifferentismus" was equated with "tolerantismus".[99] The lively polemic between Bossuet, on the one hand, and the Protestant defenders of tolerance, Basnage, Burnet and Jurieu, on the other, produced an abundance of tracts on the question of indifference and religious liberty which were familiar to Lamennais.[100] Chr. Maréchal has discussed in detail the writings of Feller, Regnier, du Voisin and Bergier, Catholic apologists of the late 18th century who continued to center their apologetics upon the necessity of refuting a skeptically based neutrality towards the claims of religion.[101]

Although most Catholic writers of the period were quick to distinguish various meanings of the word tolerance, equating only dogmatic tolerance with systematic indifference,[102] a new element had been added to the discussion by J.-J. Rousseau. In Rousseau's religious testament, *Profession de Foi du Vicaire Savoyard*, he reiterates his rejection of any such distinction in the notion of tolerance. "The distinction between civil tolerance and theological tolerance is vain and puerile".[103] He does no more than re-affirm the principle of complete tolerance of all beliefs and cults, except those which maintain doctrinal intolerance, which he had already established in *Contrat Social*, Livre IV, chap. VIII. This new affirmation of tolerance as a positive value, however, is made in the context of a vigorous criticism of the religious indifference erected into a system by the "philosophes". This position is taken in defense of religions, that is, the natural religion developed throughout *Profession de Foi*..., and of religious sentiment.[104]

As is clear from the numerous citations in the four volumes of the *Essai sur l'indifférence*..., Lamennais had an extensive knowledge of the history of the problem which he proposed to treat and of its

[99] See P. Richard, "Indifférence religieuse", *Dictionnaire de Théologie Catholique*, T. VIII, Paris, 1923, col. 1580-1594.

[100] A review of the literature emanating from this dispute may be found in Chr. Maréchal, *La jeunesse*..., p. 576.

[101] Chr. Maréchal, *La jeunesse*..., pp. 550-576.

[102] An example of this classical distinction may be found in Bergier, *Traité historique et dogmatique de la vraie religion*, (T. IV), Paris, 1780; confer Chr. Maréchal, ibid., pp. 572-574.

[103] J.-J. Rousseau, *Profession de Foi du Vicaire Savoyard*, (ed. P.-M. Masson) Collectanea Friburgensia, Paris, 1914, Fasc. XVI, p. 423.

[104] Ibid., pp. 449-469.

literature. Abbé Teysseyre not only provided Félicité with the inspiration to undertake the work but also with a collection of notes and materials on the subject whose value and importance have been studied elsewhere.[105] There are strongly traditional lines of approach in the writings under consideration, but these are united to the original insights of the author producing a literary result which is both eloquent and pregnant with possibilities of more radical developments.

Quite apart from the succeeding additions to the *Essai sur l'indifférence...*, the first volume may be considered as a whole, a self-sufficient unit.[106] Within this volume, there is a natural division which can be made, following the methodology and logic of the author, between the series of chapters dealing with the various systems of indifference, namely, Chapters I through VIII, and the concluding chapters, IX through XII, which contain the positive elements of a philosophy of religion and a concomitant social theory. The book is well structured in that the first part furnished Lamennais with a state of the question, that is, with a problem and with historical data for the constructive enterprise of the second part. It is important to bear in mind that the author did not consider his work as an apology for Christianity but, rather, as a pre-apologetic, a work that would establish the conditions for a theological explication of the claims of religion.[107]

There is a fundamental assumption at the outset of Lamennais's theorizing through which he gives priority to moral affirmation over psychological description. He does not attempt to describe the nature of human motivation nor its operational stages but assumes that men act because of their beliefs. Both the individual and the masses react on the basis of what they believe since their very passions are determined by these beliefs.[108]

> If the belief is pure and true, the general tendency of actions is correct and in harmony with order: if the belief is erroneous, the actions, on the other hand, are degrading for error viciates and truth perfects.[109]

Taking this assumption as a base, it becomes obvious that social and

[105] These manuscripts have been partially published with commentary by Chr. Maréchal, *La jeunesse...*, pp. 598-633.

[106] Ibid., p. 636.

[107] *Essai sur l'indifférence...*, T. I, pp. 57, 197.

[108] Ibid., T. I, p. 2.

[109] Ibid.

political change parallels a change in belief. "The logic of nations is as rigorous as the very truth of God."[110] Every doctrine is necessarily true or false and, consequently, has good or evil effects upon the individual and upon society. Thought and action are subject to a general law of conservation of intelligent beings which is founded on truth and which is the basis of the spiritual order. Although he does not explain this law at the preliminary stage, Lamennais attempts to show how it works by recalling some examples from history to demonstrate the interaction of beliefs and events.[111]

The noble beliefs of the Christian peoples have, in fact, produced beneficial results for society. But, if history clearly shows the effect on the social order of the tendency within Christianity towards perfection, it reveals as well the dire results of the rejection of religion and of the principle of authority. By substituting the contrary principle of private judgement or individual reason for the authority of superior reason, a theory of revolution had been introduced into the social organism which tends to destroy order, annihilate the spirit, and reduce all to chaos.[112] Such is the lesson to be learned from the fall of the Roman Empire and the French Revolution.[113] Following the experience of history, how is it possible to consider any religious, social, or political doctrine as indifferent to society?[114]

When one holds that a doctrine is neither true nor false, that is, the subject is not compelled by the internal veracity or falsity of the object of his thought to accept or to reject it, the object under consideration is indifferent to the subject. If there were such a condition of the intellect and will as absolute indifference, it would be a final de-humanization for "it is the extinction of all sentiment of love and of hate in the heart due to the absence of all judgement and belief in the spirit".[115] But is it not inherent to man to judge, to love, to hate? What is indifference but the domain of ignorance and of matter? There is nothing indifferent to pure spirit. The partial indifference

---

[110] *Essai sur l'indifférence...*, p. 4.

[111] Ibid., pp. 2-5.

[112] Ibid., pp. 5-9.

[113] Ibid., Lamennais devotes much of Chapitre II, (T. I), "Considérations sur le premier système d'indifférence, ou sur la doctrine de ceux qui, ne voyant dans la religion qu'une institution politique, ne la croient nécessaire que pour le peuple", pp. 21-43, to an analysis of the fall of Rome and its likeness to the French Revolution.

[114] Ibid., p. 9.

[115] Ibid.

which man experiences with regard to certain realities is a result of human limitations; but it is not for man to glory in this material restriction proper to the human condition. Lamennais emphasizes the role of the will and the relationship between morality and knowledge. Indifference is as much a product of moral degradation as it is indigenous to the human condition. This moral atrophy of the will to overcome doubt is both individual and social, a progressive expansion of evil vertically and horizontally across governments and down through the levels of society.[116] The result of this "fatal disposition" is a "new genus of persecution and trial under the name of tolerance" which Christianity must suffer.[117]

Error no less than truth is subject to the laws of logic. Once a false principle is avowed as the cornerstone of an intellectual edifice, it becomes systematized. To be sure, there is an indifference of hatred and an indifference fostered by apathy; but these are not the major concerns of the *Essai sur l'indifférence*... The author wishes to engage in discussion the proponents of the three systems of indifference which he identifies as atheism, deism, and heresy, three types of opposition to the principle of authority.[118]

The burden of the following seven chapters is to expose and to demonstrate the internal contradictions of three systems, which, in the opinion of Lamennais, allow for areas of indifference or of tolerance in matters of religious belief. Interestingly, he proceeds from the ultimate degree of indifference, which is also the final stage of philosophical skepticism, to the lesser degrees to be found in the theories of natural religion and in Protestantism. Quite simply, he attempts to show the futility of any effort to save some degree of authority once the subordination of reason to authority has been rejected in principle.

There is no need to enter into a detailed analysis of Lamennais's treatment of the various systems or to recount in detail his refutation of each. Summarily, for our purposes, it will be sufficient to point out the important elements which open the way for the elaboration of his own theory concerning the relationship between religion and society. Methodologically, however, it would be worthwhile noting that, although he makes ample use of history, he gives priority to logic.

[116] *Essai sur l'indifférence*..., T. I, pp. 10-17.
[117] Ibid., p. XXX.
[118] Ibid., pp. 18-19.

> In opposing philosophical doctrines, the only difficulty is to reduce
> them to precise and fixed terms. Once this is done, everything is done:
> they refute themselves.[119]

"Religion is found near the cradle of all peoples, as philosophy is found near their tomb".[120] First, he speaks of religious unity for it is precisely the primitive religious spirit which is at the source of nationhood; when the principle of action or faith is subverted by the philosophical spirit, there is a proportional decline in social unity. This unifying and vitalizing function of religion is acknowledged even by the political theorists who are categorized by Lamennais as atheists or advocates of political indifference. Under this designation, he refers particularly to the political theorists such as Hobbes who regard religion as both a political institution and the product of political inventiveness.[121]

To prove the purely hypothetical character of the various theories concerning the purely human or legislative origins of religion,[122] Lamennais relies upon the traditionalist doctrine concerning the absolutely primordial character of the religious and social realities.

> Society is the natural state, the necesary state of man: outside of
> society, he can neither reproduce nor conserve himself. Thus, religion,
> without which society could not exist, is as necessary as society: thus,
> religion is not a human invention.[123]

What is this religion that has always existed? It is the ground or the pre-existing background against which the legislators have worked. The grand legislators of the ancient peoples desired to give law a sanction vested with a sacred character; but this was not an artificial construction. They founded their laws upon a deeper source of obligation, the religious sentiment proper to man and to peoples. The laws and rules of a society may manifest multiple variations; but the fundamental dogmas of the universal religion upon which they are based are always the same. No sentiment in man is more natural and more indestructible than that of religion.[124]

An internal contradiction plagues all theories of political

---

[119] *Essai sur l'indifférence...*, T. I, p. 87.

[120] Ibid., p. 21.

[121] Ibid., p. 33.

[122] Concerning the reaction of German and French scholars in the early Romantic Period to the Enlightenment theories of religion, see J.-R. Derré, *Lamennais, ses amis et le mouvement des idées à l'époque romantique*, Paris, 1962, particularly, Chapitre I, "Les nouvelles composantes de la pensée religieuse", pp. 5-66.

[123] *Essai sur l'indifférence...*, T. I, p. 45.

[124] Ibid., T. I, pp. 46-48.

philosophy which postulate that the political order, formed on the basis of a contract or a free association, is the source of religion. On the one hand, religion is considered as necessary, while, on the other hand, neither its truthfulness nor falsity can be vouched for. While insisting that religion is required for the social and political control of the people, the politically atheistic theorist would exempt those who may not believe, usually, the intellectual and social elite. Could there be a greater disregard for the rights of man and for the demands of the human spirit than this purely utilitarian treatment of religion? The religious fact cannot be subordinated to the political structure for religion sustains this very structure just as it does morality and social cohesion. By emphasizing the contradiction which he finds in the utilitarian notions of political philosophy, Lamennais logically reduces such theories to what he considers to be a condition of absolute indifference or complete liquidation of human liberty. This goal achieved, he leaves the final refutation of absolute indifference for the second part of the first volume.

Rousseau, more than any other modern thinker, was aware of the dangers of the purely political approach. He rejected the atheism and the merely functional role of religion implicit in Hobbes and in the utilitarian theories. He founded his critique upon his own concept of the universality of religion. There is a pragmatic approach at the core of Rousseau's objection which Lamennais enthusiastically adopts.

> ... in matter of doctrine, truth is inseparable from utility... in other words, every doctrine advantageous to mankind, and, with greater reason, every necessary doctrine is a true doctrine. I ask the reader to keep this observation in mind.[125]

This correlating of utility and truth, which Lamennais finds so valuable in the religious instruction of *Émile*, is a reversal of the doctrines of naked utilitarianism. For Lamennais and Rousseau a doctrine is useful because it is true and necessary which is not quite the same as saying that it is simply efficacious without regard for its veracity or falsity. Lamennais considers that Rousseau was the very "organ of universal tradition"[126] when he spoke in defense of the anteriority and the universality of religion and of religious sentiment.

Although the Vicar of Savoy stoutly professes both the necessity and ultimate truthfulness of religion, he finds it impossible to recognize

---

[125] *Essai sur l'indifférence...*, T. I, p. 65.
[126] Ibid.

this religion in any of the existing institutions. He subordinates positive religion to a natural ethic founded upon an interior conscience and religious sentiment. At this point, Lamennais takes issue with the mentor of his youth. Both Rousseau and the English Deists, in trying to save religion, fall into a contradictory position of positive and negative indifference. All religions are simultaneously true and false. Insofar as all religions are manifestations of a universal religion, they are true; but since no particular religion is free from prejudice and error, all religions are also false. For Lamennais, the key to the difficulty lies in the inability of Rousseau and the Deists to rely upon any other criterion for accepting the one, true religion than individual sentiment or reason.[127]

The apparently tolerant and generous attitude displayed in this second system of indifference, or as Lamennais calls it, that of natural religion, is the result of subordinating dogma to ethics and of emptying cult or worship of any meaning beyond the purely political or ceremonial. The universal religion of which they speak is itself void of content. There is no agreement among the Deists on the dogmatic symbol of their universal religion, thus, they can only advise that men lead moral lives and that they be tolerant. Lamennais objects strongly to the priority granted to the ethical among the Deists. Does not morality become as problematic as dogma once the same rational critique is applied to the natural ethic as it has been applied to dogma? Again, the real difficulty lies in the rejection of authority and in the unique reliance upon individual reason. Philosophy, contends Lamennais, has never understood the real nature of the "noble faculty" of reason. The attempts of Rousseau and the Deists to save something of the authority of a natural religion degenerate into absolute indifference.[128]

As a final preparation to his positive exposition, Lamennais undertakes a confrontation with the various systems within Protestantism which had been proposed to re-establish Christian unity on the basis of a common symbol of faith containing only the necessary, fundamental articles acceptable to all Christians. The need for unity in the fundamental, as a means of stemming the growing dis-memberment of the Protestant communion, and the recognition of variety in ecclesial manifestations of Christianity following the

---

[127] *Essai sur l'indifférence...*, T. I, pp. 63-85.
[128] Ibid., pp. 87-128.

Reformation, gave birth to a certain ecumenism which was very much a matter of discussion in the late 17th century.[129]

Lamennais resurrects the famous polemic between Jurieu and Bossuet for the purposes of analyzing Jurieu's doctrine of the fundamental articles. In spite of the French Protestant theologian's effort to save something of the doctrinal content of Christianity as a basis of unity, Jurieu failed completely because his rules for recognizing which dogmas are actually fundamental — quite like the elements of Rousseau's natural religion —[130] are ultimately subject to a rational control or a purely human authority which can give no guarantee of infallibility. The fundamental error, the negation of any authority superior to individual reason, remains in the system of Jurieu; thus universal tolerance, a "general and necessary law of error",[131] cannot be avoided. In showing how Protestantism must arrive at skepticism and, consequently, absolute indifference, Lamennais sustains his central thesis, "every religious system founded upon the exclusion of authority contains within its womb atheism and, sooner or later, will give birth to it".[132]

"Libertas indifferentiae" cannot be applied to matters of religion. Recalling Pascal, the ardent Breton finds it impossible to accept the notion that the judgement to be made in the big questions concerning the existence of God and the immortality of the soul can ever be a simple choice between two doubts. Eternity and momentary joy cannot be equated. Since prudence itself requires that man investigate the claims of religion, Lamennais proposes as a working hypothesis with which to introduce his positive pre-apologetic, the following:

> ... If there is a true religion, it is of infinite importance to the individual and to society; thus, there is an infinite interest to find out which religion is this true religion.[133]

All systems of indifference in matters of religion can be refuted by demonstrating the absurdity of the two principles which he sees at the origin of indifference, namely, man has no interest to assure or to inform himself of the truth of religion, and, it is impossible to discover

[129] Concerning this movement see P. Hazard, *The European Mind, 1680-1715*, London, 1964, particularly, Chapter 5, "An Attempt at Reunion and What Came of It", pp. 253-274.
[130] P. Janet, *La Philosophie de Lamennais*, Paris, 1890, p. 24.
[131] *Essai sur l'indifférence...*, T. I, p. 184.
[132] Ibid., p. 136.
[133] Ibid., p. 222.

the truth in such matters. The plan of Lamennais is quite simply to prove the contrary of these two positions by making evident the overwhelming importance of the religious fact for man and for society, and by showing that it is not only possible to discover religious truth, but also, that every man has the infallible means to do so.[134] Lamennais's refutation of the first principle will be treated in section "b" immediately following, "Religion and Society", while the treatment of the problem of certitude will be studied in Part 2 of this Chapter, "A Social Theory of Certitude".

b) *Religion and Society*

An element which is at times overlooked in studies on the thought of Félicité Lamennais is the profoundly spiritual inspiration of his world-view. Greater justice has been done to the translator and commentator of one of the most popular French editions of the *Imitation of Christ* in more recent writings.[135] The religious anguish which hovered over his meditations and dominated his thoughts removes him from an easy categorization under the wing of political traditionalism. It is imperative to be aware of this profoundly spiritual concern when attempting to interpret his political and social ideas.[136]

Due to his emphasis of the social and collective aspects of the human experience, both in his understanding of religion and in his epistemology, the fact that his point of departure in thematizing on social realities is one of spiritual interiority, is often overlooked. Lamennais begins his consideration of the relationship between religion and society by first trying to understand the significance of religion for the individual. His initial steps are those of a descriptive anthropology. In a portrait of man that is remarkably Augustinian in content and in development, Lamennais sees man as a creature of longing and desire, a seeker for that happiness which eludes him and yet is the cause of his inner dynamism.[137] Men tend, almost uni-

---

[134] This purpose is stated clearly in the Introduction, ibid., p. XXXVII.

[135] See particularly, L. Le Guillou, *L'évolution de la pensée religieuse de Félicité Lamennais*, Paris, 1966.

[136] K. Jürgensen, *Lamennais und die Gestaltung des Belgischen Staates*, Wiesbaden, 1963, pp. 8-9.

[137] Concerning, St. Augustine's religious anthropology, see *Obras de San Agustin*, Madrid, MCMLVII, Introducción General, XI, "*Las Confessiones o el genio religioso de San Agustin*" by V. Capanaga, O.R.S.A., pp. 176-210.

versally, to identify this happiness with peace, the peace which St. Augustine had accurately defined as "tranquillity of order".[138] "There is no happiness but in order; order is the source of the good".[139]

Explaining his own understanding of "tranquillity of order", Lamennais sees man as a "being in relation", thus, as a creature whose happiness or perfection would depend upon his knowledge of the essential relations which correspond to his open-ended, innate desires and upon an harmonious ordering of these desires among themselves and to the whole. The whole is an englobing, intelligible Nature which is not a construct of the human spirit but an immutable system of laws willed by an Intelligent Will. These laws, which, when observed, produce peace and harmony, are not invented but are recognized through their antiquity, universality, simplicity and durability.[140] The mennaisian theory of knowledge, the actual explanation of just how this recognition or discovery takes place, was not elaborated in the first volume of the *Essai sur l'indifférence...*, nonetheless, the famous theory of common sense pervades the evolving social metaphysics.[141]

Like Rousseau, Lamennais attempted to restore a metaphysical meaning to the word "nature", that is, some idea of a rationality and a teleology in creation, but he avoided the confusion which surrounds the use of this term in the works of Rousseau by refusing any fictional or mythical employment of the term.[142] Nature is not an imagined primitive state but is the totality of that which is given in human experience and which reveals an underlying reasonableness. It includes both physical and cultural realities.

> Religion, morality and society are general facts, like weight; general laws independent of our ideas, such as the laws of equilibrium...[143]

---

[138] *Essai sur l'indifférence...*, T. I, p. 224.

[139] Ibid.

[140] Ibid., pp. 224-226.

[141] Lamennais had already expressed the thematic of his apologetic and his concern for the epistemological foundations of the act of religious faith in his *Lettres à un Anglais sur le Protestantisme*, (1815), published in A. Blaize, *Œuvre inédite de F. Lamennais*, Paris, 1866, T. II, pp. 271-284.

[142] Concerning the idea of Nature in Rousseau, confer J. Maritain, *The Social and Political Philosophy of Jacques Maritain*, (ed. J. W. Evans and L. R. Ward), New York, 1955, pp. 106-108; and P. Arnaud, et al., *Rousseau et la Philosophie Politique*, Paris, 1965, particularly, "Hors des ténèbres de la Nature", by Pierre Burgelin, pp. 21-34.

[143] *Essai sur l'indifférence...*, T. I, p. 227.

Into this already constituted world comes man whose very being is "to know, to love, to act".[144] These powers or faculties of man are ordained to objects beyond themselves and are subordinated the one to the other. In a quite traditional fashion, he holds knowledge precedes love as love precedes action. It is important, however, to recall this fundamental intellectualism of Lamennais in the light of the severe criticism to which he has, at times, been subjected.[145] As E. Faguet has so clearly noted, charges of skepticism are not quite accurate when addressed to Lamennais.[146] Man must know the good which he is to love; the will must be under the guidance of the intellect. Without this harmony between intellect and will, disorder arises. So central is knowledge of the essential laws of the Divine order of Nature in Lamennais's view that sin is identified with ignorance.[147] The real question is, how does man obtain this essential knowledge?

Can philosophy tell man about the truths of his deepest nature, about the good to be sought, or about obligations to fulfill? The tragedy of man, expressed in Rousseau, is that he is possessed of this innate desire for happiness but seeks it through philosophy alone where it is not to be found. Lamennais attempts to demonstrate the bankruptcy of what he calls "irreligious philosophy"[148] in its efforts to elaborate an adequate anthropology and ethic for man. The multiplicity of the philosophical opinions on the end of man and the meaning of happiness is compared unfavorably to the unitary teaching of religion that "God is the sovereign good of man".[149] If the desire for happiness is not a vain illusion, and if life has any meaning, only religion can offer that knowledge and perfection which man seeks.[150] Philosophy fails to recognize the "essential law of order"[151] which is the requirement of human nature to believe. The phenomenon of faith is introduced as a connatural to finite man in his quest for the infinite; the psychology of belief had been singularly neglected by the

---

[144] *Essai sur l'indifférence...*, T. I, p. 227.
[145] See L. Le Guillou, *L'évolution de la pensée religieuse de Félicité Lamennais*, "Les adversaires", Paris, 1966, pp. 199-222.
[146] E. Faguet, *Politiques et Moralistes du XIXe siècle*, Paris, 1898, T. II, pp. 91-92.
[147] *Essai sur l'indifférence...*, T. I, pp. 228-229.
[148] Ibid., p. 251.
[149] Ibid., p. 256.
[150] Ibid., p. 257.
[151] Ibid., p. 260.

rationalists and underlies their failure to attain certitude in questions of religion.[152]

Up to this point, Lamennais's method is largely descriptive. He simply announces a priori positions which are somewhat negatively proved by showing that the alternatives are untenable. Blondel strongly criticized this "propensity to interpret all in function of the attitude of the adversary".[153] Nonetheless, it should be pointed out that Lamennais's method, not yet fully achieved in the first volume of the *Essai sur l'indifférence...*, was limited by his own purposes. First, he was more concerned with giving his readers cause to reflect than with presenting them with a finished whole;[154] second, being conscious of the historical inter-relationship of ideas, he sought to discover as much as he could in the arguments of his adversaries to support his own position;[155] and, third, he was determined to show throughout the first volume, in terms both stark and vivid, the confusion of opinions which reigned in the France of the Restoration.[156]

If it has been shown, at least by applying a pragmatic measure, that philosophy cannot aid man in his search for happiness, it is equally powerless to bring society to a knowledge of those essential relations which form its natural constitution and which conserve it in a state of order and peace. Quite the contrary, philosophy is destructive of the happiness of peoples and of the stability of order for it has substituted fictive constructs of the spirit for social reality.

> One of the most dangerous follies of our era is to imagine that one can constitute a State or form a society from one day to another just as one builds a factory. Man does not make societies; nature and time, working together, create them.[157]

The necessity of religion is a "truth of fact as ancient as the world".[158] The mennaisian approach, which the author identifies with common sense, is to observe the facts of history, the beliefs and customs of all times and societies in order to discover the laws which

---

[152] Concerning the adaptation of the psychology of belief, see A. Fonck, "Le Menaisianisme," *Dictionnaire de Théologie Catholique*, Paris, 1925, T. XVIII, 2ième Partie, col. 2513.

[153] M. Blondel, "Une note inédite de La Mennais contre la Religion naturelle et le 'Semi-déisme'", *Annales de philosophie chrétienne*, Paris, sept. 1912, T. XIV, p. 617.

[154] *Essai sur l'indifférence...*, T. I, p. 302.

[155] Ibid., p. 342.

[156] Ibid., passim.

[157] Ibid., p. 272.

[158] Ibid., T. I, p. 271.

are expressed in these facts. Facts are the "abbreviated expression" of principles which are rooted in time and in peoples.[159] Certainly, the desire of peoples for peace, like the desire of man for happiness, is a principle revealed by an acute observation of history and of the social realities. Is this peace not the result of order and is not unity the very essence of order?[160]

When disorder is present, such as in the case of a revolution, a reason must be sought; a society has become dislocated, de-naturalized. The study of the political philosophers reveals that they have been unable to provide man with a basis for political power, liberty and morality. A remarkable critique of the *Contrat Social* is made by Lamennais in this context which will be treated in a more detailed fashion in III, 1, a, b, of the following part "Elements of Transition". Not only do such theories produce contradictions when internally examined but they also generate an unavoidable chaos and de-humanization when applied.

The evidence of fact, which enables the observer to discover the necessity of unity in the social order and to discern the causes of disruption when fundamental truths of tradition or common sense are ignored, is not yet the demonstration of the ultimate reason for this necessity of an ensemble of laws and relations called religion. The proof that religion alone conserves societies and conducts them to happiness is not uniquely dependent upon a study of the results of religious influence in history. The first cause of these results is to be discovered on the level of metaphysics.

> Order, taken in its widest sense, is the ensemble of relations which derive from the nature of beings; and these relations are truths, since they exist independently of the thoughts of the spirit which considers them. Every truth flows from God because *He is the One Who is*, that is, being par excellence without restriction and without limit, or infinite truth; and when He decided to produce the entire creation, it could only be a magnificent manifestation of a part of the truth included in the Divine Being.[161]

The above doctrine might well be considered the basic ontological thesis undergirding Lamennais's expanding synthesis. It is simply stated as a theoretical principle which can explain the first cause of that necessity of religion which the facts of history point to. This

---

[159] *Essai sur l'indifférence...*, T. I, p. 161.
[160] Ibid., pp. 271-275.
[161] Ibid., pp. 348-349.

affirmation remains undemonstrated; a sufficient demonstration, within the framework of mennaisianism, would still require the development of the epistemological criteria for establishing the truth of such theoretical positions which is the burden of his famous second volume. It should be remembered that, although Lamennais speaks with assertativeness in describing the ontological foundations of religion and, in turn, the religious source of society, he remains on the level of hypothesis until he can show that man has the means of attaining to a certain knowledge of the universal spiritual society whose existence he presumes.[162]

If such a religion, emanating from God, can be assumed, it is readily apparent that order proceeds from a higher, immutable source beyond the particular wills of individuals. In this conceptualization, there is no society without the primordial religious bond with God; "... it is necessary that man be first in society with God in order that he may be able to enter into society with his fellow-creatures".[163] Given this universal order, power or the right to command and the duty to obey, necessary functions in any society, are founded upon a sovereignty which is not arbitrary force but the just and necessary Will of the Supreme Intelligence in which order originates.[164] More will be said concerning this in the section "Liberty and Order". In a similar fashion, law becomes the expression of justice and love rather than the will of the strongest or the mere legal protection of particular interests.[165] Since religion renders possible the sacrifice of self, the essential factor of the true social union, an ethics of service and love, supported by the religious eschatology of Christianity, becomes meaningful.[166]

The dogmas of this hypothetical religion, in this case, Catholic Christianity, are truths of the highest metaphysical importance. In his final chapter, Lamennais proposes that the close harmony between the natural and the supernatural, upon which his theory of society hinges, is verified in the fact of the Incarnation.[167] The Mediator, Christ, is the bond of that spiritual society which is the original spiritual reality uniting mankind and the Divinity.[168]

---

[162] *Essai sur l'indifférence...*, T. I, p. 449.
[163] Ibid., p. 276.
[164] Ibid.
[165] Ibid., p. 365.
[166] Ibid., pp. 376-385.
[167] Ibid., p. 446.
[168] Ibid., pp. 420-421.

We have passed over the many proofs from historical experience which Lamennais evokes to establish the necessity of religion for law, morality and society in order to arrive at the fountainhead of his synthesis, the idea of the existence of God contained in the primitive revelation. Volume I of the *Essai sur l'indifférence...*, which was to establish Lamennais among the first generation of the Romantic thinkers, ends with an eloquently descriptive theodicy. To the general reader of the time, he simply added brilliant form to traditional apologetical arguments, but, as time would prove, there were also raised several disquieting notes concerning the role of reason and the nature of faith.[169] The more properly philosophical treatment of the problem of certitude will be the subject of the following section.

2. *A Social Theory of Certitude*

Writing to his uncle, Robert des Saudrais, in 1818, the widely acclaimed author of the enthusiastically received Volume I of the *Essai sur l'indifférence...*, was keenly aware that he was about to launch much more revolutionary concepts in the second volume which he was in the process of preparing.

> It will be of less popular interest than the first but newer and more important. With God's help, I hope to reduce these individuals so proud of their reason to this alternative, either not to say *I am* or to say, I believe in God and the rest of the Symbol even to the last syllable.[170]

The vision of Lamennais was both ambitious and clearly philosophical as he undertook the task of socially reconstituting human certitude. Lamennais sought "to produce a work of truth, a new Christian philosophy... above all in the second volume of the *Essai* and in the *Défense de l'Essai*, both published in 1820".[171]

It has been shown how, in Lamennais's view, the three systems of indifference proceed from one another and how all equally repose on the false principle of individual judgement as the ultimate measure of truth. Volume II was conceived to prove what had already been concluded in Volume I, namely, that anyone who searches for truth with the aid of reason alone is necessarily bound to arrive at

---

[169] L. Foucher, *La Philosophie Catholique en France au XIXᵉ Siècle*, Paris, 1955, pp. 33-34.

[170] Letter from Lamennais to Robert des Saudrais, 25 janvier, reproduced in A. Blaize, *Œuvres inédites de F. Lamennais*, Paris, 1866, T. I, p. 320.

[171] L. Foucher, *La Philosophie Catholique en France au XIXᵉ Siècle*, Paris, 1955, p. 35.

skepticism.[172] His task is not, however, uniquely that of criticism; his purpose is also constructive. The much controverted second volume of the *Essai sur l'indifférence*. . . contains the famous mennaisian method of authority conceived to be a sweeping reversal of the Cartesian method of reason. It was not to be considered a new method for it was the method that had always given men the basis of their certitude, the common sense of mankind.[173]

The philosophical justifications of the various systems of indifference might be reduced to what Lamennais considers the three general systems of philosophy. Materialism, idealism and modern dogmatism are logical developments of the principles of certitude chosen by the inventors of these systems. Sense, sentiment, or reason, the normally accepted human sources of knowledge, have been isolated and taken as the loci of the principle of certitude in the various philosophies following Descartes. Lamennais dismisses rather summarily the possibility of accepting the senses or sentiment as sources of certain knowledge on the basis of the utter relativity of our experiences on these levels.[174] It is the philosophical method of Descartes, as is plainly clear from the clarifications contained in *Défense*. . ., which offers the principal target for Lamennais's critique. Descartes was to philosophy what Luther had been to religion. As Lamennais explained to Maistre, "since reason has declared itself sovereign, it is necessary to go straight to it, to seize it upon its throne and force it under pain of death to prostrate itself before the reason of God".[175]

> The originality of Abbé Lamennais was to see that which was seen by neither Bonald nor Maistre nor by the apologists of the 18th century; namely, if the authority of the Church was to be saved, it was necessary to return to the source of modern skepticism that is, to the principle of free examen, to the rule of evidence, to the authority of individual reason.[176]

The alleged distinction, attributed to Descartes, between the method of authority employed in theology and the method of reason or free examination used in philosophy and science, established, correctly or incorrectly, for the succeeding generations a certain antinomy between

---

[172] *Essai sur l'indifférence*. . ., T. I, passim.

[173] Ibid., T. II, p. 21.

[174] Ibid., pp. 4-11.

[175] Letter from Lamennais to Maistre, 2 janvier 1821, reproduced in A. Feugère, *Lamennais avant l'Essai sur l'indifférence*, Paris, 1906, p. 288.

[176] P. Janet, *La philosophie de Lamennais*, Paris, 1890, p. 27.

authority and liberty which had innumerable consequences in the areas of ethics and politics.[177] The trajectory of this evolution cannot be traced here; it is simply to be noted that Lamennais was acutely aware of the epistemological roots of the problem of authority. In granting priority to the problem of certitude in his own philosophizing, Lamennais remained true to the Cartesian tradition; indeed, he re-opened the question exactly "where Descartes had posed it at the beginning of his doctrine with the methodic doubt and his notions on the criterion of evidence".[178]

As early as 1815, in a letter to a young Anglican under religious instruction, Félicité had indicated his preoccupation with the problem of certitude and of its relation to religious belief.[179] Having affirmed the importance of religion to man and to society in the first volume, he must now show that the true religion can be known with certitude. Reason alone, the reason of Descartes' "Cogito", is insufficient. Our experience clearly shows us the frequency with which our reason errs. Human judgements are relative to environment, to temperament, to prejudices and to innumerable factors which tend to relativize human knowledge. In the pages in which Lamennais paints such a somber picture of human reason, he does little more than repeat notions from Montaigne and Pascal.[180]

His critique of Descartes is more original. Trying to avoid skepticism and to break through the methodic doubt, Descartes announced his famous "Cogito ergo sum" which for Lamennais was an illicit leap across an "immense abyss".[181] Lamennais justifies his position more amply in the *Défense*...

> ... in his celebrated passages, he [Descartes] recognizes that his certitude depends upon the certitude of the existence of God, and of the impossibility that he will deceive us. Whoever says, *I am*, before being certain that God is and that he cannot deceive us, thus affirms without any reason to affirm.[182]

The basic error in the Cartesian approach is to isolate the subject from anterior social reality by means of a systematic elimination of all

---

[177] Chr. Maréchal, *La dispute...*, p. 235.
[178] P. Janet, *La Philosophie de Lamennais*, Paris, 1890, p. 28.
[179] See footnote 141.
[180] *Essai sur l'indifférence...*, T. II, pp. 11-15.
[181] Ibid., p. 16.
[182] Lamennais, *Défense de l'Essai sur l'indifférence en matière de la religion*. Œuvres Complètes, Paris, 1836-1837, T. V, p. 101 (In subsequent citations this work will be referred to simply as T. V...).

beliefs arising from the authority of others through universal doubt. For Lamennais, this is an unrealistic fiction for in order to say "I think" one must be in possession of language, a social reality which cannot be put into brackets. In trying to find truth in the individual reason, Descartes has failed to take into account the primordial faith which englobes and precedes acts of the reason.[183]

Since our study is not essentially connected with the total technical development of Lamennais's theory of knowledge but rather its influence in his political and social thinking, it will be impossible to enter into the details of Lamennais's refutation of Cartesianism. The discussion on this point continues to the present time, an important discussion, since it concerns the correct understanding of Lamennais's own theory of knowledge and, from the historical point of view, the validity of such charges as "skeptic" and "fideist" to which he has been subjected.[184] For the purposes of this study, it will be sufficient to continue with a brief exposition of the theory of common consent or superior reason.

There is a method available and easily accessible to all men by which they may come to have certain knowledge. "Common consent, sensus communis, is for us the seal of truth; there is no other".[185] While Lamennais uses the same term, "common sense", as the Scottish critics of Hume, there is a notable difference in meaning. Reid, the principal figure of the Common Sense school in Great Britain, adhered to an introspective, psychological approach to show the inconsistency of skepticism with the lived experience of the thinking subject. Every man experiences innumerable "common sense" assurances.[186] With Lamennais, the term "sens commun", as will be seen shortly, has a more sociological signification.

Universal doubt as held by the skeptics is a fiction, for all men, even the skeptics, believe countless truths which are presupposed by life itself. We believe irrevocably in our own existence, in our senses and in our ability to think before we even reflect upon the nature of these

---

[183] *Défense de l'Essai sur l'indifférence en matière de la religion...* pp. 102-103, also T. II, p. 87.

[184] Chr. Maréchal has contended at the conclusion of his long research on Lamennais that the charge of "fideism" is incorrectly attributed to Lamennais; confer "La vraie doctrine philosophique de La Mennais", *Revue Philosophique*, Paris, 1949; and "La Mennais, Descartes et St. Thomas", *Revue Philosophique de la France et de l'Étranger*, Paris, 1947, pp. 443-451. For a critique of Maréchal's thesis, see L. Foucher, *La Philosophie Catholique en France au XIXᵉ siècle*, Paris, 1955, pp. 42-50.

[185] *Essai sur l'indifférence...*, T. II, p. 21.

[186] Chr. Maréchal, *La Dispute...*, pp. 221-222.

realities. Even the physical sciences depend upon a primordial, unquestioned faith in unproven principles and in the very possibility of a science.[187] The fact of faith in the daily lived experience of all makes it evident that, first, the tendency to believe is connatural to man, and, second, the general reliance upon that which is universally held for certain is itself the natural or "common sense" criterion of truth.[188] The act of faith is simultaneous with all human actions; even in denying faith, the skeptic admits it for he uses language and believes in the liaison between word and thought and in the possibility of communicating his denial.[189]

A descriptive psychology justifying the priority of faith as the already given in any process of human reasoning was provided by Bonald and Rousseau, from the one a theory of language and from the other an enriched notion of sentiment.[190] Reason is described in the mennaisian psychology as a double faculty, the faculty of knowing and the faculty of reasoning. The faculty of knowing is the very basis of the intellectual life; it is prior to and makes possible the operations of the faculty of reasoning. We know before we can reason about what we know. Using Tertullian's definition of man as "animal rationale, sensus et scientiae capacissimum", Lamennais sees the human intellect as the capacity to receive truth.[191] There will be an important refinement of this notion of the double faculty of reason in Gerbet's *Sommaire d'un système des connoissances humaines* which was adopted by Lamennais and which had im-

---

[187] *Essai sur l'indifférence...*, T. II, pp. 20-25.

[188] Ibid., p. 131; also T. V, pp. XVII; 105.

[189] Ibid., T. V, p. 103.

[190] Chr. Maréchal, *La Dispute...*, p. 257.

[191] *Essai sur l'indifférence...*, T. II, pp. 3-4. Although in later years, Lamennais was to acquire a certain knowledge of Kant and even to undergo a certain influence from neo-kantian currents, his basic distinction between the faculty of knowing and the faculty of reasoning does not seem to emanate from kantian sources. Historically, the distinction is due to the multiple influences on his thought of his early readings. Malebranche was certainly the source of his notion of a superior reason which both illuminates and supports individual reason while Rousseau's teachings on the importance of sentiment as a counter-weight to skepticism had undoubtedly given Lamennais the inspiration for his idea of a natural faith serving as the existential layer supporting the operations of the individual reason through its unquestioning adherence to a superior reason. It should not be forgotten either that Bonald dealt with very similar ideas and from the same sources. For an excellent discussion of the genesis of the mennaisian doctrine of common sense, consult, Chr. Maréchal, *La dispute...*, particularly, Chapitre III, pp. 233-259. A shorter, but, nonetheless, interesting account is given by L. Foucher, *La philosophie catholique en France au XIXe siècle*, Paris, 1955, pp. 42-47.

portant repercussions upon his valorisation of the role of reason.

There are no innate ideas in man but rather an inborn capacity to receive certain sentiments and necessary ideas.[192] The faculty of knowing is passive and leaves us open to the only source of our thoughts, social experience. Likewise, society provides us with the only criterion of truth possible to man, the authority of general reason or the common consent of mankind. For Lamennais, all philosophers previous to him, with the exception of the Fathers of the Church, particularly Augustine, and Bonald, had failed to fully grasp the social character of human knowledge and the authority which is proper to universal belief.[193]

The unique, ultimate object of our thoughts is that which is, the ontological to be. The most natural and illuminating thought is that of unlimited Being; it is the very basis of our intellectual life. Every time an atheist declares that something is, he is implying the existence of the infinite Being whom he explicitly denies.[194] Although this approach seems like that of a traditional ontologism, it is necessary to advance in our description in order to see the originality of Lamennais on this point.

The idea of being in no way arises spontaneously in man; it is spoken to him. Language is metaphysics since it is the general expression of being. When man speaks, he necessarily employs the verb "to be", but how could he have an idea of the word "to be", which expresses infinite Being, if this word were not given to him?[195] The verb "to be" is the "reason of language as the Substantial Word is the reason of infinite Being".[196] Through language, man's most social experience, God is in the discourse of the universe which unites, while unfolding, all that is. Bonald's thesis on the origin of language through revelation is broadened by Lamennais to support his own theory of common consent.

Just as the idea of the existence of God is the ultimate guarantee

---

[192] *Essai sur l'indifférence...*, T. II, p. 138.
[193] See the summary but interesting chapters of critique on Descartes, Malebranche, Leibnitz, Bacon, Pascal, Bossuet, Nicole and Euler in *Défense de l'Essai sur l'indifférence...*, T. V, pp. 19-74; Lamennais finds the source of the *"méthode chrétienne"* in the quotation from St. Augustine, "Naturae ordo sic se habet, ut, quum aliquid discimus, rationem praecedat auctoritas" (De morib. Eccl. cathol., cap II), ibid., pp. 43, 47.
[194] *Essai sur l'indifférence...*, T. II, p. 6.
[195] Ibid., pp. 79-80.
[196] Ibid., p. 79.

of truth for Descartes, so it is for Lamennais; but, with this difference, man attains to a knowledge of God, implicit in any linguistic communication, through the universal testimony of mankind. All thought is a participation in the thought of God, similarly to the doctrine of Malebranche who discovered the great truth that "human intelligence is and can only be a participation of the Divine intelligence".[197] If, however, Malebranche had pushed his analysis further and had considered the means by which God enlightens man, he would have, in the opinion of Lamennais, arrived at the true philosophy which is religion.[198] The illumination of the human intellect by the Divine Word is not particular but social, for man is, by definition, a social being bound to God and to other by word or by language which is the organ of common or general reason. Revelation is thus in conformity with the very nature of man. Being, the idea of the existence of God, and the laws of being, the fundamental and necessary relations binding contingent beings to one another and to their Source, are revealed to man through tradition, the transmission of the primitive revelation of God.[199] For the traditionalists, therefore, the common sentiments of mankind, since they reflect the infallible Divine Reason revealing itself in history, become the criteria of certain knowledge.

Everything is rooted in the past; words of authority go back to the Divine Word and are unerringly believed by succeeding generations. The certitude of witness is substituted for the certitude of evidence. Universal reason is expressed in the "multiplicity of uniform testimonies" which "constitutes ... the certitude of knowledge".[200] It is not necessary nor possible to fix rigidly the number of testimonies bearing witness to a certain truth in order to consider it universal. The authority of the witness proposing, his truthfulness and disinterestednes, all these are factors which give credence to a certain proposition. Ultimately, certitude is not found in the most evident proposition, that is, in terms of clarity and distinctness, but in the testimony of the witness of the greatest authority.[201] Lamennais attempts to identify, logically and historically, the Roman Catholic Church as the authority which expresses and conserves the tradition

---

[197] *Essai sur l'indifférence...*, T. V, p. 30.
[198] Ibid.
[199] Ibid., T. II, p. 85.
[200] Ibid., p. 38.
[201] Ibid., T. II, pp. 40-55.

of mankind.[202] Within the limits of this study, it will be sufficient to simply state Lamennais's conclusion in this matter, that is, the role of the Church as the infallible teacher of humanity, without entering into the details of his arguments for this proposition. The principal notion to be kept in mind from the point of view of political philosophy is the centrality of the doctrine of common consent in the mennaisian structure. The political implications of this doctrine will be discussed in III, 2, of this Chapter.

III. ELEMENTS OF TRANSITION

1. *Liberty and Order*

The striking contrasts between the doctrines of "L'Avenir", which inaugurated Catholic Liberalism and which will be discussed in Chapter Five of this dissertation, and the doctrines espoused by Lamennais in the period of early Romanticism, which coincides with the publication of the *Essai sur l'indifférence*..., hold a perpetual fascination for all who attempt to undertake a study of the thought of this remarkable figure. A serious question arises concerning the unity and the seriousness of Lamennais's ideological evolution. Could he justifiably, in a philosophical sense, change in a short period of time from an openly accused theocrat who held tolerance in contempt to a champion of liberty, including religious liberty, as indeed, he was to become? To accuse Lamennais of charlatanism or vulgar opportunism would be patently incorrect and unjust. Quite the contrary is true; except for the brief period of wide acceptance following the publication of Volume I of the *Essai sur l'indifférence*..., he experienced only dismal sufferings both of mind and body as well as increasing hostility both inside and outside the Church for the positions he defended.

The reasons for the dramatic changes and the unusual evolution of mennaisian philosophy must be sought, therefore, within the thought itself. Given a certain organic law of thought, what are the elements in the conceptualizations of the early Lamennais which admit of progress and logical growth? Where are the open gaps in the notional structure of the *Essai sur l'indifférence*... which would allow new light

---

[202] See T. III Chap. XXI, "Première conséquence du principe de l'autorité: la vraie religion est nécessairement révélée de Dieu", pp. 1-19; and Chap. XXII, "Seconde conséquence du principe de l'autorité: le christianisme est la religion révélée de Dieu", pp. 20-31.

to penetrate? Which are the links which connect the principles defended and formulated between 1809 and 1823 with those of 1830? This concluding section of Chapter Three is an attempt to show which are, in the opinion of the writer, the elements underlying the transition, the principles of liaison within this period.

a) *Priority of Social Unity*

The ontological monism supporting Lamennais's world vision leaves both state and society without a reason for being beyond the context of religion. On the level of theory, he developed an epistemology which had its complement in a theory of society. His theory of knowledge reposes on faith and revelation; thus, society is indefinable outside of religion. Adopting a "totally social and historical conception of religion,"[203] Lamennais made of it the very basis of social solidarity. Given the essentially social definition of man, which we have seen already,[204] the problem of union in society is raised to the first rank as the principal problem of the political order.

> Society means union; whenever someone separates and becomes individual, at that moment, each finds it impossible to exist whence it follows that self-sacrifice, the only principle of order, is also the only means of conservation.[205]

This unity implies hierarchy, a relationship of the parts to the whole. The whole trajectory is lineal from man to family to particular society, that is, the state, and, thence, to general society or the union of intelligent beings with and under the sovereignty of God. If God is not recognized as the source and ruler of the social union, there is no society.[206]

> There is no social order without social hierarchy, without power and without subjects, without the right to command and the duty to obey.[207]

Such a unity goes far beyond simple social instinct; it is based upon truth itself and is thus metaphysical in origin. Unity is the "character of all that is true".[208] Social unity, if it is to be truly one, must be

---

[203] J.-R. Derré, *Lamennais, ses amis et le mouvement des idées à l'époque romantique*, Paris, 1962, p. 56.
[204] See Chapter Three, II, 1, b, "Religion and Society".
[205] *Essai sur l'indifférence...*, T. II, p. XI.
[206] Ibid., T. I, pp. 275-276.
[207] Ibid., T. I, p. 275.
[208] Ibid., T. III, p. 140.

founded upon truth; this truth is known through revelation. "Religion is a law, the first of all laws";[209] it is a law which "includes all truth and order; all that should rule the reason, the heart and the actions of man".[210] Religion is not then a matter of choice. Either religion is accepted through faith or social disintegration and death ensue.[211] Not only is religion necessary but this religion is the one, true religion. It is contradictory to speak of religions.[212]

The unity, necessity and truth of religion leave no place for that strange "state of suspension between contrary probabilities" or religious indifference.[213] Were such a state possible without social implications, the indifferent soul could be left to his unhappiness and doubt; but such is not the case. Through the imposition of tolerance, indifference, in fact, becomes the fundamental ideology of society. Since, however, indifference is no position at all, society is emptied of its content and meaning. In this connection, Lamennais comes to grips with the enormous problem of the multiplicity of religious beliefs in society. He does not propose a solution in the practical order but he seeks to provide the important, if negative, service of clarifying the problem. If toleration is based upon religious indifference, the only option open to the believer is to remain intolerant. Truth is the sovereign authority which cannot be rejected in order to make living more comfortable.

The strong position taken by Lamennais in the first volume of the *Essai sur l'indifférence...* was vigorously objected to by a Protestant minister, M. Vincent. The exchange between them was published by Lamennais in his second volume. M. Vincent accused Lamennais of confusing tolerance with indifference, a charge frequently repeated. Man is tolerant, argued the pastor, because opinions pertain to the conscience of the individual; no one is safe from error; all must hold one another in mutual respect. This position, for the unrelenting Breton, is nothing more than religious indifference. Religion is not opinion and the true believer cannot regard himself as open to error in this fundamental matter. Such an attitude of tolerance, although benevolent, could never lead to true unity.[214]

---

[209] *Essai sur l'indifférence...*, T. II, p. 176.
[210] Ibid., p. 193.
[211] Ibid., T. I, p. 44.
[212] For the formulation of Lamennais's argument see ibid., T. II, p. 102.
[213] *Essai sur l'indifférence...*, T. I, p. XXIX.
[214] Ibid., T. II, p. XXIX-LI.

The basis for social and religious unity cannot be established by a concord among men; they have no power to establish the limits of what may be tolerated and what may not.[215] Such an intransigent position on the level of the theoretical could not possibly be advanced without strong objections in a milieu that had long been habituated to plurality of fact if not of spirit. The liberals immediately discovered dangerous tendencies. Royer-Collard saw law subordinate to power and morality to religion as inevitable consequences of the author's premises. The less moderate liberals, such as Benaben and Senancour, questioned the theocratic character of the political theories embedded in the *Essai sur l'indifférence*... Order, in their view, is erected into a fundamental political principle simply to promote intolerance. A more perceptive critic, Ch. Loyson, discovered an important principle in Lamennais's staunch defense of religion as the source of all liberties but expressed wonder that the Breton priest had not seen positive and traditional values in the very institutions being advocated by the liberals.[216]

The theory of certitude, core matter of the second volume, brought forth more serious criticisms. Even those who could hardly be considered as opponents to the idea of theological intolerance were shaken by the seemingly, totally extrinsic character of certitude in the mennaisian epistemology.[217] It seems apparent that Lamennais leaves the subject without a proper identity or without subjective density. Individual judgement, the crucial issue in the scholastic discussion of the problem of tolerance,[218] is reduced to a secondary function of the reason by Lamennais. It becomes the operational activity of the faculty of reasoning which is already dependent upon the faculty of knowing.

> To judge is nothing other than to compare new ideas to ideas already existent in us —[which ideas]— are not themselves to be judged since they cannot be compared to anything anterior.[219]

The essential truths are within the reach of all. To believe or not to believe is basically an act of the will. "It is the will, a free will, which determines your beliefs."[220] The problematic of tolerance is shifted by Lamennais from the level of a correct or incorrect judgement to that

---

[215] *Essai sur l'indifférence*..., T. I, pp. 172-175.
[216] Chr. Maréchal, *La Dispute*..., pp. 33-60.
[217] L. Foucher, *La Philosophie Catholique en France au XIXe Siècle*, Paris, 1955, p. 48.
[218] L. Janssens, *Liberté de conscience et liberté religieuse*, Paris, 1964, pp. 9-15.
[219] *Essai sur l'indifférence*..., T. II, p. 90.
[220] Ibid., T. IV, p. 147.

of good or bad will. The moral emphasis is quite obvious. Error always implies a certain moral degradation, inherited or personal.[221] What becomes of the spiritual autonomy of the person within the mennaisian system of knowledge and in its complementary social cosmos? What is the consequence on the level of political theory of such a monistic social theory derived from the primacy of religion?

b) Christian Liberty

Certain key concepts present themselves to the researcher attempting to reconstruct the genesis of Lamennais's political thought, namely, his idea of equality, considerations on the nature of power, notion of spiritual society, definition of Christian liberty, doctrine of Church and State relations, and his epistemological theory of common consent. We will discuss briefly the first four ideas in this section since they are inter-connected facets of his doctrine of liberty and the implications for Church-State relations in the following section. Common consent, because of its pivotal position in the whole notional structure, will be treated separately.

The principal theoretical objection to the mennaisian theory of certitude is that it de-substantiates the individual.[222] The concentration on social solidarity and the close-knit mechanism of the whole moral universe seem to reduce the individual to being simply a cog in a geometric whole. The rigid organicism present in Lamennais's universal sociology does not leave, at first view, much autonomy to the participating subject. While he certainly did not conceive of the relationship between person and society, as, for example, Jacques Maritain, who sees the problem as one of relating a whole, the person, to another whole, society,[223] there is a definite indication in the *Essai sur l'indifférence...* of a profound concern for the integrity of the individual. It is well to remember that he makes his own, within limits, Rousseau's anthropology, particularly, the latter's idea of human equality.

---

[221] *Essai sur l'indifférence...*, T. III, p. 48.
[222] For a summary of these objections see L. Foucher, *La Philosophie Catholique en France au XIXᵉ siècle*, Paris, 1955, pp. 47-50; also L. Le Guillou, *L'évolution de la pensée religieuse de Félicité Lamennais*, Paris, 1966, pp. 199-222.
[223] J. Maritain, *The Social and Political Philosophy of Jacques Maritain*, New York, 1955, p. 85.

> What is it then when man himself presumes empire over man, his equal in right and, often, his superior in reason, enlightenment and virtue?... Certainly, I do not hesitate in the least to say with Rousseau: a great alteration of sentiments and ideas is necessary before one can reconcile himself to accepting his fellow creatures as master.[224]

If he had conceived of society as had the philosophers, he would have agreed with Rousseau that civilly constituted society was against Nature.[225] In contrast with the more pessimistic Hobbesian conception, Lamennais places himself in complete accord with the more democratic thinkers on the original equality of men. "Every created being", he affirms, "is in a natural independence from all other created beings".[226] The principle of fundamental equality of origin and destiny among men is the essence of the idea of humanity, an ideal born of Christianity.[227] C. Carcopino considers this notion of equality to be "at the base of the social concepts of Lamennais ... without which there could not logically be any question of liberty and fraternity".[228] Once accepted as an ideological point of departure, equality demands that the relations between men be governed by law and that power be exercised by right.

The elaborate efforts to show the dependence of man on society through a theory of certitude were not directed against the liberty of man. Lamennais, like Rousseau, was concerned with freeing man from the arbitrariness of opinion and from domination by brute force. Lamennais was temperamentally and ideologically opposed to constraint while, at the same time, incapable of living in doubt. Although he defiantly proclaimed the rights of truth and the obligation to believe, he repeatedly refrained from an advocacy of force to impose belief. A remarkable text reveals the nuance of his thought.

> If religion were to become a simple political institution and faith a law of the State, whoever publically professed a different faith ought to be considered as a rebel against the law and an enemy of the State.[229]

But religion is not a "simple political institution".

---

[224] *Essai sur l'indifférence...*, T. I, p. 351.
[225] Ibid.
[226] Ibid.
[227] Ibid., p. 434.
[228] C. Carcopino, *Les doctrines sociales de Lamennais*, Paris, 1942, p. 73.
[229] *Essai sur l'indifférence...*, T. I, p. 35.

> The Church, as a spiritual society, only considering the diverse religions under a spiritual rapport, that is, as true or false, is supremely intolerant of errors but pronounces only spiritual punishments against persons.[230]

The political society, on the other hand, may be tolerant of errors but it is intolerant of persons.[231] Against the charge of intolerance, he states, "no one is more convinced than I that we cannot in the least bring men to truth by violence".[232] As a priest, he is a "stranger" to the ways of political intolerance; his duty is charity.[233] He agrees with his Protestant adversary, M. Vincent, that only teaching and neither ignorance nor persecution could lead to a union of Christians. To reassure M. Vincent, he explains that the method of authority is "a pacific approach as far removed from... the way of constraint as a doctrinal judgement is from the death sentence".[234] Yet, it must be agreed that, although he began to see the implications of freedom of conscience and opinion in some of the articles written in this period, there was no profession of tolerance nor recognition of it as a necessary attribute of liberty.[235]

In comparing these passages in defense of non-violence and the integrity of the non-conformists with the rigorous attack throughout the *Essai sur l'indifférence*... on the very notion of tolerance, a contradiction seems apparent. Indeed, it would be so were it not for the mennaisian theory of power which gives him an ideological bridge across the chasm between liberty and authority. Starting, as Rousseau, with the doctrine of basic human equality, Lamennais, like his adversary and mentor, is forced to seek a justification for the submission of men to authority and for the exercise of political power in society.[236] Rousseau, however, in Lamennais's opinion, had failed to recognize that liberty must be considered, not as completely individual, but as a relationship to power.[237]

Liberty is not the autonomy of the subsisting ego but a relationship between creature and Creator. All of man's dignity comes from this

---

[230] *Essai sur l'indifférence...*, T. I, p. 35.
[231] Ibid.
[232] Ibid., T. II, p. XXVI.
[233] Ibid.
[234] Ibid., T. II, p. XLIX.
[235] K. Jürgensen, *Lamennais und die Gestaltung des Belgischen Staates*, Wiesbaden, 1963, p. 16.
[236] *Essai sur l'indifférence...*, T. I, p. 371.
[237] Ibid., p. 354.

relationship of obligation and obedience to law which alone enables him to act freely. The law is religion and this religion is Christianity. The perfect law of liberty is the Gospel. At this juncture, he freely quotes from the New Testament to explain what he understands by liberty.[238] Psychologically, liberty is still the ability to choose; it is exercised in an act of the will. Theologically, it is salvation from self-interest and egoism.

> It is by this noble obedience that we are delivered from the slavery in which the children of Adam weep, men of pride; it [obedience] gives us the true liberty. Once we abjure the sovereignty of self, we depend only on God, He is our unique Master.[239]

With the Gospels (Mark, X, 42, 45), "all changes, power established for the interest of all, becomes a burden and obedience a right".[240] Slavery becomes insupportable and "man becomes sacred for man".[241] In the political order, force, which is only physical ability to impose, cedes place to authority which is the "right to command".[242] Man does not fear power which is the expression of true authority; he loves it because there is nothing arbitrary in truth and order.[243]

The parallels between the mennaisian device of achieving a political and social order founded on God as source of the primitive legislation and, therefore, the only legitimate source of authority, and Rousseau's structuring of the social order among essentially equal beings through the mechanism of the "General Will" are most striking.[244] Contrary, however, to the totalitarian character of the political state attained through the "General Will", the state loses its density or "esse proprium" in the mennaisian theory. Unlike Rousseau or even Bonald, Lamennais was not a philosopher of the state. "What Lamennais desired was to indicate the means whereby the Catholic Church might regain her institutional integrity".[245]

Perhaps, too much has been made of the authoritarian aspects of the political theory indirectly present in the *Essai sur l'indifférence...*[246]

[238] *Essai sur l'indifférence...*, T. I, p. 354.
[239] Ibid., T. IV, p. 332.
[240] Ibid., T. I, p. 383.
[241] Ibid., p. 5.
[242] Ibid., p. 280.
[243] Ibid., pp. 356-357.
[244] For a recent discussion of Rousseau's "General Will", see P. Arnauld et al. *Rousseau et la Philosophie Politique*, Paris, 1965, particularly, "Volonté Générale, Volonté Particulière" by Hans Barth, pp. 35-50.
[245] H. Laski, *Authority in the Modern State*, New Haven, 119, p. 201.
[246] P. Janet, *La Philosophie de Lamennais*, Paris, 1890, p. 15.

Certainly, he said "authority can do everything, either for good or for evil",[247] but this should not be understood as an absolute, totalitarian political authority. Even at this stage of his evolution when he had few liberal sympathies, he was anxious to show that the state did not have unlimited power over its subjects, either individuals or moral bodies. For Lamennais, particular authority loses its power to command when it is in conflict with general authority. This is the source of all tyranny. Using Rousseau's distinction between power and force, Lamennais distinguishes arbitrary despotism or force from legitimate sovereignty or power which comes only from God.[248] This distinction is of capital importance in understanding the traces of Lamennais's later liberalism.

The Will or "power" of the Supreme Intelligent Being maintains order in creation and is the source of order in society. When particular authority, the government of the state, acts in conformity with the claims of the Divine Will, it exercises "power"; when it does not, it must employ "force" since it has no claim on the conscience of men. When the individual acts in harmony with the Divine Will, whose demands are known through religion, and with the dictates of particular authority, which exercises legitimate power, he enjoys his true liberty. At this stage, Lamennais failed to deduce the theory of revolution which is present in his distinction.

c) *Towards a "Free Church"*

The unity of the spiritual and the political orders would seem to be the natural consequence of Lamennais's social ontologism. There is no doubt but that the spiritual supports the political order; but, as K. Jürgensen has clearly established, Lamennais actually remained vague as to what this political order should be during this early phase of the Bourbon Restoration.[249] This is a most significant point. Lamennais's theorizing was not simply a repetition of the traditional Church-State thesis. Quite in conjunction with his distrust of Gallicanism, he is trying to insure, first, the liberty of the spiritual, that is, the Church, and, secondly, the elevation of the physical order by the spiritual or moral. He asks only that governments "ally themselves sincerely to religion."[250]

[247] *Essai sur l'indifférence...*, T. I, p. 15.
[248] Ibid.
[249] K. Jürgensen, *Lamennais und die Gestaltung des Belgischen Staates*, Wiesbaden, 1963, p. 10.
[250] *Essai sur l'indifférence...*, T. II, p. XVIII.

One would search in vain throughout the four volumes of the *Essai sur l'indifférence*... for any recognition on the author's part of secular values or for any open acceptance of an independent temporal sphere. The very character of the political order and the degree of union attained by it depend upon the state of belief of the citizens. The State becomes a non-State when its citizens and its rulers become separated from the eternal law of beliefs which is the Christian religion. Indeed, "in ancient times, no one could even conceive of either purely human societies or of a legislation which did not repose upon the authority of God".[251] The Church alone is the perfect society which serves as the "model" for lesser social entities and which "communicates its force and its life to purely human societies which might be established among Christians".[252] Both the "smallest school" and the "greatest empire" require that power which comes from a higher law of which religion is the guardian in order to function.[253] The State, like the family, is a necessary and a natural social unit but not an entity unto itself; State and family are functions within a higher social organism.

Although "religion and politics" together embrace "the highest interests of men",[254] there can be no question of an equality between the two. The metaphysical and theological priority of religion over political entities is abundantly clear throughout the various chapters of the *Essai sur l'indifférence*... which treat of this matter. If there is in any sense an element present in the *Essai sur l'indifférence* which would forecast in some way the future doctrine of separation, it is to be found in the effort which Lamennais expends to liberate the spiritual from that sort of temporal interference which he found so worthy of condemnation in the theories of Hobbes and Shaftesbury, and, in a similar way, in the final reliance of Jurieu upon princely power to achieve religious unity. His tenacious anti-Gallicanism grows out of a similar dislike for religio-political theories which tend to treat of the Church-State question as a matter of accommodation between two sovereignties, each supreme in its own sphere.

The ultramontanism advocated by Lamennais is really a radical departure from the traditional Church-State debate in that, for him, there is no longer a confrontation between two spheres on a certain basis of equality but rather the problem becomes one of the proper

---

[251] *Essai sur l'indifférence*..., T. IV, p. 32.
[252] Ibid., p. 351.
[253] Ibid., T. I, p. 42.
[254] Ibid., p. 272.

functioning of lesser powers within an englobing spiritual society. What Lamennais accomplishes, in effect, through his broad generalization which unites the two powers in a common society is the de-emphasizing of the sacral character of the temporal power such as was attributed to it by the various divine right theorists. While remaining fundamentally religious in origin, political authority becomes no more than another association in a universal theocracy for which the Pope is the articulate representative. Yet, it must not be thought that Lamennais conceived of this supremacy of the spiritual in terms of political domination. He reiterated several times his conception of the spiritual power as that which is exercised over the intellects of men, not over their persons and goods. Certainly, his theory lacks realism on this point but, in his view, a just and well-functioning State would be to the Church what an obedient body is to the soul.

Underlying this somewhat overly theoretical approach to the philosophy of power is a strain of utopian thinking, already present in the *Essai sur l'indifférence...*, which will become so strongly manifest in the Lamennais of later years. It is, in the opinion of J. Poisson, a "form of romanticism" which "dreams, above all, of new syntheses in which a spiritual domination would be the source and the fulfillment of terrestrial powers".[255] The ambivalence of Lamennais's attitude towards the State proceeds from his disillusionment with governments and his suspicion of independent political sovereignties. This pessimistic evaluation of the realities of political power is matched by a metaphysical optimism which leads him to pin his hopes upon the spiritual leadership of the Papacy. The most practical consequence of this ultramontane position is to be found in the movement of his thought towards the open advocacy of the idea of a "free Church"[256] with all of the implications which this idea holds in relation to the question of Church and State.[257]

The problem of adjusting the relations between the secular and spiritual powers is not the central theme of the *Essai sur l'indifférence* ... Such an adjustment would take place almost mechanically once his

---

[255] J. Poisson, *Le romantisme et la souveraineté*, Paris, 1932, p. 103.

[256] Chr. Maréchal, *La Dispute...*, p. 19.

[257] For an interesting discussion concerning the problem of the "free Church" idea in the context of English Church-State debates confer H. J. Laski, *Political Thought in England from Locke to Bentham*, Tenth Printing, London, 1961, particularly, Chapter III, "Church and State in the Eighteenth Century", pp. 54-85.

principal thesis concerning the unique spiritual society of intelligent beings were accepted and the re-Christianization of society accomplished. This extreme subordination of concrete realities to the rules of logic reveals both the metaphysical character of his social thinking and the weakness of his political theory. Through such an extreme generalization "the essentially concrete character of authority, without which powers and societies are no more than metaphysical abstractions", tends to disappear.[258]

What is clear for Lamennais is the necessity of not allowing the spiritual to become subservient to the political for if the spiritual "is subordinate to the institutions of the State, the political society itself will fall into chaos".[259] Governments have shown that they are incapable of saving themselves from the destructive effects of error and, thus, cannot be relied upon.[260] The salvific action of the Church takes place on the level of ideas through the communication of its message and, as such, does not require the aid of the secular arm. Obedience for Lamennais, as for Rousseau, is achieved through consent and not through force. Indifference, in his view, "disappeared eighteen centuries ago before a nascent Christianity; it will disappear again before a fully developed Christianity".[261] To achieve this development, he sought, before all else, those conditions of freedom and non-interference which would allow the Church to preach her message and to win men to the authority of the higher law. He does not advocate a reciprocal independence for the temporal powers since the spiritual must be free not only to teach but also to judge the acts of secular authorities. Temporal power de-humanizes man if it is not constituted on the priority of the spiritual.[262] At a later date, he would conclude that only a complete separation of the Church from the State would allow for the necessary conditions of freedom required by the Church to accomplish her salvific role.

2. Political Implications of Common Consent

In discussing the question of certitude, Lamennais simply elevated to the level of theory the time-honored, day-to-day experience of the pre-critical mind. The unreflective belief and trust of everyman in the

---

[258] J. Poisson, *Le romantisme social de Lamennais*, Paris, 1931, p. 81.
[259] *Essai sur l'indifférence...*, T. II, p. XVIII.
[260] Ibid., pp. II-IV.
[261] Ibid., T. I, p. 43.
[262] Ibid., p. 29.

world around him and in the words of normal social intercourse are the unquestioned, practical supports of everyday life, a certitude, which, in the eyes of Lamennais, is a "social production".[263]

> ... "the intelligent being can only conserve himself in society... society tends to break up when the basis of certitude and intelligence is reversed by submitting authority or general reason to individual reason.[264]

Nothing is more clear than the end intended by Lamennais in his efforts to re-establish the foundations of human certitude within the context of the common sense tradition. "Authority and love", he states, "are the two great characteristics of the Church and the two great needs of society;"[265] it is in defense of these principles that he sought mightily to overcome the prevailingly critical spirit which had destroyed the habits of obedience of Christian peoples. Authority in the mennaisian lexicon, it is well to remember, is not irrational, nor anti-rational; it is simply a higher or purified reason, the social check on the individual reason as well as the source of its operations.[266] It is not necessary, indeed, it is impossible, to disregard the role of individual reason. What Lamennais demands is that, methodologically, the philosopher should begin, just as he does in the ordinary activities of life, with faith and not with doubt being assured that his individual reasonings are formed within and developed by a general reason.[267]

The difficult question is to properly identify this general reason, to find its locus. Lamennais affirms, and attempts to prove through what he esteems to be the universal beliefs consented to by all men, in all times, that this general reason is an original religion which can be identified with the Church.

> Christianity, before Jesus Christ, ... was the *general reason manifested by the testimony of mankind*. Christianity after Jesus Christ, a natural development of intelligence, is the *general reason manifested by the testimony of the Church*.[268]

[263] *Essai sur l'indifférence...*, T. II, p. 42.
[264] Ibid.
[265] Ibid., p. XXII.
[266] Chr. Maréchal, "La vraie doctrine philosophique de La Mennais", *Revue philosophique*, Paris, 1949, p. 329. In Maréchal's view, authority in its deepest sense is inseparable from reason as seen by Lamennais. From this union, springs the intimate relationship between theology and philosophy.
[267] *Essai sur l'indifférence...*, T. II, p. 159.
[268] Ibid., p. LXVIII.

Although this assumption, in spite of the historical evidence marshalled by the author to sustain it, may appear to be entirely gratuitous,[269] it was, nonetheless, a new and radical notion in apologetics. We will discuss the mennaisian idea of the universality of Christianity and history in the section immediately following. The claims of the Church to be the true Church revealed by God and the infallible teacher of Divine Revelation are proved by the common agreement of mankind. A subsequent step is to regard the teaching authority of the Church and the tradition of humanity as one and the same expression of the primitive religion.[270] The older methods of apologetics, which followed the classical approach of first proving the historicity and the compatibility of certain supernatural phenomena such as miracles and prophecies as preliminary to proving the Divine nature of the Church's origins, are replaced by a methodology which situates the Church within a natural context and recognizes in it a fulfillment of a connatural revelation.[271]

There are within the method of common consent certain characteristics which have generally been recognized as the sources of Lamennais's future liberalism and eventual disassociation from the hierarchical Church. His efforts to equate the magisterium of the visible Church with the voice of humanity, in spite of his ambitious desire to do so, remain tentative and not final in the *Essai sur l'indifférence*... The high-point of his ultramontane doctrine will be achieved in *De la Religion considérée dans ses rapports avec l'ordre politique et civil* (1826). It is interesting to bear in mind, however, that he was attempting to tailor the Church to fit his description of the Church and vice versa.

Bonald correctly observed that the doctrine of his contemporary was "an explanation and a positive application of one axiom as ancient as the world, and true, when one encloses it within the proper limits,

---

[269] Baron Eckstein, a German intellectual and an important figure in the Catholic intellectual revival in France during this period, criticized the *Essai sur l'indifférence*... for the inconclusiveness of the effort and for the author's lack of proper technical and critical apparatus for historical studies. See, J.-R. Derré, *Lamennais, ses amis et le mouvement des idées à l'époque romantique*, Paris, 1962, pp. 138-140.

[270] See footnote 202.

[271] Through this effort to eliminate all contradictions between faith and reason, Lamennais runs the risk of "naturalizing the Christian religion in putting on the same level the truths received from the general reason and those properly revealed or supernatural", L. Le Guillou, *L'évolution de la pensée religieuse de Félicité Lamennais*, Paris, 1966, p. 71.

112

Vox populi, Vox Dei".[272] But what are these limits which Bonald had in mind? Lamennais had gone much beyond Bonald and Maistre, both of whom had championed the cause of tradition, by calling tradition itself the common consent of mankind and by making of it the sole principle of certitude.[273] In the mennaisian conceptualization of a moral universe based upon the knowledge, through language, of a series of revealed axioms or principles which constitute the deposit of the primitive gift, the political order becomes a manifestation of the people's fidelity to the original truths. But, ultimately, the people themselves through their common agreement will speak these truths to each generation. Once the universal beliefs of mankind became for Lamennais the ultimate criterion of truth, the possibility of an evolution towards democracy would seem to be inevitable.[274] Given the nature of history, these universal beliefs are subject to an evolution. What the majority of men hold to be true, which is man's greatest authority, is essentially bound up with a profoundly historical, and consequently, relative notion of truth.

Truth is no longer the province of an endowed elite and faith the lot of the masses. Truth is available to all men and faith is the only means to attain it. Just as all in Rousseau's community must accept the "General Will" in order to be truly free, so also, for Lamennais, all men must believe and accept the religion of mankind which is the rock upon which the social order is built. It would seem that, as in the case of the author of *Contrat Social*, an embryonic democracy is engendered by an egalitarian epistemology.[275]

Although Lamennais steadfastly refused to admit the theory of popular sovereignty, at least as it was then held, in order to leave no doubt about the absolute sovereignty of the Divine Will, his peculiar position on the value of the testimony of mankind makes possible, in the ideological order, a certain fluidity concerning the actual seat or incarnate representation of the superior authority which emanates from the voice of humanity. Once the key doctrine of common consent is united to the englobing character of a socializing and liberating Christianity, would he not one day be forced to question the

---

[272] M. De Bonald, "Sur un dernier ouvrage de M. l'abbé De La Mennais", published with the "Pièces relatives du second volume de L'Essai sur l'indifférence en matière de la religion" in *Défense de l'Essai sur l'indifférence...*, T. V, p. 194.

[273] E. Faguet, *Politiques et Moralistes du XIXe siècle*, Paris, 1898, T. II, pp. 98-100.

[274] Ch. Calippe, *L'attitude sociale des catholiques français au XIXe siècle*, Paris, 1911, T. I, p. 223.

[275] H. Laski, *Authority in the Modern State*, New Haven, 1919, p. 212-213.

validity of his ecclesiology? Could the visible authority of an hierarchical Church which, in his mind, ignored the voice of humanity be the genuine representative of the religion of mankind?[276] Such a possibility was quite evident to the earliest critics of the *Essai sur l'indifférence...*, particularly, Abbé Paganel.

> ... between J. J. Rousseau affirming that the General Will is sovereign and the rule of all others, and Lamennais pretending that public reason ought to be the basis of individual reason, he [Paganel] didn't see the slightest difference.[277]

To better understand, however, the possibility of such an evolution, it will be necessary to consider briefly the relationship between dogma and history and the nature of history itself as seen by Lamennais at the time of the completion of the *Essai sur l'indifférence...*

3. *History and Truth*

In order to understand the possibility of Lamennais's intellectual journey, it is both convenient and necessary to have some notion of the importance of history in his world-view. It can be agreed that "when a man treats of universal history and either gives a finalistic interpretation of historical development or concerns himself with universally-operative laws, it is not improper to speak of him as a philosopher of history".[278] The role of history and the importance of history-writing within the romantic period have already been mentioned.[279] Lamennais shared in the spirit of his times; he felt impelled by a particular mission accorded to him by Providence. It is an element quite common to the psychology of the Romantics.[280]

> Convinced... of the temporal government of Providence, he believed himself authorized by the progress of events to create an order capable of culling from the Divine message the interpretation required for his times.[281]

---

[276] Concerning the genesis of Lamennais's rupture with Rome, see the recent and well-documented study by L. Le Guillou, *Les Discussions Critiques Journal de la Crise mennaisienne*, Paris, 1967.

[277] M. Deschamps, Souvenirs Universitaires: "L'Université et Lamennais", *Mémoires de l'Académie des Sciences, Inscriptions et Belles-Lettres de Toulouse*, Tome V, Toulouse, p. 38.

[278] F. Copleston, *A History of Philosophy*, Volume 4, *Modern Philosophy: Descartes to Leibniz*, Garden City, New York, 1963, p. 62.

[279] See Chapter Two, III a, "Revival of the Old".

[280] C. Carcopino, *Les doctrines sociales de Lamennais*, Paris, 1942, p. 42.

[281] J.-R. Derré, *Lamennais, ses amis et le mouvement des idées à l'époque romantique*, Paris, 1962, p. 302.

Like his senior contemporary, Maistre,[282] Lamennais sought to grasp the hidden significance of the events which constitute the history of man. He saw men who were so dominated by opinion that "they are incapable of grasping with the spirit alone a vast ensemble of relations and of uniting the present to the past".[283] The materialized offspring of the 18th century were unable to take distance and to go beyond the surface.

> They see facts and seek the cause of these facts but they are too close to them; they are spectators of the storms which rock society, simply of the coming and going of events which make up its history. They explain each wave by the wave which pushes it instead of going first to the impulse which has produced all events.[284]

First, therefore, it must be observed that events take on an overwhelming importance for the romantic spirit in search of the inner law connecting temporal happenings. The false systems of philosophy, taking their inspiration from Aristotle, "throw spirits into vacuity by substituting pure abstractions for the reality of things".[285] Just as the empirical fact, the relation of word and thought in language, plays a key role in the traditionalist psychology, the events of history reveal more about man and his destiny than the solitary abstractions of the philosophers. The daily event cannot be ignored. "Often", notes Lamennais, in a newspaper article written during this period, "it is a circumstance, unimportant in itself or unexpected, which suddenly reveals to society that which it ignores or that which it must know".[286] How else can the sensus communis of mankind be known except through a knowledge of the components of history?

Lamennais was not, however, an historiographer; he sought to interpret the historical facts which so interested him. To interpret or to understand the content of a present fact or of a primitive myth, he had to have a method of deciphering governed by a set of rules which might be called his philosophy of history. Since events are vectors which point beyond, to what do they point? Writing a Preface to a collection of articles published contemporaneously with the *Essai sur l'indifférence...*, he asserts the first principle or rule of interpretation.

---

[282] Concerning Maistre and the importance of history, see D. Bagge, *Les idées politiques en France sous la Restauration*, Paris, 1952, "La Fécondité Historique", p. 247.
[283] *Essai sur l'indifférence...*, T. I, p. 2.
[284] Ibid.
[285] Ibid., T. IV, p. 4.
[286] Lamennais, "Sur la Poursuite Judiciaire dirigée contre le Drapeau Blanc au sujet de l'Université", Œuvres Complètes, Paris, 1836-1837, T. VIII, p. 364.

Our century has this of particular, that its history is bound up essentially, in all of its details, to the history of the doctrines which stir the spirits and which could not be separated from it. One would never understand anything concerning even the apparently most simple events of our epoch if one did not go back to the moral causes of which events are but the effects.[287]

There is a perfect parallel between the history of dogma and the history of secular events, "everything is joined, everything is connected in history as in the dogmas of religion".[288] The idea of the existence of God, the first revealed truth, is also an historical happening. The history of nations and the history of religious beliefs have the same source in the revelation of the primitive religion. The whole is not imponderable; the temporal can be explained. If one can grasp the dialectic between the immutability of dogma or the first truths and the manifestations of these truths in history, one would be able to see a "logical filiation of events".[289]

History is important because it is the arena in which the truths of revelation are passed from one generation to another. Since events and generations are continuous, it is imperative to know the law which governs the movement inherent in time. The history of dogma becomes the point of reference or the background of secular history. When he speaks of dogma, he means the doctrines of Christianity which he identifies with the whole.

Christianity began with the world; developed according to promise, without changing basically, without varying, it has remained in diverse states and will remain perpetually one.[290]

Remaining one and basically the same, Christianity admits of growth. This evolution is not the addition of anything new; it is similar to the physical growth of a child into adulthood or like the truth present in our reasonings which remains always true although it develops.[291] With metaphors such as these, Lamennais attempts to reconcile the immutability of dogma with the fact of change.

Christianity is unlike the impatient philosophers since it allows for imperfection; God has revealed to man but man, as temporal, is in the

---

[287] Lamennais, *Mélanges religieux et philosophiques*, Œuvres Complètes, Paris, 1836-1837, Préface, T. VIII, pp. 1-2.
[288] *Essai sur l'indifférence...*, T. I, p. 200.
[289] Ibid., T. I, p. 199.
[290] Ibid., T. III, p. 28.
[291] Ibid.

process of growth.[292] Truth becomes clear with time for its profound unity becomes more evident.[293] There have been three stages of the Divine Revelation of the same essential truths, namely, the primitive, the Mosaic, and the Christian. Each revelation has deepened and illuminated the original truths; they are parallel to the three ages of mankind, infancy, adolescence, and the era of human maturity.[294] Following the thoughts of Bossuet, he emphasizes the inner-connection and teleology of events.

> ... all is prepared in advance, and develops according to laws which do not allow us to fix rigorously the precise epoch in which the passing from one state into another is attained.[295]

Although Lamennais considered that he had found the first principle governing history in his theory of the universality of Christianity,[296] he was forced to explain in some way the opacity of the temporal. Clearly, although man could grasp the meaningfulness of the whole, it was not transparent to him. Due to the profoundly historical nature of revelation and the temporality of man, there is an evolution of dogma; there is a revelation within revelation of that which is hidden in the ancient truths.[297] In this context, the role of error is seen as a positive spur to the unveiling of truth. They fulfill a function within the movement of history towards the last days "when figures will give way to reality".[298]

> Everything is supernatural in what we see, and the evils, as remedies, derive immediately from a higher order of causes, as elevated as impenetrable to the view of man...[299]

This attitude, underlying the main lines of thought in the *Essai sur l'indifférence*..., frees Lamennais from a static, non-historical posture in reference to error. Error is not an absolute, abstract evil; error becomes a vehicle of history. This is possible because history is oriented towards the future. The future is unimportant for the materialists whom he opposes; they fail to see that the future is the

---

[292] *Essai sur l'indifférence*..., T. I, pp. 368-369.
[293] Ibid., p. 151.
[294] Ibid., T. IV, p. 96.
[295] Ibid., p. 390.
[296] F. Brousse, *Lamennais et le christianisme universel*, Paris, 1963, pp. 23-24.
[297] *Essai sur l'indifférence*..., T. IV, p. 104.
[298] Ibid., T. III, p. 373.
[299] Letter from Lamennais to his brother, Jean-Marie, Londres 12 septembre 1815, reproduced in A. Blaize, Œuvres inédites de F. Lamennais, Paris, 1866, T. I, p. 222.

"inflexible will of God".[300] By incorporating Christian eschatology into his system, Lamennais becomes essentially optimistic about history in spite of the dark forebodings which pervade his correspondence during this period.[301] Although he may speak of the coming revolutions in the bleakest terms, it cannot be doubted that he sees these upheavals in function of a future order which will be the apotheosis of truth.[302] It is not difficult to see within this framework of ideas a re-absorption into a Christian theology of the idea of progress which had become secularized in the previous century.

What is worthwhile noting here is that Lamennais placed himself ideologically in a position of attributing positive importance to error and to opinion, in spite of the seemingly strong attack against any liberality in reference to these weaknesses of the human spirit. Two conclusions would seem to result from Lamennais's understanding of history. First, he could not, without contradicting his principles, fail to be impressed by the presence of wide-scale historical phenomena such as liberalism and the struggle of people for liberty. Secondly, if he were radically certain of the triumph of truth in history and, as we have seen, ideologically opposed to arbitrariness and force, it would not be too great a step for him to take to come to an open advocacy of a free, un-hampered, interplay of ideas. Such a turn of the spirit and its justification will be the matter for the subsequent chapters.

[300] Lamennais, "De L'Avenir", Œuvres Complètes, Paris, 1836-1837, T. VIII, p. 284.

[301] Lamennais gives a great deal of importance to the purgative value of suffering; see letter from Lamennais to Baroness Cottu, Saint-Brieuc, 18 juillet (1820), "If I were with you, I would speak to you of an important law to which, in general, little attention is paid, and which I admire more and more as I reflect upon it: it is the law of suffering without which there is nothing beautiful, nothing great... The happiness of men does not unite them one to another. It is necessary that they suffer together in order to love one another...", reproduced in d'Haussonville, Lettres inédites de Lamennais à la baronne Cottu, Paris, 1910, p. 93.

[302] K. Jürgensen, Lamennais und die Gestaltung des Belgischen Staates, Wiesbaden, 1963, p. 20.

CHAPTER FOUR

THE YEARS OF TRANSITION (1825-1829)

I. THE MEDIEVALISM OF LAMENNAIS

1. *The Romanticists and the Middle Ages*

Romanticism, as it has already been pointed out,[1] is characterized, in part, by its attitude towards the past. Historiography was not the unique invention of the Romantic movement, for, certainly, the thinkers of the century which preceded the romantic reaction were not without a keen historical interest and were indeed responsible for the introduction of the scientific method into historical research.[2] The Romanticists, however, added the dimensions of sentiment and empathy, products of a poetic exaltation, which were lacking in the norm-governed historical efforts of the rationalists. The age of Romanticism was, in the opinion of C. Dawson,

> ... an age of History, when for the first time men set themselves to re-create the past, and sought to enter with imaginative sympathy into the life and thought of past ages and different peoples.[3]

While the historians of the Enlightenment were more concerned with the past as an object of study for the pedagogical value contained therein, the romantic spirit tended to present the past as an ideal, almost as something of a meaningful myth. "This idealization and spiritualization of the past is one of the distinctive characteristics of romantic thought".[4]

For some observers, the romantic attitude towards the past is a flight from the reality of the objective world into the realm of the frankly subjective and imaginative. In the provocative opinion of C. Schmitt, "romanticism is a subjectivized occasionalism; the romanticist", he contends, "treats the world as a pretext or an occasion for romantic activity".[5] The prevailing literary character of romantic writings, even when treating of history or of philosophy, complicates considerably

[1] See Chapter Two, III a, "Revival of the Old".
[2] E. Cassirer, *The Myth of the State*, New Haven, 1963, p. 181.
[3] C. Dawson, *Progress and Religion*, New York, 1938, p. 26.
[4] E. Cassirer, *The Myth of the State*, New Haven, 1963, p. 181.
[5] C. Schmitt, *Romantisme Politique*, (Translation of *Politische Romantik*), Paris, 1928, p. 31.

any attempt to uncover the real meaning or doctrinal content of these writings. Such an undertaking would require a study of the particular psychology of the romantic soul which is beyond our limited purposes; nonetheless, it will be important to our exegesis of Lamennais's thought to have some understanding of the romanticists' reconstructions of the past. Indeed, as C. Dawson notes very perceptively,

> ... we cannot fully understand an age unless we understand how that age regarded the past, for every age makes its own past, and this re-creation of the past is one of the elements that goes into the making of the future.[6]

The attitude towards the past held by the post-revolutionary romantic generation was a radical departure from that of its immediate ancestors. Although not limited to a rehabilitation of the Middle Ages, romantic historiography displayed a marked propensity for that period of Europe's history which was representative for them of a "golden age of mankind".[7] The motivations behind this phenomenon bespeak the deep anxieties among the disillusioned heirs of the Jacobin experience for that medieval religious unity embodying the whole social and political order and for an artistic inspiration closer to the mysterious and the primitive.[8] It would also seem quite logical that the groups of expatriates dispossessed by the Revolution should turn hopefully to a past which had known the certitudes of belief and the stabilities of an integrated social order.[9]

Contrary to the disdainful attitude held in reference to the medieval epoch by the rationalist historians and philosophers, the new German and French schools of history rejected the tendency of the classicists to evaluate the past on the basis of the roles of reason and form within a particular period thereby dividing past ages into eras of enlightenment or of darkness. The critical approach of a Gibbon or a Voltaire was replaced by an *organic* concept of history in which the unity of the culture and the inter-connection of the whole were stressed. "The underlying historical premise of the historiography of Romanticism was the doctrine of the gradual and unconscious nature of cultural evolution in any nation".[10]

[6] C. Dawson, *Dynamics of World History*, New York, 1957, p. 352.
[7] E. Cassirer, *The Myth of the State*, New Haven, 1963, p. 185.
[8] H. Schenk, *The Mind of the European Romantics*, London, 1966, pp. 36-40.
[9] J. Oechselin, *Le mouvement ultra-royaliste sous la Restauration*, Paris, 1960, p. 16.
[10] H. Barnes, *A History of Historical Writing*, New York, 1962, p. 178.

The restoration of the past, principally the Middle Ages, was manifested not only in the historico-literary works of a Chauteaubriand or a Walter Scott, but also, and more significantly for the study of political theory, in the appearance of the new theorizing on the nature of law and of institutions. A profound reaction to the natural law theories based upon reason and to the deductive application of abstract norms unrelated to history in concrete cases found expression in an Historical School of Law which was dedicated to the principle of historical and traditional right as the source of legitimacy and legality. Whether the approach was politico-historical, as was the case for Burke, Bonald, and Maistre, or, juridico-historical, as represented by the German jurist, Savigny, the same spirit of reaction to the postulates of the political contract theories and the same endorsement of an organic concept of society, of which medieval society was a most vibrant example, binds the variously historically oriented groups together.[11]

The disenchantment with Cartesianism and, consequently, rationalism, already palpable before the Revolution of 1789, has been identified as a four-fold reaction, namely, philosophical, mystico-religious, historical and traditionalist, and, finally, aesthetic. All four forms of opposition are found to be represented in the Romantic movement although it is difficult to find all in the same romantic figure.[12] Among those personalities which are clearly identified as Romanticists — there is much discussion concerning the status of such theorists of politics as Bonald and Maistre[13] — the aesthetic opposition to the idea of nature as held by the empiricists and to the rigidity proper to classicism in art and literature becomes mixed with a nostalgia for religious experience and for the re-integration of the socially and economically uprooted into a genuine social unity. René Chateaubriand, a leader of this sort of aesthetic opposition in literature, was also the principal literary innovator of the new religious apologetic aptly described as a "sentimental and aesthetic theology".[14] His enormously popular paeans to the marvels of Christianity, Génie du christianisme, and Les Martyrs, "did more than any other books to destroy for a time the

---

[11] G. Del Vecchio, *Philosophy of Law*, (Translation of *Lezioni di filosofia del diritto*), Washington, 1953, pp. 121-134.

[12] C. Schmitt, *Romantisme Politique*, Paris, 1928, pp. 59-62.

[13] Ibid., p. 51.

[14] R. Duhamel, *Aux sources du romantisme français*, Ottawa, 1964, p. 66.

Rationalist notion of the Middle Ages".[15] Chateaubriand's return to the Middle Ages was a religio-literary expression of the same general current which became torrential in post-revolutionary Europe.

Lamennais participated in this upsurge of romantic fever and succumbed, for a time, to the charm of the Middle Ages. More profoundly philosophical than Chateaubriand, he is nonetheless deeply indebted to the author of *Génie du christianisme* for many of the insights into the Christian past which add a note of lyricism to his defense of historical Christianity in the *Essai sur l'indifférence* . . .[16] His concept of the Middle Ages, however, was not a simple re-make of Chateaubriand's idealization of the age of gothic faith. Before, and, especially, after the publication of the *Essai sur l'indifférence* . . . , Lamennais was in the very center of a vast and complex eruption of new ideas fed principally by German erudition and discussed avidly in the many journals and newspapers whose volume and importance were so characteristic of the period. The "Catholique", founded by Baron Eckstein, served as a transmission belt for many of the ideas and findings of the German romanticists into France and as an important point of contact between the young French Catholics and the leaders of the German Catholic revival.[17] Lamennais had become familiar with the works of the important figures of German Catholic thought of this period and it is interesting to note that it was in Germany that "the idealization of the Middle Ages reached its greatest intensity".[18]

It was also in this period, 1824, that the "Mémorial Catholique" was inaugurated by Gerbet and Salinis, two young clerical followers of Lamennais, as a sounding board for mennaisian doctrines and, in some measure, as a French Catholic counterpart to the Catholic journals of Germany, particularly, the Catholic publication of Mainz, which were contributing so energetically to the Catholic intellectual awakening which accompanied the early period of Romanticism.[19] J.-R. Derré has treated in considerable detail the complex interchange

---

[15] H. Barnes, *A History of Historical Writing*, New York, 1962, p. 182.

[16] A. Viatte, *Les interprétations du catholicisme chez les romantiques*, Paris, 1922, pp. 97-136.

[17] For a discussion of the part played by Baron Eckstein in the Romantic movement confer Chapter III, "les idées du Baron Eckstein", in J.-R. Derré, *Lamennais, ses amis et le mouvement des idées à l'époque romantique*, Paris, 1962, pp. 115-167.

[18] H. Schenk, *The Mind of the European Romantics*, London, 1966, p. 37.

[19] Concerning the interesting history of the "Mémorial Catholique" consult Chapter IV, "Luttes et doctrines du Mémorial Catholique", in J.-R. Derré, *Lamennais, ses amis et le mouvement des idées à l'époque romantique*, 1962, pp. 169-225.

of ideas between French and German Romanticists and, as such, need not be repeated here. What is important to recall, in our limited context, is that Lamennais, in the principal works of this period, *De la Religion considérée dans ses rapports avec l'ordre politique et civil* (1826) and *Des progrès de la révolution et de la guerre contre l'Eglise* (1829), attempted to fashion his politico-religious theories within the framework of a broad movement of ideas which was watered from many fountains and which was singularly eclectic in character. The medievalism of the Romanticists is singled out because, as a principal feature of this ideological current, it will help to explain, at least partially, the most salient characteristics of Lamennais's political thought in this period of transition. He reinforced and expanded the global value system undergirding a hoped-for restoration of Christianity and, consequently, of society, first outlined in the *Essai sur l'indifférence...*, and, subsequently, evaluated the actually existing social and political order against this notional backdrop. Accordingly, our purpose in this chapter is to treat, first, his positive idea-structure concerning the principles and the organization of society; second, his criticism of the dominant theories and of the actual state of society; and, finally, the conclusions which he drew from these observations.

2. Lamennais's "Political Theology"

a) Religion and Law

Various historical and political events of the decade between 1820-1830 profoundly influenced the romantic thinkers of this period leading them to reverse positions in reference to the restoration theories of the Bourbon monarchy and, in general, to a transferral of political and ideological loyalties from reaction to revolution. The Greek movement for independence aroused an unusual display of sympathy throughout young Europe which was in direct opposition to the policies of the Holy Alliance and, consequently, to the political stance of the Restoration governments.[20] The romantic generation which had been royalist and Catholic was deeply moved by this popular struggle for liberty and national identity against the archaic Turkish despotism.[21] Another factor, in the case of the French

[20] J. Droz, *Restaurations et Révolutions (1815-1871)*, Paris, 1953, pp. 579-581.
[21] R. Duhamel, *Aux sources du romantisme français*, Ottawa, 1964, pp. 194-198.

Romanticists, was the failure of the government of Villèle, prime hope of the ultra-royalists, to achieve what the younger generation had considered as necessary for a true re-establishment of a re-integrated Christian society. The right-wing governments, once in power, were caught between the demands of the theoretical purists of the monarchical party and the very real presence of a strong tendency to maintain and continue the work of liberalization springing from the Enlightenment and the Revolution of 1789.[22]

The abiding interest of Lamennais in the events of public and political life is one of his most notable characteristics and an important factor in understanding his thought.

> It is very evident that, after 1820, scarcely a day passes in which he does not comment, in long letters to his acquaintances, on the interior and exterior events ... for him, politics is the area of experimentation, the laboratory of his theories ...[23]

He was sensitive to the phenomenon of change and shared in the apocalyptic preoccupations of the whole romantic world.[24] As early as 1821, he confessed his inability to share the optimism of his distinguished correspondent, Joseph de Maistre.[25] While in Rome during the summer of 1824, where he had been so well received by Pope Leo XII,[26] he wrote to his brother,

> ... all is dying; life is slipping away everywhere. The social body is no more than a cadaver which one must leave rot.... This fact is well established for me; and I will take from it the rule for my future conduct.[27]

For Lamennais, the sickness of European society and, in particular, that of the French Restoration monarchy, is a disease at the very marrow of the political structure, a spiritual blindness to the religious realities which alone support the social order. In a most remarkable letter written to his faithful correspondent, Baron Vitrolles, a leader in

---

[22] J. Droz, *Restaurations et Révolutions (1815-1871)*, Paris, 1953, pp. 86-88.

[23] C. Carcopino, *Les doctrines sociales de Lamennais*, Paris, 1942, p. 40.

[24] For a discussion of this psychological aspect of the Romanticists confer H. Schenk, *The Mind of the European Romantics*, London, 1966, particularly, "Forebodings and Nostalgia for the Past", pp. 30-45.

[25] Letter from Lamennais to Maistre, Saint-Brieuc, 2 janvier 1821, reproduced in R. De Maistre, *Lettres et Opuscules inédites du comte J. De Maistre*, Paris, 1869, T. II, p. 120.

[26] A. R. Vidler, *Prophecy and Papacy*, London, 1954, p. 102.

[27] Letter from Lamennais to his brother, Jean-Marie, Rome, 28 juin 1824, reproduced in A. Blaize, *Œuvres inédites de F. Lamennais*, Paris, 1866, T. II, p. 15.

the ultra-royalist party, he outlines the problematic which will occupy his attention during the years leading up to the publication of "L'Avenir".

> I have thought extensively about this subject [jus gentium] and, consequently, I have certain ideas, acceptable or unacceptable ... I believe firmly that there has never been a true law of nations for the reason that nations, totally independent or separated one from the other have never been united in a general society. Christianity attempted to form this society so necessary to civilization which will always be incomplete without it. Europe feels vaguely the need of it but she is far from taking the steps which would lead her there in time. The absence of a true law, and, as a consequence, of recognized duties, has produced a politics of interests which leads directly to barbarism and even to anarchy ... Are there laws which bind the nations as nations? What are these laws? Who has made them and how does one know them? Who has the right to declare them and to impose them? I defy anyone to answer these questions without arriving at a result which would be either the abolition of society or the establishment of an order as different as possible from the reigning ideas of today.[28]

In an unedited Mémoire addressed to Pope Leo XII concerning the revitalization of studies in the Church and the principal errors to be opposed, Lamennais emphasizes that the moral sciences must receive special attention, particularly, the science of law.

> There are only Protestant or philosophical theories [of law] which have not a little contributed to produce and which continue to perpetuate the disorders which we are witnessing.[29]

As a contribution to the re-building of sound political thought, Lamennais conceived of preparing a politico-religious study while visiting in Geneva in 1824. Writing to Count Senfft, he declares that some effort must be made in this direction;

> ... for it seems to me that until now neither ancient society nor Christian society has been well understood. Those who have seen most

---

[28] Letter from Lamennais to Baron Vitrolles, La Chênaie, 28 mai 1822, reproduced in Eugène Forgues, *Correspondence inédite entre Lamennais et le Baron Vitrolles*, Paris, 1886, p. 99. (These letters were left unpublished in the editions of E. D. Forgues due to litigations with A. Blaize, the nephew of Lamennais, on behalf of Lamennais's family.)

[29] There are two versions of the Mémoire which Lamennais was believed to have sent to Pope Leo XII. One was reproduced by A. Blaize, *Œuvres inédites de F. Lamennais*, Paris, 1866, T. II, pp. 312-339. The other, a fragment, was published by P. Dudon, "Fragment inédit d'un mémoire de Lamennais à Léon XII", *Recherches de Sciences religieuses*, T. I, Paris, 1910, pp. 476-485. The citation made above is from an extract of the Dudon article, No. 894, F.I.C. Archives,Highlands, Jersey, C.I., p. 13.

clearly have recognized that there are intimate, necessary relations between religious society and political society; but they have not perceived that religion is the whole of society considered under diverse relations . . .[30]

The first attempt of Lamennais to attain his aspirations concerning the rehabilitation of political theory and to analyze the wrongs of the current social and political order appeared in two parts, (May 1825 and February 1826), under the title, *De la religion considérée dans ses rapports avec l'ordre politique et civil.* In order to first clarify the positive content of this publication, it will be necessary to reverse somewhat the order employed by the author. Lamennais begins with a description of what he considers to be the democratization of the Restoration government and follows with a declaration of ultramontane principles which furnish the basis for the critique. For our purposes, it will be more logical to, first, disengage these principles in order to show the continuity and evolution of his key doctrines without losing our way in a myriad of particular issues.

Initially, *De la religion* . . . seems to entail simply a reiteration of the themes of Chapters X and XI of Volume I of the *Essai sur l'indifférence* . . . concerning the necessity of religion for any durable social order.

> Instructed by the experience and the universal tradition of peoples, ancient wisdom had understood that no human society could either form itself or perpetuate itself if religion did not preside at its birth and had not communicated to it that divine force, foreign to the work of man, which is the life of all durable institutions.[31]

This theme, already established in the *Essai sur l'indifférence* . . . , is repeated throughout the text but with considerable expansion, particularly, in reference to the very nature of the spiritual and temporal orders and the relation between the two. As a leit-motiv for the book, Lamennais adopts intact the central notion of Maistre's "metaphysics of sovereignty",[32] namely, "without a Pope, no Church;

---

[30] Letter from Lamennais to Count Senfft, Genève, 15 mai 1824, reproduced in P. Dudon, "Lamennais en Italie", *Études*, Paris, 29 février 1933, p. 431.

[31] Lamennais, *De la religion considérée dans ses rapports avec l'ordre politique et civil*, Œuvres Complètes, Paris, 1836-1837, T. VII, p. 1. (In subsequent citations, this work will be referred to simply as *De la religion* . . .)

[32] Nomenclature given to Maistre's ultramontanism by Camille Latreille and cited in R. Aubert, "Géographie ecclésiologique au XIXᵉ siècle", published in *L'ecclésiologie au XIXᵉ siècle*, Paris, 1960, p. 18.

without a Church, no religion; without a religion, no society".[33] On the occasion of the publication of Maistre's *Du Pape*, Lamennais had accorded the layman's ultramontane thesis an enthusiastic welcome. Separating himself more definitely from Bossuet, he rejects with Maistre any sort of conciliarism which might tend to lessen Papal authority. Only such a unitary and monarchical concept of Papal sovereignty, based upon the doctrine of infallibility, could insure temporal societies of the necessary stability upon which to build the political order.

> It is sovereignty which makes society: thus, sovereignty ought to be permanent as society itself. An intermittent sovereignty is, as M. de Maistre observes very well, a contradiction in terms.[34]

The reasoning behind Lamennais's ultramontane position can be most clearly and completely seen in the refutation of the first proposition of the Declaration of 1682, that is, "temporal sovereignty, by divine institution, is completely independent of spiritual power", in Chapter VII, "Des libertés gallicanes", of *De la religion ....*[35] His first principle is that God is not only the Creator of man but that He is also the Author of society. It is evident that man is social; therefore, it follows that the Creator of this social being has also willed the proper order for the conservation of these social beings. There are two fundamental necessities or conditions for the very existence of a union of intelligent beings. First, there must be a law uniting the members and, secondly, a power to insure the observance of this law.[36] Thus, out of an inner necessity stemming from man's sociability, he deduces that "there is a divine law, the basis of all society, an immutable law ... a law as universal and perpetual as society itself".[37]

If the law governing society is divine, that is, a necessity emanating from the very order of creation, the power or obligatory character which is implied in the very definition of law is also divine in origin. This is evident not only from Sacred Scripture which teaches that all power comes from God but also from the very idea of power or the right to obligate which cannot be isolated from the source of all rights, the Creator. Power, like sovereignty, is one; it is impossible to hold

[33] *De la religion ...*, p. 121.
[34] Lamennais, "Sur un ouvrage intitulé *Du Pape* par M. le Comte De Maistre", Œuvres Complètes, Paris, 1836-1837, T. VIII, p. 128.
[35] *De la religion ...*, pp. 167-194.
[36] Ibid., p. 167.
[37] Ibid.

that an intelligent Creator could have willed a multiplicity of contending powers capable, in right, of opposing or reversing the very law of Creation.[38]

> Power, ordained to an end which is the conservation of society by the reign of justice or the divine law, always implies the idea of a right and of a divine right; and this is that which distinguishes it from force, which, being completely material, is incapable of constituting a right and, thus, cannot be a true power or sovereignty.[39]

Insofar as Lamennais rejects the natural law tradition such as it was held, for example, among the Thomists, he might be said to be an advocate of that "political theology" which H. Rommen considers as particularly characteristic of the traditionalist movement.[40] Instead of grounding the natural law in natural reason and experience, Lamennais and the other traditionalists find the origin of the supreme law in an original, divine revelation which is not apart from but the very reason for being of the natural order. Thus, Lamennais speaks of a "divine law" and not of a natural law. The reasoning behind this position can be clarified by an explanation of the traditionalists' understanding of the "natural" which Lamennais had given to a friendly critic of the *Essai sur l'indifférence* . . .

> Only revelation, without which man ... would never know anything concerning that which is necessary for him to conserve himself as a moral and intelligent being, or even as a physical being, is truly *natural* and in conformity with *nature*.[41]

Maistre, although recognizing the Divinity as the source of all sovereignty, sees history as the matrix of legitimacy, that is, the actual right to govern is a product of time.[42]

> Duration is the most natural argument of the conservatives and traditionalists. Permanence is that which justifies a state of affairs and the *longum tempus* is, in itself, the ultimate argument which establishes right.[43]

In *De la religion* . . . , Lamennais makes an important break from this conservative dogma. He began to consider the historical justification

---

[38] *De la religion* . . . , p. 168.
[39] Ibid.
[40] H. Rommen, *The State in Catholic Thought*, St. Louis: London, 1955, pp. 111-115.
[41] Letter from Lamennais to Canon Buzzetti, Paris, 22 décembre 1821, reproduced in P. Dudon, "Lettres inédites de Lamennais au chanoine Buzzetti", *Études*, Paris 20 janvier 1910, p. 214.
[42] D. Bagge, *Les idées politiques en France sous la Restauration*, Paris, 1952, p. 293.
[43] C. Schmitt, *Romantisme Politique*, Paris, 1928, p. 69.

of legitimacy as insufficient and honed a more sharply theocratic criterion for judging the claims of rulers to the right of exercising power. The mere exercise of power gives neither the people nor the ruler the right to declare themselves sovereign for both are subject to a higher law.

> Thus, there is a spiritual law, a religious law to which God Himself has submitted all sovereignty, a law which obliges the ruler not only as man but also as ruler.[44]

The people have always recognized, in the opinion of Lamennais, that once a ruler violates this divine law of justice, they are no longer obliged to obey him. When a ruler acts against the divine law, legitimacy or power is forsaken and replaced by force or tyranny.[45] Lamennais supports these really remarkable conclusions, which seem to imply, at least embryonically, the justification of revolution, by pointing to the existence of "a universal, perpetual fact, and, consequently, an indestructible law of the moral order"[46] which would allow for the refusal of allegiance to the unjust ruler.

> ... in all times, in all places, unjust, oppressive power, which, when governing by mere caprice, has trampled under foot the law of God, has no longer been regarded as power, and, considering it fallen ... society has believed itself right in substituting for it a true and legitimate power in order to insure its own existence.[47]

It is noteworthy to remark that the democratic and populist sentiments implicit, if unspoken, in his doctrine of common consent begin to lead him to a position quite similar to that of the advocates of popular sovereignty. Although this tendency is quite clearly present in *De la religion* ..., Lamennais was bent upon avoiding any acceptance of popular sovereignty by means of his ultramontane thesis which locates the unique spiritual sovereignty in the Papacy. What is taking place, however, in *De la religion* ... is an evolution towards a closer identification of the Papacy and the people. Before discussing this aspect, it will be necessary to further clarify Lamennais's concept of divine law which is at the basis of his ultramontanism.

What is this divine law which rules the exercise of sovereignty and which constitutes the rights and duties of men? Who makes it known

[44] *De la religion* ..., p. 170.
[45] Ibid., p. 169.
[46] Ibid.
[47] Ibid., pp. 169-170.

to us? Who guards it and protects it from violation? Lamennais unhesitatingly calls this divine law "religion". Deepening the political significance of the traditionalism which he espouses in the *Essai sur l'indifférence* ... , the Breton spokesman for a total spiritual restoration binds his theory of divine sovereignty to the basic notions of the primitive revelation and the universality of the true originally revealed religion. This divine law or primitive religion, containing the truths necessary for the correct moral order, had been maintained before Christ in the "general sentiment" of mankind; with the coming of Christ, the older order was completed and perfected.[48]

> Jesus Christ established a spiritual society, an infallible guardian of doctrine, and invested it, in the order of salvation, with a power independent of governments. Accordingly, all of the great questions of social justice, all of the doubts concerning the divine law, sovereignty and duties, previously decided by the people, ought to be decided by the Church ... unique depository of the divine law.[49]

The theoretical elaboration and political ramifications of this ultramontane option will be treated in the section immediately following, "Lamennais and Unam Sanctam".

In his theory of the divine law, Lamennais resurrects a political theory not unlike certain medieval theories which were held chiefly by the representatives of the Augustinian tradition.[50] He also tended to see a great similarity in his position concerning the relationship between religion and law to that of Plato and Cicero whose texts he frequently cites as supporting evidence.[51] Society is fundamentally and uniquely spiritual and the precepts of religion are the source of the public law of the nations. Although critics might ridicule religious sentiment as mere prejudice, it is representative, even when manifested in pagan forms, of the most primitive recollections and impulses of mankind. Only religion can create a city and only Christianity, the very incarnation of the universal beliefs of mankind, can bring order and unity to the nations. It was Rousseau who had remarked that "perfect Christianity is a universal social institution".[52] Lamennais finds in this text a verification and, perhaps, the inspiration of his own philosophy

---

[48] *De la religion...*, pp. 170-171.

[49] Ibid., pp. 170-171.

[50] For an interesting treatment of the Augustinian influence on the political doctrines of sovereignty confer M. J. Wilks, *The Problem of Sovereignty in the Later Middle Ages*, Cambridge, 1964.

[51] *De la religion ...*, pp. 1, 2; 240.

[52] Quoted by Lamennais in *De la religion ...*, p. 245.

of religion. Just as Rousseau had based the Social Contract upon the union between the State and the natural religion, Lamennais finds a common source of the religious and political spheres in a primitive revelation of which Roman Catholicism is both the fulfillment and the guardian.[53]

The attribution of all sovereignty to God constitutes the central mennaisian thesis of this period; all theories of sovereignty which separate temporal power from its spiritual source destroy society, rights and the rule of law. Although democracy and Christianity are seen as mutually exclusive,[54] the mennaisian attack, particularly in the second part of *De la religion* . . . , is directed chiefly against the divine right theory of monarchical government which he held to be the basic ideology underlying Gallicanism. Under such theories, the people and non-governmental institutions have no recourse against the abuses and excesses of government.[55] Similarly, the relations between nations are governed not by the universal law of justice but by "force directed by interest".[56] Democracy and royal absolutism are, in effect, dual manifestations, both despotic, of the same error, the rejection of religious authority.

> The State does not *create* nor determine truth by its judgement; but, as the individual, it *recognizes* this immutable *law* of the spirit and submits to it while being attentive to that which the independent, universal, and perpetual authority teaches . . .[57]

In this period of the re-discovery of the Middle Ages, Lamennais was not so much defending the new liberties inspired by the Enlightenment as speaking out in behalf of the ancient liberties which the Church and the various orders of society had known under the feudal organization.[58] Time will make quite evident, however, that Lamennais's return to the more socially based concept of liberty of medieval political theory was not merely anachronistic. The synthesis attained at the period of "L'Avenir" reveals a positive enrichment of

[53] W. Gurian refers to the traditionalist political philosophers as "Catholic Rousseaus", in his *Die politischen und sozialen Ideen des französischen Katholizismus*, Münster, 1929, p. 62.

[54] This is the theme of Chapter I, "État de la société en France", *De la religion* . . . , pp. 1-29.

[55] Ibid., p. 190.

[56] Ibid., p. 116.

[57] Ibid., p. 42.

[58] K. Jürgensen, *Lamennais und die Gestaltung des Belgischen Staates*, Wiesbaden, 1963, p. 15.

the liberal ideals through the critical efforts of the political theocrats. Lamennais placed the debate on tolerance and liberty on a level quite beyond that of pure legalism.

> Where, indeed, there was much to be said for his attitude was in his firm refusal to base his theory of social organization upon no other consideration than that of public policy. Here it is true, he was obviously medieval; for the abandonment of the attempt to discover a natural order founded upon divine right is the chief political characteristic of the modern world . . .[59]

b) *Lamennais and "Unam Sanctam"*

Metaphysically, the idea of being, an unlimited original being which is one, lies at the core of the mennaisian philosophical thought.[60] Political and social theorizing within the mennaisian school must be evaluated in the light of this primordial metaphysical choice. The principle of unity, as has already been mentioned,[61] represents both the source and the goal of history and of all human existence. "In religious matters, and even, in any order of ideas whatsoever", affirms Lamennais, "only through a violation of the catholic principle can there be *two truths contradictory to one another*".[62] As will be seen in Chapter Five, this catholic principle refers to the ontological priority of the one within the metaphysical system which he begins to elucidate more clearly during this period.

Faced with an insupportable chaos in the realm of religion and, consequently, discord in moral and political conduct, Lamennais reacted somewhat as those kindred souls of the later Middle Ages who were confronted with the first pre-Reformation movements away from the ideal of Christian unity which had achieved its apex in the 13th century.

> The formula for so many hierocratic treatises in this period thus becomes the need for *reductio in unitatem*, a constant stress upon the necessity for what Augustinus Triumphus calls a single "caput et director fidei christianae".[63]

[59] H. J. Laski, *Authority in the Modern State*, New Haven, 1919, p. 224.
[60] F. Ravaisson, *La Philosophie en France au XIXe siècle*, Paris, 1889, pp. 34-35.
[61] See Chapter Three, III 1 a, "Priority of Social Unity".
[62] *De la religion* . . . , p. 41.
[63] M. J. Wilks, *The Problem of Sovereignty in the Later Middle Ages*, Cambridge, 1964, pp. 44-45. It is curious to note that among the books auctioned by Lamennais from his personal library in 1836 are two copies of the principal treatise of Augustinus Triumphus. Catalogue Number 701 refers to *Augustini Triumphi, de Ancona, summa*

The parallels between the pro-Roman publicists who inspired "Unam Sanctam" in the reign of Boniface VIII and the leader of the early ultramontane movement of the 19th century are quite striking; but, as is obvious, an entirely new historical frame of references enclosed the attempted mennaisian rehabilitation of the Papacy. Not political hegemony, but the unity of peoples, the christian revitalization of a society based upon the defense of spiritual values, particularly, religious liberty—as Lamennais then understood it—are the ideals which sustain his ultramontane thesis.

In his opinion, the philosophers who have ignored the universal beliefs of mankind and who have relied upon the principle of private, free examination as their unique methodology in their search for truth have never been able to grasp the true nature of either religion or society. What is this Church whose authority they refuse? It is "the depository society of the true religion, that is, the true faith and the true cult".[64] The Church of Rome embodies the universal creed of mankind, the truths of common sense which are to be found among all peoples and races. Not only Sacred Scripture but also eighteen centuries of history in which the Church has exercised power render testimony to the veracity of its claims to be a spiritual society and the unique authority in questions of religion. From the scriptural account of the conferral of the keys to St. Peter, Lamennais deduces his theory concerning the monarchical and infallible character of the Papacy.[65] Since for the traditionalist the given in revelation is a necessity of nature as well as a supernatural intervention, the data of theology and of philosophy are easily joined in one and the same theoretical development.

Since the power given to the Church is independent of and above all other powers, it is a unique sovereignty, therefore, monarchical. Any attempt to place some power over the Papacy would undermine ecclesiastical society and, with it, the whole social order. This is so because without the sovereignty of the Church which alone is infallible all other sovereignties cease to exercise rightful power. This infallibility can be recognized in the Church because the signs of

de Ecclesia potestate, Augustae (per Joh. Schuszeler), 1473, petit in-fol. goth. v.m.; and Number 702, Augustini Triumphi, summa de potestate ecclesiastica. Romae, 1584, pet. in-fol. v.m. Confer, Catalogue de Livres rares et précieux provenant de la Bibliothèque de M. F. de la Mennais, Paris, 1836, p. 44.

[64] De la religion ..., p. 129.
[65] Ibid., pp. 122-132.

unity, universality, perpetuity and sanctity point to it and are only found in the Church. The most perfect embodiment of these signs is the Papacy.[66] Lamennais's reasoning becomes clearer if one reverses the formula inspired by Maistre to read, "no society without Christianity; no Christianity without the Church; no Church without the Pope".[67]

As a reference to the sources employed by Lamennais to construct his ultramontane thesis on Papal prerogatives and infallibility would seem to indicate, there is nothing unusually radical in his argumentation. What is original in Lamennais's ultramontanism, and important for our study, is the definition of the Church and of its politico-social mission which begin to emerge in *De la religion* . . .

"It seems to me", states Maistre, "that every true philosophy must choose between two assumptions, either that it is going to fashion a new religion or that Christianity will be revived in some miraculous way".[68] As D. Bagge has pointed out, Auguste Comte chose the first option while Lamennais took the second.[69] There is an element of newness in Lamennais 's theocracy and ecclesiology which is often overlooked. Although he made much of "Unam Sanctam", to the scandal of the Gallicans, and even added the text of the famous bull to *Des progrès* . . . as a justifying supplement, Lamennais conceives of Church-State relations less in terms of juridical ties and distinctions and more in terms of a metaphysical relationship between two orders reducible to the one source. The Church, in particular, the Papacy, symbolizes the ontological unity of all that is in the Divine Being; its mission is to evoke this truth and to lead mankind to its realization. This unity is a unity in liberty just as the Trinity represents unity in multiplicity. The Church is a guardian of rights and of justice not only a protector of order.

> Considered particularly from the political point of view, its [the Church's] action . . . tended [in the Middle Ages] to lead all to unity, to coordinate nations, as members of a family, in a system of universal fraternity through obedience to a common father, and to establish the

[66] *De la religion* . . . , pp. 122-132.

[67] L. Le Guillou, *L'évolution de la pensée religieuse de Félicité Lamennais*, Paris, 1966, p. 97.

[68] J. de Maistre, *Considerations on France* in *The Works of Joseph de Maistre*, (ed. Lively), London, 1965, pp. 73-74.

[69] D. Bagge, *Les idées politiques en France sous la Restauration*, Paris, 1952, p. 233.

pre-eminence of right over interest by substituting everywhere justice for force.[70]

In *De la religion* ... , Lamennais succeeds in separating the Church from any close identification with the legitimist regime governing France. Monarchical governments which themselves refuse the direction of the Church in matters of the spirit are preparing for their own destruction. Lamennais does not, at this point, ally the Church with any particular form of government; his almost obsessive concern becomes that of the freedom of the Church, a complete independence of the Church from the administrative control of governments. In the face of the inevitable revolution which will come to governments, such as that of France, which have violated the divine law, the Church must take the following steps.

> ... courageous exercise of its divine authority, order and life within itself, fearing nothing of men, expecting nothing from them, waiting in patience and in peace for that which God will decide for the world.[71]

This amazing conclusion of *De la religion* ... reveals the doubt and the disillusionment with which Lamennais was confronted concerning the fate of the Restoration; but there is no hesitancy on his part to demand, at least, implicitly, the separation of the spiritual society, the Church, from the reigning political order. Contrary to the more rigidly authoritarian and juridical notion of the Church which was dominant in the texts of canon law and theology of the period, Lamennais presents a broader vision of the Church, that is, a Church which becomes the herald of the people, the protector and liberator of the weak, and the guardian of divine law.[72] This spiritualization of the Church and its identification with freedom, even if only, at this stage, with freedom for itself, is a highly significant advance in the forward thrust of Lamennais's thought towards Catholic liberalism.[73]

In his mind, there is the ever-present idea that something must be done to save society; there must be a social and political redemption. But this renewal will not be accomplished by the forceful intervention of governments. The use of the secular arm through civic intolerance and religious persecution cannot attain the ends envisioned.

[70] *De la religion* ... , pp. 110-111.

[71] *De la religion* ... , p. 301.

[72] L. Le Guillou, *L'évolution de la pensée religieuse de Félicité Lamennais*, Paris, 1966, p. 100.

[73] K. Jürgensen, *Lamennais und die Gestaltung des Belgischen Staates*, Wiesbaden, 1963, pp. 12-13.

> It [Christian society] is the fruit, not of violence but of conviction; its
> base is faith not the sword. It exists when one believes in it; it ceases
> when one ceases to believe; laws can only restore [his society] by aiding
> to re-establish it in thought and in conscience.[74]

The interrogating tone, the questioning of the future, which colors the
conclusion of *De la religion* ..., simply opens the problematic which
Lamennais will treat during the period leading up to the publication
of *Des progrès* ... in which he will announce for the first time in clear
and unequivocal terms his declaration in favor of the complete
separation of Church and State and his whole-hearted identification
with the cause of liberty. The principles concerning spiritual
sovereignty and freedom of the spiritual order, although still narrow
in conception as established in *De la religion* ..., are fundamental to
the positions taken in *Des progrès*...

3. *The End of "Societas Christiana"*

No matter how strongly some authors have tended to criticize
Lamennais as a theorist, there is generally considerable agreement in
admitting that he correctly assessed the process of secularization
which was taking place in Western Europe in the early 19th century.
In the years preceding the final admission in *De la Religion* . . . that
France had, in fact, become a "vast democracy"[75] Lamennais had
detected various signs of importance which he considered to be
harbingers of an inevitable neutralization of the nations of Western
Europe which had been originally organized under Christian inspiration. To him, such a process was catastrophic; nonetheless, he
displayed great honesty and a keen sociological sense in his ability to
seize upon certain political events and social phenomena as
symptomatic of deeper processes at work in the whole culture.

In a sense, *De la religion* ... is both a summing up of and a
conclusion drawn from the agitated journalistic debates which had
won for him both renown and the unhappy reputation of being an
extremist. As the final pages of *De la religion* . . . indicate, he had
not yet fashioned a positive program for the preservation of religious
values and spiritual unity in face of the frankly recognized process of
desacralization which was taking place. Before the publication of this

[74] *De la religion* ..., p. 299.
[75] Ibid., p. 17.

work, as his sharply phrased articles establish, he could but warn of the dangers and foster a certain resistance; he had not yet seen the clear possibility of either adjusting his principles to the historical realities or of finding any positive value in the prevailing tendencies. Although we have already discussed in Chapter Three Lamennais's theoretical opposition to the ideas of tolerance and temporal sovereignty emanating from the Enlightenment, it would further clarify our investigation if some consideration were given to his more important journalistic reactions, genuinely representative of philosophical orientations, to certain political happenings. There is a sharpness of focus in Lamennais's journalism which is enormously enlightening and helpful in uncovering the true direction of his thought.

A most interesting legal case arose in 1818 concerning the rights of a certain non-Catholic French citizen to abstain from any outward participation, in this instance, by decorating his property, in a religious festival of a definitely public character which had been sponsored by the dominant Catholic majority of the region. The case of Jacques-Paul Roman, defended by Odilon Barrot, became famous in the annals of French legal history and occasioned a sharp debate between Barrot and Lamennais concerning religious liberty. The plea of the non-conformist's lawyer hinged upon the interpretation to be given Articles 5 and 6 of the Charter, namely, liberty of cult for all religion and the official recognition of Roman Catholicism as the State religion. The decision of the lower court, which had condemned the defendant for failing to show proper respect for the religion of the State, was reversed by the higher court which accepted the reasoning of Barrot that "liberty is equality in rights, it is the neutrality of the law".[76]

The position of the higher court was, for Lamennais, the confession in public of the neutrality or atheism of the law in France, an admission that there is no "public religion" underlying the political and legal structures.[77] Lamennais had proposed that a true application of the principles of religious liberty could not have required of the defendant any act against his conscience; but, if there was truly a State

---

[76] For a brief, but concise, modern treatment of this important case confer J. Lecler, "Les controverse sur l'Église et l'État au temps de la Restauration", published in *L'ecclésiologie au XIXᵉ siècle*, Paris, 1960, pp. 297-307. Barrot's argument is quoted by Lecler on p. 301.

[77] Lamennais, "Sur un arrêt rendu par la Cours de Cassation", (1819), Œuvres Complètes, Paris, 1836-1837, T. VIII, pp. 162-167.

or public religion in France, civil authorities had the right to demand a certain outward respect for that religion. He accepted the necessity for a sort of civil tolerance as a concession to an unfortunate diversity of beliefs and to individual conscience but not as a political and philosophical position which would require that the law and the police authority of the public power be blind to the truth or non-truth of religion. At this phase of his thinking, 1818-1819, Lamennais was chiefly concerned with establishing the limits of religious toleration in order to safeguard the public religion, Roman Catholicism.[78] In *De la religion* ..., he returns to this famous decision upholding the argumentation of the lawyer, Barrot, as the official recognition of a conclusion which he finds himself forced to admit if not accept.

> ... the State which grants equal protection to opposing cults has evidently no cult; the State which pays ministers to teach contradictory doctrines, has evidently no faith; the State which has neither faith nor cult is evidently atheistic ...[79]

The attitude of the French court in the case of Jacques-Paul Roman had become, in the judgement of Lamennais, the prevailing consensus of the government in all of the hotly disputed proposals of legislation which touched upon questions of religious importance. He had never advocated constraining individuals to practice the religion of the nation; but, in the early years of the Restoration, he had hoped that the government would refrain from acts which would be an implicit denial of the traditional religious character of the nation.

To his chagrin, he had ample occasion to observe the contrary. In a group of articles on the religious and social conditions of the workers in Paris, whose importance for the initiation of Catholic social thought in the 19th century has been emphasized by J.-B. Duroselle,[80] Lamennais observes that the poor are not even protected from exploitation on Sundays; they are forced to work because the State, in the name of religious liberty, refuses to recognize the moral and social purposes of protective legislation. A neutral law is a mockery of law.

> The zeal of impiety uses everything, even hunger, in order to corrupt the people without any opposition from authority, and this is called protection of liberty of conscience and of opinion.[81]

[78] Lamennais, "Sur un mémoire pour le sieur Jacques-Paul Roman par M. Odilon-Barrot", (1818), Œuvres Complètes, Paris, 1836-1837, T. VI, pp. 251-258.
[79] *De la religion* ..., pp. 32-33.
[80] See Footnote 50, Chapter One, II, "Lamennais as a Philosopher".
[81] Lamennais, "Sur l'observation du dimanche", Œuvres Complètes, Paris, 1836-1837,

Not only does the State refuse to provide adequate social legislation out of fear of violating the liberties of certain sectors of the population, powerful interests, but it actually coerces the majority, particularly the Church which is recognized as the religion of the State. Against the dictates of their consciences and the laws of their religion, Roman Catholic priests are frequently required by public officials to grant Christian burials to known violators of Church laws,[82] or to suicides.[83] What then, asks Lamennais, is the meaning of tolerance if it is applied one-sidedly? But the crusading journalist began to make important discoveries. As Chr. Maréchal has pointed out, Lamennais started to make the distinction between the situation of a believer and that of a citizen in his article, "Sur la prétention de l'autorité civile de forcer le clergé à concourir à l'inhumation de ceux à qui les lois de l'Eglise défendent d'accorder la sépulture ecclésiastique".[84]

Throughout this series of articles, particularly, in "Observations sur la promesse d'enseigner ler Quatres Articles de la Déclaration de 1682", (1818), Lamennais pinpointed the inconsistencies of the government in interpreting the articles of the Charter of 1815 which formed the constitutional base of the renewed monarchy. There seemed to be a double standard to be used in applying the freedoms granted in the Charter within the area of tolerance. On the one hand, minority groups were, in the eyes of Lamennais, vigorously protected while the majority group, the Roman Catholics, were administratively shackled. If the political power professes to be blind or neutral in religious matters—really an admission that social faith has vanished—what right has the government to require seminary professors to teach certain Gallican propositions concerning the nature of the Church? Some of the comments in this article are extremely enlightening. "In order to dictate orders to the intellect",

---

T. VIII, p. 325. To this article must be joined two other articles which demonstrate the keen sociological insight of Lamennais. An earlier article, 1816, under the same title, "Sur l'observation du dimanche", was written in defense of the poor who were forced to work on Sunday (T. VI, pp. 243-250). "Association de Saint-Joseph", 1821, contains an excellent description of the conditions of the workers in the cities and expresses an awareness of their need for associations similar to the ancient guilds. (T. VIII, pp. 250-257).

[82] Lamennais, "Sur la prétention de l'autorité civile de forcer le clergé à concourir á l'inhumation de ceux à qui les lois de l'Eglise défendent d'accorder la sépulture ecclésiastique", Œuvres Complètes, Paris, 1836-1837, T. VI, pp. 259-266.

[83] Lamennais, "Sur le suicide", Œuvres Complètes, Paris, 1836-1837, T. VIII, pp. 186-192.

[84] Chr. Maréchal, La dispute . . . , p. 161.

states Lamennais, "it is necessary to possess the power to enlighten it".[85] Political agencies have no such power; the ministry cannot dictate to the Church in matters of doctrine.

> When the civil authority seeks to act on the spirit of man by way of constraint, it misjudges both itself and men. There is something in man which rejects opinions presented to them, not as an object of examination, but as a test of their obedience; human reason is and can only be passive before God.[86]

It is most interesting to read these statements in favor of liberty of conscience in light of the remarks which Félicité made to Jean-Marie in a letter about this article. "I have united to my subject", he informs his brother, "an entirely new theory of *spiritual power,* the development of which would require a book".[87] The elucidation of this new theory was achieved in *De la religion...* where he disengages spiritual authority from the temporal trappings of privilege and legal status demanding for it an unfettered liberty of action. To be sure, Lamennais had not yet arrived at a full acceptance of a modern theory of liberty; much refinement of his thought was necessary before attaining the open social and political philosophy of "L'Avenir".

The question of public education probably did more than any other issue to force the emergence of some sort of Catholic liberalism.[88] Education was a pivotal question for the French Catholics such as Lamennais who readily saw that the path to the future survival of Christian values was intimately bound up with the preparation of the present generation. Lamennais, future founder and superior of a religious congregation established to modernize the apostolate, was keenly aware of the struggle for the minds of men that was behind the whole issue of education.[89] Treating of this matter, which was to become and to remain a central issue in Church-State relations even to our own day, Lamennais saw with remarkable clarity both the weaknesses and the strong points of the doctrinaire liberal position.

As early as 1814, he bitterly, and somewhat unjustly, assailed the

---

[85] Lamennais, "Observations sur la promesse d'enseigner les Quatre Articles", Œuvres Complètes, Paris, 1836-1837, T. VI, p. 167.

[86] Ibid., pp. 167-168.

[87] Letter from Lamennais to his brother, Jean-Marie, Paris, 15 mars 1818, reproduced in A. Blaize, Œuvres inédites de F. Lamennais, Paris, 1866, T. I, p. 345.

[88] G. Weill, Histoire du catholicisme libéral en France, 1828-1908, Paris, 1909, p. 10.

[89] L. Le Guillou, L'évolution de la pensée religieuse de Félicité Lamennais, Paris, 1966, pp. 73-86.

university system inherited from the Napoleonic era of re-organization which was based upon the principle of state monopoly in higher education.[90] He correctly analyzed the totalitarian character genuinely embedded in any theory of education which makes of public instruction a state function allowing for no other participation in this domain. It was, to his way of thinking, a perpetuation of the principle of statism enunciated by the revolutionary, Danton, in 1793, to the effect that the state has prior rights over parents in the education of children. Bonaparte had succeeded in preserving and in institutionalizing this philosophy through his administrative unification of the university and the upper schools. Such an idea was new to civilized states and rife with dangers for within it are the seeds of tyranny. Absolute and exclusive government control of education is, for Lamennais, a direct violation of the "natural" rights of parents to educate their children.[91] "Teaching, which, at bottom, is nothing more than the communication of ideas, will always remain as free as thought itself".[92]

The advocates of this state monopoly theory in the field of education were, strangely enough, generally to be found among the so-called liberals. According to Lamennais, there is a contradiction in a philosophy which, on the one hand, weakens the social bonds built upon a common religious creed in order to safeguard individual reason while, on the other hand, it grants the State the exclusive right to educate the young. Lamennais envisioned possibly dire consequences emanating from such a gesture; "society itself will be made a species of automaton".[93]

The reasoning behind this rather stark conclusion is to be found in Lamennais's philosophy of education which is, it should be noted, perfectly consistent with his epistemology. Education consists in the formation of spiritual habits in the youth through the teaching of social beliefs and, as such, is prior in importance to mere instruction which is the teaching of the arts and the sciences. Since education is the preparation of the "moral" man, it cannot be left to political society; it is the obligation of the parents and the Church. The State

[90] Lamennais, "De l'Université Impériale", (1814), Œuvres Complètes, Paris, 1836-1837, T. VI, pp. 308-328.
[91] Lamennais, "Du Droit du gouvernement sur l'éducation", (1817), Œuvres Complètes, Paris, 1836-1837, T. VI, pp. 356-368.
[92] Ibid., p. 358.
[93] Lamennais, "De l'éducation considérée dans ses rapports avec la liberté", (1818), Œuvres Complètes, Paris, 1836-1837, T. VI, p. 370.

may instruct but instruction without education has a de-moralizing effect upon the youth.[94]

Familial right is undermined and true liberty of thought endangered by such monopolistic tendencies. "Science, the common property of all spirits and often the bitter fruit of their labor, is in no way within the domain of authority".[95] Similarly, "to know is to think, and what is more free than thought? What is more independent of all human power?"[96] The fundamental liberal error, as well seen by Lamennais, was to atomize society into individuals while forgetting social unities. The rights of individuals became a passionate liberal concern but the rights of families and natural associations were ignored. Basically in the question of rights, it is not possible to hold that the government grants or denies rights. Governments defend justice; they do not invent it. This is so because they are not the source of truth; they do not create their own sovereignty. It is the duty of the government as of the individual to recognize truth and to provide the conditions necessary for its maintenance and propagation. In the question of education, the State should recognize the parental right to educate and should support those free associations, such as religious communities, which serve to fulfill this parental right.[97]

Education was only one, albeit a most important one, of the sensitive areas of discussion which stimulated the public and parliamentary life of the Restoration governments. The debate concerning the projected governmental law designed to punish perpetrators of acts of sacrilege was another cause célèbre of the mid-1820s. This particular debate had considerable influence in the future orientation of French political life. "There is surely a bond", in the opinion of J. Lecler, "between the controversies of 1825 concerning the law of sacrilege and the new orientations of liberalism".[98] The discussion in the Chamber of Deputies, which had provoked the involvement of various luminaries, seemed only to verify for Lamennais the growing realization that the State is basically incompetent in treating of religious matters. Both in an article for the

---

[94] Lamennais, "De l'éducation du peuple", (1818), Œuvres Complètes, Paris, 1836-1837, T. VI, pp. 329-346.
[95] Lamennais, "De l'éducation considérée dans ses rapports avec la liberté", Œuvres complètes, Paris, 1836-1837, T. VI, p. 371.
[96] Ibid.
[97] Ibid., p. 381.
[98] J. Lecler, "Les controverses sur l'Église et l'État au temps de la restauration", published in L'ecclesiologie au XIXᵉ siècle, Paris, 1960, p. 305.

"Mémorial Catholique"[99] and in Chapter II of *De la religion* ... ,
Lamennais discusses the great debate. His doubts concerning the
sincerity of the alliance between the Restoration government and the
Roman Catholic Church are affirmed by the parliamentary impasse
over the legislation. In the course of the discussions, religious dogma
had been treated as mere opinion; no distinction had been made
between a sacrilege, that is, a crime committed against the true
religion, and similar acts perpetrated against the other sects. In simply
designating all such acts as sacrilege, the government had again
avowed its atheism.

Royer-Collard, chief spokesman for the system of government
under the Charter, attempted to defend the idea of an equal,
undifferentiated protection of all cults as the correct application of the
concept of civil tolerance contained in the Charter. This equal
protection is not, in his opinion, an admission of the fundamental
atheism of the law. In his comments reproduced by Lamennais in *De
la religion* ... , he contends that law requires a religious ground or
foundation for without it morality has no sanction. Against an
either/or position of the type advocated by Lamennais, the scholarly
parliamentarian pointed out that the relationship between a state and
religion is not the same as that between an individual and his religious
beliefs. Lamennais, however, with rigorous logic, refuses to admit that
a State can be at the same time neutral in religious matters and, at
base, founded upon religion. Since there is no such thing as a neutral
religion, no true society can be religiously undetermined. The basis of
the mennaisian argument is another aspect of the "Catholic principle"
which, epistemologically considered, requires that religious truths be
recognized, not created, through faith and common consent. There is
no middle position, such as that proposed by Royer-Collard; the unity
between Church and State is either one of a spiritual penetration of
the secular sphere, such as had been the case in the Middle Ages, or
one of no alliance at all. The latter is made necessary when there is
a real danger of the use of religion by temporal rulers for subservient
ends. The discussion concerning the law of sacrilege was, for

[99] Lamennais, "Du projet de loi sur le sacrilège présenté à la Chambre des Paris",
Œuvres Complètes, Paris, 1836-1837, T. VIII, pp. 422-445. In the Daubrée et Cailleux
edition of the Œuvres Complètes employed here, the date of this article is given as 1832.
This error is averted to and corrected in J.-M. Querard, *Notice bibliographique des
ouvrages de M. de La Mennais*, Paris, 1849, p. 39. The correct date of the first publication
of this article is 1825, a date contemporaneous with the actual debate.

Lamennais, another example of the failure of the Restoration.[100] This debate with Royer-Collard underlines a certain ambivalence in Lamennais's position which has been noted previously.[101] Metaphysically, no State, just as no individual, has a reason for being outside of the divine law and, for him, this means outside of Catholic Christianity. But it would seem that the official recognition of the Roman Church would not, in itself, be equivalent to a genuine religious foundation of political power. The ancient formulae of legal history such as "recognition" and "State Church" had become, in the opinion of Lamennais, devoid of meaning, and, therefore, the political order must be reconstituted as the religious order itself is revitalized. Lamennais does not, for the moment, venture any prognostications as to the nature of the future liaison.

To understand the new direction taken by Lamennais towards an open declaration in favor of the separation of Church and State, such as is evident in the conclusions drawn from *De la religion* . . . , it has been useful to review the positions taken by him in reference to critical political events of the epoch in the many short articles he has written. Chr. Maréchal has been the principal advocate of the theory that these early newspaper articles betray "the first symptoms of an alliance between Mennaisian and liberal ideas which will be wedded later on".[102] Although K. Jürgensen correctly hesitates to speak of any mennaisian "liberalism" for this period, as is implied by Maréchal,[103] the dispute seems to be one of words. Whatever one may call the protests which Lamennais made in the name of a higher, more spiritual liberty, they all reveal a pattern of thought and a certain coherency which is logically consistent with the whole of his intellectual evolution. The ideas contained therein cannot be overlooked as source material for a future and more favorable re-evaluation of liberalism. These arguments formed in the context of controversy provide the linkage between Lamennais's fundamental political philosophy of the unique spiritual sovereignty, a genuine authoritarianism, and his espousal of a philosophy of liberty compatible with his theological presuppositions.

---

[100] *De la religion* . . . , Chapter II, "Que la religion, en France, est entièrement hors de la société politique et civile, et que par conséquent l'État est athée", pp. 30-52.

[101] See Chapter Three, III 1 c, "Towards a Free Church".

[102] Chr. Maréchal, *La dispute* . . . , p. 82.

[103] K. Jürgensen, *Lamennais und die Gestaltung des Belgischen Staates*, Wiesbaden, 1963, p. 15.

During this decade, Lamennais struggled mightily to balance the exigencies of his theology and philosophy based upon a unitary conceptualization of spiritual reality with a growing awareness of the actual requirements of a pluralistic society. With the publication of *De la religion* . . . , he had re-asserted, more clearly than ever, his lofty idea of spiritual sovereignty, incarnate in an historical institution, while, at the same time, recognizing the need for an order that would be truly one of liberty. He had not resolved the antinomy of the one and the many such as history presented it to him.

There are, however, three characteristic features of Lamennais's intellectual and spiritual development, revealed principally in his correspondence, which seem to dominate during the turbulent decade preceding the appearance of *Des progrès* . . . These might be described as: (1) a profound pessimism regarding the durability of the Restoration and the monarchy; (2) a resolute desire to find a new solution for the re-organization of society; and, (3) an unshakable confidence in the power of truth. Concerning the imminent triumph of what he had consistently designated as the revolutionary principle, he had no doubt whatsoever.

> The proof that kings understand absolutely nothing concerning all that is taking place is that they combat everywhere the effects and never the causes . . . This universal idiocy convinces me that the evil has not yet sufficiently developed, that the people have not been sufficiently instructed and chastized to accept the remedy which will save them.[104]

To his acquaintance, Berryer, he reveals that the doctrines espoused by the new liberal group gathered around the "Globe" and by the followers of Saint-Simon publishing the "Producteur" are clear signs of the coming universal revolution "which more and more, I believe to be absolutely inevitable".[105] He brooded continually over the widespread agitation which he saw about him.

> Society moves on shifting foundations; we are approaching a catastrophe . . . be assured that everything is beyond man in what is taking place today.[106]

---

[104] Letter from Lamennais to Baron Vitrolles, La Chênaie, 17 octobre 1820, reproduced in Eugène Forgues, *Correspondance inédite entre Lamennais et le baron de Vitrolles*, Paris, 1886, p. 70.

[105] Letter from Lamennais to A. M. Berryer, 22 décembre 1825, reproduced in E. D. Forgues, *Œuvres Posthumes de F. Lamennais*, Paris, 1859, T. I, p. 150.

[106] Letter from Lamennais to Countess Senfft, Paris, 8 avril 1826, reproduced in ibid., p. 174.

As has been pointed out, prophetism was endemic to Romanticism.[107] While it may be seen as simply a derivative of feverish imaginations, it was, nonetheless, part and parcel of the romantic psychology and must be taken as a contributing factor in the elaboration of the romantic philosophies. In the case of Lamennais, the presentiment of doom, so common in his letters, did not mean inactivity or fatalistic resignation. If evil must have its day, it is because Providence has permitted it for a salutary effect. The believer's role is to search out the meaning of these catastrophic events and to learn from them while preparing for the new order. In his quest for political and social redemption and salvation, Lamennais turned his attention to the very elements which he had considered as the most representative of the revolutionary spirit. As early as 1825, he makes known in his letter to Berryer his interest in the ideology of the Saint-Simon group and his search to find a new center around which to unite the just cause.[108] The interest was reciprocal. Auguste Comte was quick to recognize the direction which Lamennais's thought was taking in *De la religion* . . . "M. de la Mennais", according to Comte, "has recently been led to a most grievous infraction of the fundamental principles [of the ultra-royalist party] in formally invoking liberty of cults".[109] For his part, Lamennais found the writings of Comte in the "Producteur", "quite remarkable".[110] He also expressed his admiration for the young liberal, Victor Cousin, to whom he gave his assurance that Catholicism, contrary to many opinions, does not stifle the honest inquiry after truth. "All men of good faith who seek the truth, no matter what inevitable differences of opinion they may have, are made to love one another and to join together".[111]

Pessimism concerning the irremediableness of the existing situation without great suffering and turmoil is entirely compatible, in the romantic complexity of Lamennais's mind, with the optimistic proclamations of the new society to come. The liaison between these two seemingly opposed emotions is provided by his profound belief in the power of truth. Lamennais is not a fatalist but a believer in the

[107] See Footnote 21, Chapter Four.
[108] Letter from Lamennais to A. M. Berryer, 3 novembre 1825, reproduced in E. D. Forgues, *Œuvres Posthumes de F. Lamennais*, Paris, 1859, T. I, p. 139.
[109] C. Calippe, "Les relations d'Auguste Comte et de Lamennais", *Revue du clergé français*, Paris, 1er octobre 1918, p. 24.
[110] Ibid., p. 19.
[111] Letter from Lamennais to Victor Cousin, 30 juin 1825, reproduced in part in A. Feugère, *Lamennais avant l'Essai sur l'indifférence*, Paris, 1906, p. 302.

free action of men to bring about the restoration of an order willed by Providence, the necessary condition of true liberty. The Church, guardian of the primitive and essential truths, must show the way to the new society. "Society awaits a new action of Christianity, a grand act, as elevated as Christianity itself, in order to be regenerated".[112] Providence, the law of history, will have its way but man is free to bring about the order of justice and truth willed by Providence or he must suffer the consequence of being forced to do so by revolutionary chaos. For W. Gurian, the idealistic appeal of Lamennais to the Church and for the Church in his conclusion to *De la religion ...*, contains the germ of the coming association of the Church with the cause of freedom. The mission of the Church must become immanent in history through an identification with a specific social and historical movement which Lamennais will soon discover in the growing and evident desire among the peoples, especially, those in Catholic nations, for liberty and political justice.[113]

II. Religious Liberty—Source of all Liberties

1. *Christian Liberty in a Secularized World*

The theological sources of Lamennais's doctrine of liberty as developed in the *Essai sur l'indifférence...*[114] remained basically constant during the years of transition which would bear witness to an energetic application and refinement of this doctrine. In an earlier essay on the particular problem of liberty, "De la Liberté", (1820), Lamennais made it quite clear that he was not concerned with a psychological definition of liberty but with a description that is essentially ethical and ontological. Rejecting all equating of liberty with the idea of independence, he sees in liberty "a state of being in which nothing separates man from his end nor prevents him from arriving at that perfection which is proper to man".[115] Although he sees liberty as a "sentiment" and as a "desire" common to all men, this sentiment or desire is but the immanent counterpart of a relationship to transcendental truth. Liberty in this intellectualist view consists in

---

[112] Letter from Lamennais to Ventura, Paris, 14 mai 1826, reproduced in P. Dudon, "Lettres inédites de Lamennais à Ventura (1826)", *Études*, Paris, 5 mars 1910, p. 612.

[113] W. Gurian, *Die politischen und sozialen Ideen des französischen Katholizismus*, Münster, 1929, p. 105.

[114] See Chapter Three, III 1, "Liberty and Order".

[115] Lamennais, "De la liberté", Œuvres Complètes, Paris, 1836-1837, T. VIII, p. 234.

the possession of truth but, since truth is achieved only in and through a communicating society, liberty depends upon power which is the first condition of both society and liberty. Power in the mennaisian lexicon retains the more generic sense of "capacity" or "ability to" avoiding any limitation of its meaning to a restrictive sense of "force". In the perfect society, power is one because truth is one and perfect liberty is expressed through the impeccable conformity of the individual with perfect society.[116]

The declarations of *De la religion* ... render quite obvious the observation that the conditions for such a perfect society and, hence, perfect liberty, were no longer present in the political order of the later years of the Restoration. In light of the continuing disintegration of the social order it became necessary to re-define the nature of political and civil liberty. The fundamental idea of liberty as perfect conformity of will and intellect in obedience to truth does not undergo any alteration but the attainment of this perfect liberty will require the actualization of particular liberties within the political sphere in a manner which had not previously been tolerated.

De la religion . . . is both the end of one phase of thought for Lamennais and the beginning of another. What he had principally sought to re-establish up to this point were the "ancient liberties", the rights and privileges of the Church and of related social organisms such as they had existed in the Middle Ages. Although displaying some concern for the rights of the individual conscience, he does not show himself concerned about the rights of the other cults to practice and to promulgate their doctrines. In this sense, K. Jürgensen refers to *De la religion* ... as "perhaps the most intolerant of all of his writings".[117] There was no apparent shift in his opinion concerning tolerance from that which he expressed in an article on that subject in 1823, in which he maintained that "the religion of Jesus Christ is intolerant".[118] There is an important difference, however, between "De la Tolérance" and *De la religion* ... in reference to the part to be played by civil authority in the affairs of religion; and, con-sequently, elements of a new appraisal of civil toleration begin to

---

[116] Lamennais, "Dela liberté", Œuvres Complètes, Paris 1836-1837, T. VIII, pp. 233-238.
[117] K. Jürgensen, *Lamennais und die Gestaltung des Belgischen Staates*, Wiesbaden, 1963, p. 19.
[118] Lamennais, "De la Tolérance", Œuvres Complètes, Paris, 1836-1837, T. VIII, pp. 333-334.

emerge. In 1823, he found it quite acceptable that civil power intervene to protect order and truth since "society cannot tolerate those doctrines which render its existence impossible or which are incompatible with public order".[119] In the years following, however, he was forced by events and the movement of his own thoughts to re-evaluate his stand on modern liberties such as they had been formulated in the Charter. Although products of a philosophy alien to his own, he soon came to see in these liberal enactments the necessary safeguards of religious liberty and genuine values proper to the modern political order.

What brought this process about? So many factors enter into the picture between 1826 and 1829 in French history and in Lamennais's personal growth in this period that it would be impossible to cover the ground completely without writing a thorough history of man and epoch. Similarly, it is most difficult, and somewhat dishonest, to point to any one writing or event as the turning-point on the road to his dramatic espousal of the cause of liberty and democracy. But, certain facts and his written testimonies are clear signposts of the course which his ideological evolution was taking and these should be mentioned before discussing the doctrinal content of *Des progrès . . .* Contrary to the opinion of many commentators on the history of that era, the opening of mennaisianism towards liberalism was not an abrupt about-face but a consistent development. To be sure, external events became the occasions of new turns and reactions but we are dealing with a species of thought that had been hammered out on the anvil of history.

One important event was the governmental legal process against Lamennais charging him with inciting citizens to disobey ministerial regulations. In *De la religion . . .*, the priest-spokesman of the ultramontane tendency had argued that the Declaration of 1682 did not have the force of law and that French citizens, particularly, clerics and seminary professors were not obliged by its contents. Defended by Berryer, a well-known lawyer and friend, Lamennais's defense against the charges of the police was based upon the rights established in the Charter, which, Berryer contended, guaranteed his client's right to question the Declaration of 1682, considered by the government as the law of the nation, on theological grounds. The prosecution pre-

---

[119] Lamennais, "De la Tolérance", Œuvres Complètes, Paris, 1836-1837, T. VIII, pp. 338-339.

vailed, however, and Lamennais was forced to pay a minimal fine.[120]

To Lamennais, the whole affair was a confirmation of his conviction that Gallican principles were, in fact, animating the religious policies of the government and that the danger of creating a national Church was all too apparent. More interestingly, from an ideological point of view, was the fact that he had based his defense of his right to criticize on the guarantees of the Charter. Was this opportunism or a change of conviction? Probably, there is a mixture of both motives in this particular action. His correspondence of this period reveals a certain confusion, a doubting and a questioning about the implementation of his own theories on a political level. C. Carcopino sees a threefold effect on Lamennais resulting from the process of April 1826, namely, a buttressing of his opposition to the Gallicanism of the Bourbon monarchy, a realization of the widespread support of his views among the lower clergy, and an awareness of the silence of the Vatican and the hierarchy. He was also certainly cognizant of the support which he had received from the left-wing and liberal elements in his struggle with governmental censorship.[121] Could he have failed to discover a sympathy of interests with the new generation of liberals such as those of the "Globe" who, although anticlerical, were in favor of equal freedom, under the Charter, for the Roman Catholic Church and who were strongly opposed to the regalism of the Gallican ministers?[122] Apparently not, for in December 1826, Lamennais makes known to his correspondent, Count Senfft, these interesting observations.

> Among the honest liberals, and there are many of this sort even in religious areas, a spiritual disposition reigns which, in other times, would have been most fortunate. They see nothing to which to attach themselves ... and this brings them closer to the Church which alone offers that stability which can be found nowhere else. The essential task would be to show them that Christianity is compatible with all of their prudent desires, that it does not deliver the people over to power ... that it protects and maintains all rights; that it alone is the guarantee of all legitimate liberties ... The world has changed; it is looking for a master.[123]

Lamennais's encounter with the judiciary was but typical of the

[120] A. R. Vidler, *Prophecy and Papacy*, London, 1954, p. 118.

[121] C. Carcopino, *Les doctrines sociales de Lamennais*, Paris, 1942, p. 62.

[122] For this new orientation within liberalism consult J. Lecler, "Les controverses sur l'Église et l'État au temps de la Restauration", published in *L'ecclésiologie au XIXᵉ siècle*, Paris, 1960, p. 305.

[123] Letter from Lamennais to Count Senfft, Paris, 22 décembre 1826, reproduced in E. D. Forgues, *Œuvres Posthumes de F. Lamennais*, Paris, 1859, T. I, p. 217.

frequent disputes which arose in this period concerning the exercise of the police power of the state through the censorship of publication. As a journalist of long-standing, Lamennais had had occasion to both comment upon and to feel the effects of ministerial interference with the press.[124] He had approved of the right to censure anti-religious publications but had argued against the use of censorship as a political weapon with which the ministers of the government stifled political opposition.[125] His outspoken articles prepared for the conservative "Drapeau Blanc" had embroiled him in various hassles with the government and the ultra-royalist faction over his right to condemn ministerial policies.[126] It was a matter of consternation to him, at an earlier date, that he should be prosecuted for his defense of the principles of authority.[127]

Once Lamennais had accepted, however, the reality of secularization and the irrefutability of his admission to Senfft that the "world had changed", he began to see freedom of the press in a new light. Separating himself clearly and somewhat harshly from Bonald and the conservative faction, he openly admits that freedom of the press had become "a necessity of the present society".[128] His argument is two-fold in that he first assumes what is really a traditionally liberal pose of distrust towards political power and governmental administrations; the power of censorship in the hands of such a government as that which he had described in *De la religion* . . . would be tantamount to tyranny. More profoundly, he proposes that, in spite of the deleterious effects which could and would result from a total liberty of publication, the power of unrestricted truth would more than compensate for such evil as would occur. The substance of his argument is that the correction of error is a matter of time and of the free encounter of error with truth, a result unattainable by the application of force.[129] It is interesting to note that as Lamennais's conviction and belief in the universal disposition and receptability of

[124] Lamennais, "Quelques réflexions sur la censure et sur l'université", Œuvres Complètes, Paris, 1836-1837, T. VIII, pp. 193-205.

[125] Ibid., pp. 193-194.

[126] Lamennais, "Sur la poursuite judiciaire dirigée contre le Drapeau Blanc au sujet de l'université", Œuvres Complètes, Paris, 1836-1837, T. VIII, pp. 364-373.

[127] Letter from Lamennais to Saint-Victor, La Chênaie, 18 décembre (1823), reproduced by L. Barthou, "Lettres à Saint-Victor II", Revue des Deux Mondes, Paris, 15 novembre 1925, p. 425.

[128] Letter from Lamennais to Count Senfft, 19 novembre 1827, reproduced in E. D. Forgues, Œuvres Posthumes de F. Lamennais, Paris, 1859, T. I, p. 301.

[129] Ibid., pp. 300-302.

mankind to truth deepens, his rejection of the ancient systems of restrictions and privileges increases and his acceptance of modern liberties becomes more enthusiastic. There is no doubt a tactical element in Lamennais's defense of the liberty of the press but it would also seem that his doctrine of common consent, fundamentally philosophical, would permit such adjustments on the level of practical policy which before were considered as incompatible with his basic principles. Once common consent had been accepted by Lamennais as the ultimate criterion of certitude he necessarily gave greater importance to public opinion and to the shifting manifestations of the common opinion of mankind in historical movements and political facts. This matter will be treated more fully in the concluding chapter.

Not the governments but the people were to become for Lamennais the hope for the society of order and justice which was by now looming largely in his visions of the future. The pessimistic drift which had borne him to the rejection of the monarchy and of the conservatism of his earlier years seemed to have given ground to an overwhelming spirit of optimism following the mid-summer personal crisis of 1826.

> ... Is it not curious to note that the tomorrow following the day on which the poor Abbé Féli had been half taken by death, he oriented his thought in a new channel which, twenty years later, would make of M. Lamennais the director of the "Peuple Constituant".[130]

Various theories have been proposed to explain the important eschatological and evolutionary hues which begin to color Lamennais's thought during the very years in which Saint-Simon's gospel of social redemption was becoming known but a discussion of this facet of mennaisian thought will be taken up in the section of this Chapter entitled, "The Inner Dynamics of Providence", (II, 4) and, again, on the metaphysical level, in Chapter Five. It is worthwhile noting, however, that at the time during which he was working on his never-to-be finished general theory of society, he was re-reading the *Soirées de Saint-Pétersbourg* of Joseph de Maistre and began to recognize a considerable difference between his own thought and that of Maistre on the problem of evil.[131] He would soon be forced to ask himself whether or not the right to revolt which was implicitly

---

[130] C. Carcopino, *Les doctrines sociales de Lamennais*, Paris, 1941, p. 26.

[131] Lettter from Lamennais to Countess Senfft, 1er novembre 1827, reproduced in E. D. Forgues, *Œuvres Posthumes de F. Lamennais*, Paris, 1859, T. I, p. 290.

acknowledged in *De la religion* ... might not somehow be connected with the redemptive role of the people acting in history as the spokesman of common sense.

The passing of Lamennais from "conservative counter-revolution" to "revolutionary traditionalism",[132] was certainly hastened by the upsurge of a revolutionary spirit and of liberal tendencies in Catholic nations. Although the movement of unionism in Belgium between liberals and conservative Catholics has been more accurately described as tactical rather than ideological,[133] it nonetheless furnished Lamennais with an important example of new possibilities within the political order. His *De la religion* ... had been enthusiastically received by the Belgian ultramontanes and had formed the basis for the frequent contact which began to take place between Lamennais and the Catholic leaders of Belgian resistance to Holland.[134] During the subsequent years, Lamennais's thought will be profoundly influenced by both the thought and the actions of the Catholic proponents of unionism. The point to be made here is that the resistance of Belgian Catholics to their Protestant rulers had provided Lamennais with a new confidence in the good judgement of the people and a new hope for an amelioration of the French situation.[135]

The culminating blow to any trust which the Breton fire-brand may have retained for the Restoration philosophy was the series of measures taken by the government of Martignac to deal with the question of the Catholic schools. Urged on by the liberal and Gallican elements, Martignac, through his ministers, broke the tacit agreement of the previous governments which, in effect, allowed for a loose application of the still dominant policy of a state educational monopoly. The actions of the ministeries provoked a lively but short-lived resistance on the part of the episcopacy.[136] For Lamennais, the crisis had reached the point of no-return. Not only had the government usurped the rights of the majority of Frenchmen but the

---

[132] This notion originating with W. Gurian, *Die politischen und sozialen Ideen des französischen Katholizismus*, Münster, 1929, p. 112, is repeated and commented upon in K. Jürgensen, *Lamennais und die Gestaltung des Belgischen Staates*, Wiesbaden, 1963, p. 25.

[133] For a discussion of this thesis consult H. Haag, *Les origines du catholicisme libéral en Belgique (1789-1839)*, Louvain, 1950, particularly, Livre II, Chapitre II, "Qu'est-ce que l'unionisme", pp. 121-138.

[134] Ibid., pp. 86-89.

[135] A. R. Vidler, *Prophecy and Papacy*, London, 1954, p. 124.

[136] J. Droz, *Restaurations et Révolutions (1815-1871)*, Paris, 1953, p. 84.

Vatican had intervened in such a fashion as to dissuade the bishops from their almost unanimous resistance. Such would be, for Lamennais, the first of a number of set-backs to his ultramontane faith in Rome.[137] Lamennais saw in the acts of the government a direct assault against the spiritual domain of religious liberty and the real threat of a renewal of the schismatic Church in France.[138] It was an evident sign that "a total upheaval" was in store for society and, indeed, "indispensable if society is to one day be renewed".[139] Granted the inevitability of a revolution, the final working out of the errors of the past, Lamennais set about in his preparation of *Des progrès de la révolution et de la guerre contre l'Eglise* to advance upon history and to seize the initiative.[140] Liberalism must attain its full development and the Christian must make ready for this work of Providence.[141]

2. *The Phenomenon of Liberalism*

In an unedited outline entitled "De la Société", which forms the skeletal preparation for the general work on society about which he had spoken in this period and which was later partially incorporated into the *Essai d'un système de philosophie catholique*, Lamennais pinpoints his position on civil and political liberty by stating his unchanging principle as follows:

> ... They [i.e. these liberties] have their source and their guarantee in religious liberty, consequently, in the sovereignty which maintains this liberty ... [they are] independent of the forms of government.[142]

In the winter of 1828-1829, Lamennais arrived at the end of his uneasy meditations with the publication of *Des Progrès...* in February, 1829. This singular book, which has been called "the act of

[137] Ch. Boutard, *Lamennais, sa vie et ses doctrines*, Paris, 1905-1913, T. II, particularly, Chapitre Premier, "L'affaire des écoles ecclésiastiques", pp. 1-22.

[138] Letter from Lamennais to A. M. Berryer, 28 janvier 1828, reproduced in E. D. Forgues, *Œuvres Posthumes de F. Lamennais*, Paris, 1859, T. I, pp. 342-346.

[139] Lettter from Lamennais to Baron Vitrolles, La Chênaie, 15 octobre 1828, reproduced in Eugène Forgues, *Correspondance inédite entre Lamennais et le baron de Vitrolles*, Paris, 1886, p. 176.

[140] Letter from Lamennais to Baron Vitrolles, La Chênaie, 11 novembre 1828, reproduced in ibid., p. 178.

[141] Letter from Lamennais to Baron Cottu, 11 novembre 1828, reproduced in d'Haussonville, "Lettres inédites publiées par le comte D'Haussonville", *La Revue hebdomadaire*, Paris, 17 avril 1909, pp. 287-288.

[142] The unedited manuscript of Lamennais's "De la Société" was published in A. Blaize, *Œuvres inédites de F. Lamennais*, Paris, 1866, T. II, pp. 295-310. The above citation is to be found on p. 296.

birth of Catholic liberalism",[143] was an instant publishing success if not for reasons of widespread agreement with the author, certainly on account of the shock value of the author's conclusions. Lamennais makes quite clear his proposals in the Préface. He restates the factual basis of his reflections, that is, revolutions and the spirit of revolution are universal phenomena and, as such, must be somehow understood and not simply opposed.

> In this position, it is natural that one bring his vision to bear upon the future, and, by meditating upon the essential laws of society, to look for the possibilities of salvation that the future might still offer while disorder passes through the successive stages of its necessary "durée".[144]

Few statements contain, as clearly as the above, the central principle of the mennaisian methodology. The observation of the historical milieu is the crucial element, as it is for the social scientist, but, beyond observation, there is the task of defining and comparing the results of this realistic appraisal of historical data within the context of the higher laws of social theory which are metaphysical in origin. Before presenting a detailed analysis of his reasoning, Lamennais proclaims, in the Préface, the famous conclusions which, from this point forward, will form the basic platform of the Catholic liberals' program.

"We ask for the Catholic Church", he concludes, "the liberty promised in the Charter to all religions"; and, he continues, "we ask liberty of conscience, liberty of the press, liberty of education".[145] Fundamentally, *Des progrès...* is an admission similar to that of *De la religion...* that systems of privilege and juridical distinctions in Church-State relations are incompatible with the political mentality of the time and with the freedom of the Church. But, going beyond the strategy of retreat and isolation proposed in the final pages of *De la religion...*, he now advocates before a startled Catholic hierarchy the realistic acceptance of the neutral character of the modern political order and the willingness to live within the "common law" framework of a pluralistic society. Was such an endorsement of modern liberties a tactical maneuver or a philosophically based re-orientation of his thought? Before any judgment can be made, it will be necessary to

---

[143] G. Weill, *Histoire du catholicisme libéral en France 1828-1908*, Paris, 1909, p. 13.

[144] Lamennais, *Des Progrès de la Révolution et de la guerre contre l'Église*, Œuvres Complètes, Paris, 1836-1837, T. IX, p. VI (In subsequent citations, this work will be referred to simply as *Des Progrès...*).

[145] *Des Progrès...*, pp. VIII-IX.

consider the full evolution of the program of these pioneers of Catholic liberalism in the "L'Avenir" which will be treated in Chapter Five. Once this is accomplished, it will be easier to handle the question of the exact philosophical nature of what had taken place in the Conclusions. For the moment, it should be remarked that one runs the risk of disconnecting or of de-naturing Lamennais's thought if the proposals of *Des Progrès* ..., the first soundings of a new and highly optimistic Christian approach to the post-revolutionary world, are put down as simply tactical re-adjustments.

Lamennais introduces the main text of *Des Progrès* ... with a recapitulation of his theory of a unique spiritual sovereignty as the basis of a just political order. He remains faithful to his original idea concerning priority and necessity of a spiritual society as the basis of unity. Police action can only limit external acts and can never attain the domain of thought. Moral obligation, which alone can render human acts just and good, cannot be imposed by force. The only possibility of saving society from the anarchic effects of misused liberty and of saving liberty itself is to be found by means of creating a common consensus of the truths deemed necessary to preserve the social order.

Christianity had, in fact, molded a type of political and social order which can serve as a rich source of reflection for the contemporary society in search of its way. The union which had existed between men and nations in the Middle Ages when all were subject to the same "immutable law of belief" had been a valid and sound basis for both the function of liberty and the progress of the intelllect.[146] The political order itself was safeguarded from tyranny because "the submission of the people to the Prince had as a condition the submission of the Prince to God and to His law, the eternal Charter of rights and duties, against which all arbitrary and disordered wills are broken".[147]

The close rapport between the spiritual and the temporal orders in which the spiritual had been the guide of the temporal was disrupted by the absolutist tendencies of the princes who, under the guise of claiming the independence of the secular sphere, had actually refused the spiritual sovereignty of the higher moral order in favor of the

[146] *Des Progrès* ..., pp. 1-3.
[147] Ibid., p. 4.

sovereignty of interests the result of which was, inevitably, personal autocracy and despotism. Louis XIV had made "despotism the fundamental law of the State".[148] The re-examination of monarchical pretentions, already begun in *De la religion* ..., when compared with the high esteem in which he held the political order of the 17th century in *Réflexions sur l'état* ..., is a most interesting example of the importance of medievalism or the return to the Middle Ages which marks Lamennais's thinking in the mid-1820's. By discovering and evaluating, along with the other Romanticists, the religious, political, and social organization of feudal society, Lamennais was in a position to break through that close identification of Catholic political thought with monarchism which was so typical, for example, of Bossuet and Bonald. The absolutism of a Louis XIV, the ideal of the ultra-royalist and Gallicans, was now seen by Lamennais as the real source and cause of the social dissolution which had led to the Revolution and had produced such an unhappy legacy.[149] Absolutism or despotism and revolution or anarchy are both unnatural states, but, of the two, as it begins to become evident in Lamennais's thought, revolution, as an antidote to tyranny, seems to assume a purgative, if not salvific purpose.

It would not be out of context to mention in this connection that it was precisely in the latter part of this decade that A. Thiers and F. Mignet, historical apologists of the French Revolution, were defending the Revolution, principally, on the theory of the inevitability of reform once the conditions for such a reform are present. Somewhat later, J. Michelet will contribute even more effectively to this historical current. Liberal historians of the stature of F. Guizot began to place the Revolution in a proportional setting within the framework of general historical movements which is a point of view quite unlike that of the early counter-revolutionary thinkers who tended to emphasize the uniqueness and the Armageddon-like character of the events of 1789.[150]

Lamennais, acutely aware of the currents of thought in his own period, initiated his dialogue with the world about him by discussing in detail the political theory of the sovereignty of reason such as it had been fashioned, according to Lamennais, by F. Guizot, V. Cousin, and

---

[148] *Des Progrès* ..., p. 5.
[149] Ibid., p. 5.
[150] G. de Bertier de Sauvigny, *La Restauration*, Paris, 1963, pp. 340-341.

B. Constant.[151] Commenting upon a series of articles from the "Globe", Lamennais reconstructs, as he conceives the liberal position, the basic principles of the new social order. The leading idea is the confession of the demise of all religious and moral authorities beyond the admittedly fallible reason of each individual, resulting in a situation in which "nothing obliges, nothing [is] common except the liberty of admitting all and denying all without exception or limit".[152] Once this epistemological stance is held, there arises the necessity of positing a new basis for political sovereignty since the older Christian theory was rooted in the common acceptance of a divine law governing both the rights and obligations of rulers and ruled.[153] The theory proposed by Guizot in *Philosophie Politique,* which is quoted extensively by Lamennais in Chapter I of *Des progrès* ..., is really the liberal doctrine of limited authority which rejects all absolutist claims since these attribute infallibility or unquestioned perpetuity to human political sovereigns. Lamennais finds ample ground for agreement with the liberal position of Guizot and the "Globe", particularly, in the common recognition of the principles that God alone is absolutely sovereign and that all human power is only a "derived sovereignty" which has only "a conditional right: legitimate insofar as it governs in conformity with reason, truth, and justice; without authority, when it violates these".[154]

The bone of contention between Lamennais and Guizot is a third principle which Lamennais deems necessary for a perfect social equilibrium, namely, the existence of an infallible means of knowing the divine law. Since the liberals do not admit such a possibility, Lamennais finds their attribution of sovereignty to God somewhat chimerical.

> It is clear that God belongs there [in this theory] only for the form, since, in supposing that He has spoken, one cannot know what He has said; no infallible authority can teach man which are the laws which He has prescribed for them or, briefly, what truth, justice and order are.[155]

Such a doctrine as that advanced under the banner of liberalism, in spite of certain valid intuitions, is radically in error due to the rejection of a spiritual authority above the individual reason.[156]

[151] *Des Progrès* ..., p. 16.
[152] Ibid., p. 9.
[153] Ibid., p. 10.
[154] Ibid., p. 14.
[155] Ibid., p. 16.
[156] Ibid., pp. 18-19.

Nevertheless, it is not to be supposed that the followers of these movements are always conscious of the erroneous principles at the source of either Gallicanism or liberalism. Men are moved by a "sort of instinct, a sort of vague sentiment".[157] This sentiment or instinct, which "rests ordinarily on some principle of justice and truth",[158] is significative for Lamennais. A common sense philosopher could scarcely overlook the existence of extensively held political and social sentiments and be consistent with himself. There is something deeper in the liberal phenomenon than a mere ideological aberration or simple political expression of particular interests.

> ... this movement is too general, too constant, for errors and passions to be the only principle moving it. Separated from false theories and their consequences, liberalism is the sentiment which, wherever the religion of Christ reigns, raises a part of the people in the name of liberty. It is nothing other than the inability of every Christian nation to put up with purely human power.[159]

"With these words", states K. Jürgensen, "doctrinaire liberalism, in its fundamental and original claim, was approved for the first time by a Catholic priest".[160] By isolating the sentiment for liberty from the prevailing individualism of liberal theory, Lamennais began to see in this sentiment both an expression of the essentially Christian depth of the peoples, in spite of the materialism of governments, and a legitimate manifestation of the innate desire for moral perfection in mankind.[161] The situation, for him, is quite analogous to what it had been at the advent of Christianity; it was a time for a second salvation of society and a restoration of Christian "law" which is none other than the rule of right reason or the historical embodiment of divine law. Liberalism, particularly alive in Catholic nations, is this search for a public law of justice and liberty. Unfortunately, liberals fail to recognize in the Catholic principle of spiritual authority the fulfillment of their own deepest aspirations for liberty.

> ... Two things constitute liberty: the legitimacy of power and the conformity of its action with immutable justice ... thus, when the liberals ask for liberty, they also ask for order ...[162]

[157] *Des Progrès* ..., p. 21.
[158] Ibid.
[159] Ibid., p. 22.
[160] K. Jürgensen, *Lamennais und die Gestaltung des Belgischen Staates*, Wiesbaden, 1963, p. 24.
[161] *Des progrès* ..., pp. 22-23.
[162] Ibid., p. 25.

Since the liberals deny the possibility of the "transmission of divine power", they are condemned to the impossibility of ever constituting a legitimate political power. The assumption that each man is his own sovereign reason is no solution for such an assumption is destructive of society, and, actually, at the origin of arbitrary systems of order imposed by force. This theoretical betrayal of a sublime desire is simply another example of the many political idolatries which history has experienced, the substitution of material "man-power" for a spiritual "divine-power". Containing, as it does, a noxious principle, liberalism is reduced to the uncertain search, in new material forms of government, for the balance between liberty and order.[163]

Gallicanism presents the reverse side of the same coin, the half-truth which is ignored by liberalism. Just as the desire for liberty is a manifestation of a deep-seated and basically Christian sentiment so too the desire for order, the original élan of the Gallican royalist, is sound and connatural to man. But to achieve this end, the regalists place the monarch beyond the law and offer no possibility of security from his arbitrariness.[164] Liberalism and Gallicanism have really, at bottom, the same erroneous point of departure. "Power, in both, being essentially arbitrary, is never other than the variable will of man".[165] The greatest harm caused by the Gallican systems of absolute rule has been to subordinate religion and to use the Church to cloak the excesses of the system. Thus, liberalism, a natural and sound reaction to despotism, manifests an anti-religious character since it sees in the subjugated Church, "the natural ally of despotism".[166] Once Lamennais had come to see with greater clarity what he viewed as the fundamental spiritual struggle of his own epoch, he was prepared to propose a program of action which would be wedded to the highest principles of society and the laws of history.

3. The Mission of Catholicism

a) Church and State

The chief impression received from a reading of Des progrès ..., after having become familiar with the earlier writings of Lamennais, is that the author had succeeded in extricating himself from a negative

---

[163] Des progrès ..., pp. 25-31.
[164] Ibid., pp. 31-38.
[165] Ibid., p. 39.
[166] Ibid., p. 42.

attitude of opposition to the historical reality which surrounded him. Certain barriers which had retained his thought within the confines of reaction had been somehow gotten around.

> It can be said that this book, [Des progrès . . .], upon its appearance early in 1829, allowed the public to declare that a radical transformation had taken place in the ideas of the author. He, who had denounced in the *Essai* the irreducible evil of the liberalism born of the Revolution, now preaches liberty and liberation in the name of Christ.[167]

In sections 4 and 5 of this Chapter, we will discuss the sources of the author's logic which allowed for this transition and which are entirely derivative of earlier seed-ideas already recognized in the *Essai sur l'indifférence* . . .[168] In the present section, it will be convenient to show what had actually changed in Lamennais's political theory as a consequence of his new analysis of the phenomenon of liberalism backed up as it was by his stark recognition, in *De la religion* . . . , of the final death of the ancient order. To be sure, *Des progrès* . . . is but a preface to "L'Avenir" which is more thoroughly representative of an achieved synthesis of political ideas; nonetheless, our concern here is with the genetic development of elemental ideas into new patterns.

The Church in *Des progrès* . . . emerges as the intellectual and spiritual fulcrum which alone is capable of balancing opposites such as liberty and authority. But the Church does not stand aside from history; as an incarnate, historical representation of the original spiritual society of intelligent beings, it cannot be frozen by an inflexible status quo in its relationships to the secular organization of social reality. Time embodies both the temporal and the spiritual, and, as a consequence, a certain suppleness or evolutive capacity of adaptation on the part of the spiritual is necessary for the attainment of the just ordering of the whole.

Lamennais frankly admits to his admiration of the union of Church and State which once existed in Western Europe. It is entirely understandable that "when social beliefs . . . subsist in full vigor and reign without opposition in the whole nation . . . public authority trembles at the appearance of a scission and considers it a duty to prevent it and to forbid useless and dangerous controversies".[169] But

---

[167] Y. Le Hir, *"Les paroles d'un croyant" de Lamennais. Texte publié sur le manuscrit autographe avec des variantes, une introduction, et un commentaire*, Paris, 1949, p. 42.

[168] See Chapter Three, III, "Elements of Transition".

[169] *Des progrès* . . . , p. 67.

the doctrines of temporal sovereignty, for reasons discussed previously, have changed and the Church must be cognizant of this change.

> Nothing is more important for the Church than to know well the doctrines of temporal sovereignty with which she is in rapport: for these doctrines, remaining constantly the rule of administration and forming the spirit which animates it, give the ensemble of its acts an invariable tendency and determine the nature of the relations which exist between religion and the State.[170]

The unchanging core of the doctrine of the Church in reference to public power is summed up by Lamennais as the recognition of two powers in a society which is "essentially" one. This is so because society, the primordial reality, supposes both an eternal law and a constraining force; thus, the symbolism of the two swords, in the opinion of the author, aptly described, in the course of ecclesiastical history, an essential social truth. Although the swords are placed in different hands, it is impossible to speak of an independence of isolation between the spiritual and the temporal. Such a state would constitute a genuine "social Manichaeism".[171] This interesting notion of one society and two powers is emphasized as the crucial principle upon which Church-State relations must be worked out in the "Seconde Lettre à Monseigneur l'Archévêque de Paris", written in defense of *Des progrès* . . .

> Society is one, as man is one; it embraces all of the relations which exist between social beings. The ensemble of moral relations form the spiritual society, the other constitute civil society; and, since intelligent beings are and can only be united by moral relationships, the spiritual society is properly the only true society: it is to civil society what the soul is to the body, in all of the rigor of this expression.[172]

Although re-asserting and even strengthening his concept of the superiority of the spiritual over the temporal, he admits of a certain fluidity of relationships in the actual historical order due to the varying degrees of social belief at any given epoch. Speaking about the problem of education, Lamennais averts to the existence of three possible arrangements between the spiritual power, which has the undeniable right to educate mankind, and the civil authorities. True

---

[170] *Des Progrès* . . . , p. 130.

[171] Ibid., pp. 43-44.

[172] Lamennais, "Seconde Lettre à Monseigneur l'Archévêque de Paris", Œuvres Complètes, Paris, 1836-1837, T. IX, pp. 404-405. (In subsequent citations, this work will be referred to simply as "Seconde lettre . . .").

theocracy, or the complete fusion of the religious and the political orders, was the situation in ancient pagan societies in which the education was at once religious and civil. The more perfect social organization arrived with Christianity which calls for a distinction of powers with an order of "natural subordination" of the temporal to the spiritual. In matters of education, the secular arm realized clearly that its duty was to protect the right of the spiritual. Finally, when the unity born of common belief no longer exists, the spiritual and the political become independent one of the other and the spiritual has no other recourse but to opt for a universal and absolute liberty, above all, in the question of educating the youth.[173]

In a language somewhat similar to that of the thesis-hypothesis solution proposed some decades later, Lamennais expands the analysis applied to the question of the Church's rights in education to the broader problem of the Church-State connection as such. If the doctrines of sovereignty guiding the State are "pure", there is between State and Church, "perfect harmony". If this is not the case, a struggle is inevitable which can only end "by a return to the true doctrines of sovereignty which do not change, or by an open and complete separation between State and religion".[174] The State may choose to be superior, independent or submissive to the religious order just as the individual may choose between belief and dis-belief; but, whatever choice is made by the political power, it does not, by this choice, create any rights or powers over the spiritual realm.[175] If the State assumes a position of control over the Church, as, for example, the program of the Gallican-liberal alliance under Martignac, it is drifting towards the creation of a "civil theocracy".[176] Such would be inimical to the independence of the Church and must be resisted. Two points are essential to the Catholic position on the question of Church and State.

> ... 1. the sovereign possesses no legitimate authority over either spirit or conscience: in other words, truth and moral obligation are independent of his thoughts and his will ... 2. there is an immutable, universal law of justice, obligatory for sovereign as well as for subjects, and this law is the basis of his rights and of society; the Church has the responsibility of conserving it and of defending it against the abuses of force ...[177]

[173] *Des progrès* ..., pp. 104-105.
[174] Ibid., p. 130.
[175] Ibid., p. 139.
[176] Ibid., p. 107.
[177] Ibid., p. 141.

No matter what legal form of relationship exists between the two spheres, the Church must find a way of exercising its dual responsibility of teaching obedience to the laws of God and of defending the liberty of moral men against the injustices of the despotic order. In brief, the Church remains the judge of temporal powers whether or not the civil authorities recognize or reject this superior authority. The Church has the obligation to defend the just law imposed by the State to protect order but it also has the right to fix the limits when this authority is abused.[178]

Catholics should not be lulled by the official recognition of the Roman Catholic Church by the French government. At best, it is a meaningless gesture; at worst, it is a tyrannical intervention.[179] The Church must reassert her primitive independence such as she enjoyed it in the hostile pagan world before Constantine.[180] To accomplish this end, the Church and, chiefly, the clergy, should be willing to divest themselves of the honors and privileges with which the State enslaves them by separating themselves from any alliance with political powers.[181] Although remaining a theocrat, Lamennais came to the conclusion that the Church could stand on its own and enter into the free competition of ideas without fear. His exhortation on this point is a remarkable acclamation of a purified concept of tolerance.

> Renounce, therefore, the foolish idea of putting the spiritual in irons; understand that even when men go astray, one can only lead them back by free persuasion, and they will only submit to the just and the true through the use of spiritual weapons. The evil, the greatest evil, is that we have no faith in the power of truth; we believe in the violence of men and not in the force of God.[182]

Des progrès... opens a period of an amazingly intense effort by Lamennais and his followers to win the world to Christian truth by accepting the world as it was and by trying to reconcile its values with the transcendent values of Christianity.[183] In this book, there is an

---

[178] Lamennais quotes from the documents of the Council of Paris, 846, in Des progrès..., footnote 1, p. 123 as an example of the doctrine of civil obedience which he is proposing.

[179] Des progrès..., p. 148.

[180] Ibid., pp. 132-133.

[181] Ibid., p. 181.

[182] Ibid., p. 68.

[183] J.-R. Derré, Lamennais, ses amis et le mouvement des idées à l'époque romantique (1824-1834), Paris, 1962, p. 204.

important thrust forward in thought, for "he has already come to understand that the realms of church and state are by their nature distinct", but, adds H. Laski, "he had hardly, as yet, worked out the implications of his admissions".[184] The first general lines of action to be followed will be the topic of discussion in the section immediately following.

b) *The Church and Liberalism*

Having given up an "establishment" notion of the Church, Lamennais's thought began to evolve rapidly in the direction of a Christian-inspired social democracy. What, theoretically, sustains the logic of this development? Basically, the progression of his thought consists in an ever-deepening and consistent following through of his metaphysical insights even to the extent of forcing a somewhat unrealistic re-fashioning of historical reality in light of his principles. What is meant by this is that, unlike the traditionally conservative approach of his mentors, Lamennais makes the institutional and structural realities, inherited from the processes of time and history, serve an ideal order of laws and axioms which are rigorously consistent in the order of logic, but, when applied to the structured world, tend to reduce the complexity of the institutional to its minimal formal content. The Church, for example, was subjected, in his thought, to a purification from the temporal and material realities to such an extent that, as the unique spiritual community of intelligent beings, it attained, for him, a fluidity which would allow for a ready adaptation to changing political and legal structures. Thus, he began "to dream of a hypothetical accord between the Church, which would be simply the religious bond uniting souls, and the State, as the political bond uniting the wills".[185] What Lamennais is aiming at is the preservation of the presence of the Church in the world which, as he so correctly observed, did not depend upon juridical determinations but upon receiving an audience in the minds of men.

Few pages of Lamennais are as prophetic and as clairvoyant as those of the final Chapter of *Des progrès* ... The program of "L'Avenir" is sketched and the entrance of the Church into the modern world is boldly proclaimed.

[184] H. J. Laski, *Authority in the Modern State*, New Haven, 1919, p. 231.
[185] J. Poisson, *Le romantisme social de Lamennais*, Paris, 1931, p. 14.

165

> Everything has changed around you ... ideas have taken and continue
> to take incessantly new directions ... What good does the most lively zeal
> accomplish without a knowledge of the society in which it ought
> to be exercised? It is necessary to learn in another way, and to learn
> more ...[186]

The special mission of the clergy was to rid itself of old habits of
thought and to plunge vigorously into modern science and
contemporary studies. As C. Boutard has pointed out, Lamennais had
made the clergyman's first duty that of being a savant.[187] He had
already paved the way in the highly experimental approach to study
and to seminary life which he had employed in preparing the
candidates for the Congregation of St. Peter, the religious community
which he had founded.

The political program presented for the future is still somewhat
negative or hesitant as enunciated in the conclusions of *Des
progrès*.... The political aspect of his thought for the future is more
clearly in the two public letters which he had written in answer to the
pastoral letter of Msgr. de Quélen, Archbishop of Paris, which
contained a public rebuke of the author of the subversive proposals of
Des progrès.... Various commentators have agreed that Lamennais's
responses were indeed "masterpieces of polemic".[188] No doubt,
Lamennais was often much too ardent in criticism and in polemical
infighting but the heat of vigorous controversy also helped to sharpen
his thought or pushed him to the achievement of conclusions already
implicit, but unspoken, in his principles. J. Poisson, a careful student
of Lamennais's social theory, finds that the two letters mark a real
progress in his political thinking on Church and State.[189]

Reviewing the discussions of *Des progrès*..., he recalls for the
Archbishop that his purpose was to ask "of history and of religion"
both "the cause" and "the remedy" for this "frightful social
dissolution" threatening France.[190] To accomplish his ends, he had
examined from "a philosophical and political point of view the liberal
and royalist doctrines".[191] In a two-fold analysis, the errors of the

---

[186] *Des progrès* ..., p. 193.
[187] Ch. Boutard, *Lamennais, sa vie et ses doctrines*, Paris, 1905-1913, T. II, p. 47.
[188] A. R. Vidler, *Prophecy and Papacy*, London, 1954, p. 140.
[189] J. Poisson, *Le romantisme social de Lamennais*, Paris, 1931, p. 90.
[190] Lamennais, "Première Lettre à Monseigneur l'Archévêque de Paris", Œuvres
Complètes, Paris, 1836-1837, T. IX, p. 336 (In subsequent citations, this work will be
referred to simply as "Première lettre ...").
[191] "Seconde lettre ...", p. 388.

systems were first detected and explained, and, secondly, a choice was made concerning the possibilities open to the believer. He spells out the choice which Christians must make in terms which are much more direct than those which he had employed on previous occasions. If liberalism can be joined to the Catholic principle of Papal authority in spiritual matters, there could be no better response to the problem of social rehabilitation than by means of a fusion of the liberal spirit with the Catholic tradition. At base, liberalism, properly conceived, is nothing more than "an exact résumé of Catholic social doctrine".[192] Both liberalism and Catholicism are fundamentally in agreement in their rejection of political absolutism and in their concepts of delegated power and limited obedience.[193] Even more strongly, in the "Seconde Lettre" ..., he proposes that "the liberal theory is, in fact, identical to the Catholic doctrine of society".[194]

It cannot be said, however, that there is an integral acceptance of liberalism. Certainly, Lamennais adheres to a liberal anthropology such as he had previously done in earlier years,[195] but it cannot be said that he accepted a liberalistic epistemology. He held out, at this point, against popular sovereignty,[196] but not against the rights of the people to revolt against tyranny. The difference is found in his faithfulness to the ultramontane theory of Papal sovereignty over the consciences of the people and rulers. The Church will be the judge for Lamennais in the cases in which it must be decided whether or not a ruler is to be obeyed.[197]

Catholic liberalism, as the mennaisian alliance came to be designated, is really a misnomer as political labels so often tend to be. We will explain more clearly in Chapter Five and in the Conclusions that, if anything, Lamennais's doctrine was one of social democracy resulting from his rigorous criticism of both Gallicanism and liberalism. The crucial point of encounter between mennaisianism and liberalism is in their common acceptance of the forms of modern individual and social liberties as the salvific formula for the attainment of social order.

---

[192] "Première lettre ...", p. 339.
[193] Ibid., pp. 351-361.
[194] "Seconde lettre ...", p. 389.
[195] See Chapter Three, III, 1.b. "Christian Liberty".
[196] "Première lettre ...", pp. 363-367.
[197] Ibid., p. 369; "Seconde lettre ...", p. 413.

> ... in order to survive the present order, to allow for the re-birth of peace, and to permit the fulfillment of the conditions of social life, the people must necessarily return to Catholicism, which return ... can only be obtained, little by little, through the free development of truth and the lessons of experience.[198]

Even in seconding the stand of the "Globe" on civil and political liberties, including full tolerance, Lamennais remained at the opposite ideological pole from the editors of the "Globe" in his reasons for so doing. He believed, as they, in the purgative and cathartic value of freedom, but, for him, it would serve as a catalytic agent in the historical process of establishing the new Christian order in which the opposing forces, faith and reason, Church and society, authority and liberty would be united.[199]

4. The Inner Dynamics of Providence

An evolutionist conceptualization of the world order is very much in the background of Lamennais's thought in this period which marks the dawning of the ideals of "L'Avenir". Although not really formulated until the lessons given at Juilly during the academic session of 1830-31, an awareness of development in history and of the necessity of finding a key to the mystery of this development haunted his thought. Like a hovering shadow, this element of his thought remained as an imperative to his will driving him to search ceaselessly for the higher laws. Psychologically, such a feeling was very much in harmony with the emotional and ideological stirrings within the second generation of Romanticists.

> European Romanticism had begun with enthusiastic expectations of human progress but had soon become disenchanted and gloomy about the prospects for mankind. After 1830 a powerful second wave of secular enthusiasm affected the movement, and the resulting new Romantic religion of Progress all but dominated it in its final stages ... There was, above all, an unbridled emotionalism; there were the prophetic postures, the exceedingly vague yet emphatic message, and the intoxicating effect of oratorical and poetic phrases about the secularized Christian virtues of Love, Fraternity and Compassion.[200]

In the case of Lamennais, true to his basic philosophical orientation towards such classical geniuses as Malebranche, the desire for a

---

[198] "Seconde lettre ...", p. 389.
[199] W. Gurian, *Die politischen und sozialen Ideen des französischen Katholizismus*, Münster, 1929, pp. 113-115.
[200] H. Schenk, *The Mind of the European Romantics*, London, 1966, pp. 199-200.

"theoretical justification",[201] was somewhat stronger than among many of the purely literary prophets of the new religion of Progress.

By 1826, Saint-Simon had completed his *Nouveau christianisme* with its heavy accent on the coming order and the scientific reform of society. The evolutionist intuitions of this somewhat eccentric figure were not forgotten by his disciple, A. Comte, when the latter was in the process of formulating his famous law of three stages.[202] Pierre-Simon Ballanche, a liberal spirit and a traditional believer, had precociously weaved together the secular ideas of permanent progress with the Christian notion of the Fall and Redemption in his *Palingénésie sociale* (1828-1830). Even before Lamennais, he had seen the French Revolution as fundamentally a function of a deeper law, the law of Christianity which is "the law of emancipation".[203] He also made early use of the chrysalis image to explain the sometime violent unfolding of multiple forces in time towards a new harmony, an imagery which will become commonplace in later mennaisian writings.[204] Similarly, Theodore Jouffrey had already given major emphasis in his study on the philosophy of history to the decisive relationship between ideas and events: changes in thought lead to modifications of the "external facts" or institutional realities. Victor Cousin, to simply name another, introduced his French audience to the ideas of Hegel on history in his university lectures of 1828.[205]

These few examples are given as a description of the ideational milieu in which Lamennais was re-thinking his own approach to the historical process in the latter half of the decade. Both *Des progrès ...* and the "Seconde Lettre ..." contain some remarkable examples of the ingredients going into a philosophy of history that had been a-building in his mind since the *Essai sur l'indifférence ...* One does not refer here to a thoroughly consistent or even polished thought pattern but to occasional pages in which the author attempted to grasp the whole of the temporal process and to identify the directing laws which alone give reason to the chaos of events. The key, yet, not fully coordinated ideas are to be found particularly in Chapters IV and IX

[201] J. Poisson, *Le romantisme social de Lamennais*, Paris, 1931, p. 69.
[202] D. Bagge, *Les idées politiques en France sous la Restauration*, Paris, 1952, pp. 412-414.
[203] C. Calippe, *L'attitude sociale des catholiques français au XIX⁶ siècle*, Paris, 1911, T. I, p. 129.
[204] Y. Le Hir, *"Les paroles d'un croyant" de Lamennais*, Paris, 1949, p. 48.
[205] H. Barnes, *A History of Historical Writing*, New York, 1962, pp. 197-198.

of *Des progrès* ... and in the refutation of the critique of *Des progrès*
..., made by a certain French peer, M. de Frénilly, which Lamennais
included in his global answer to Archbishop de Quélen in the
"Seconde Lettre ...".

The principal characteristics of the mennaisian philosophy of
history can simply be stated as being providentialism and
evolutionism. As a general principle, a "superior cause", independent
of the thoughts and desires of men, is posited at the origin of historical
development.[206] It is assumed that this cause, which is often called
Providence, is reasonable.

> The intellectual and moral world has its laws which are as inflexible
> as those of the physical world; and, according to these laws, every idea,
> every principle, every system in action in society tends incessantly to
> realize its final consequences.[207]

When Lamennais speaks of ideas being forced to attain their final
consequences, he seems to speak, although not entirely with clarity at
this stage, of a sort of dialectic which is both internal and external to
the order of thought. Actions are reducible to an idea-content; thus,
ideas have a leverage in history. When an idea is tested by application
in the actual order, such as the implementation of regalism in the
political and legal spheres, a reaction sets in which shows the
inadequacy or untruth of the idea. General acceptance or universal
consent, the final criterion of the truthfulness of an idea, would seem
really to be attained or recognized by what amounts to a pragmatic
testing of the same idea. History is, therefore, the laboratory in which
the compatibility of the ideas of individual reason with the eternal
truths of the superior reason is discovered. The "war against religion"
of which Lamennais speaks in the title of *Des progrès* ... is precisely
this dynamic of disintegration or trial and error at work. The constant
agitation in the political order is a perfect sample of the working out
of the dialectic between truth and error. When error is present in
society, there is a state of unbalance, an unnatural situation; the
eternal logic underlying universal truths will force the correction or
purgation of an idea until a new balance is achieved. Resistance can
be offered to this disintegration, such as the resistance of the
monarchical regimes to the principle of democracy, but such
resistance cannot succeed in the long run nor prevent the anti-social

[206] *Des progrès* ..., p. 76.
[207] Ibid., p. 154.

kernel at the heart of democratic ideologies, reliance upon individual judgement alone, from attaining its final growth.

> ... there is a general, permanent attack which, without ceasing, is born anew from an ever-subsistent principle and whose success, sooner or later, becomes inevitable because it is none other than the tendency, the progressive advance of society...[208]

Movement and change are thus the hallmarks of human history; "in the world nothing stops... everything is in progress".[209] This movement is accounted for by the exteriorization of ideas which penetrate the minds of the people and the laws of institution. Democracy or the sovereignty of the people will attain its inevitable anarchic climax because all attempts to compromise with it through such legal fictions as a constitutional monarchy are actually doomed by the very incorporation of a principle which is destructive of its own stability. The "germ of revolution", once planted, serves as the active agent bringing about the purification which is necessary to any true restoration.[210]

The important change in Lamennais's analysis of this familiar idea of the instability and mobility of error, which, as has been noted, was already held by Bossuet,[211] is that the role of error becomes a positive one which makes history advance with its concomitant unveiling of truth. Although it is difficult to recognize any benefit in the unnatural state of spiritual anarchy into which Europe had fallen, Lamennais reminds his readers that there is no reason for a pessimistic attitude.

> ... the progressive development of error has produced a corresponding development of light; as a consequence, the foundations of Christian beliefs and their intimate relations with the essential laws of man, considered either as an individual or as a social being, and with the very source of human reason has never been so closely seen...[212]

Time is the "prime minister"[213] dictating the eventual regeneration of society. The law of expiation must be allowed to operate its effect through experience which both instructs and punishes. The only way open to men of good will who seek a new and just social order is to

---

[208] *Des progrès* ..., p. 84.
[209] Ibid., p. 131.
[210] Ibid., p. 78.
[211] For a brief, but expert, treatment of the themes of Bossuet's historical endeavors consult H. Barnes, *A History of Historical Writing*, New York, 1962, pp. 130-131.
[212] *Des progrès* ..., p. 190.
[213] Ibid., p. 65.

liberate truth from the trammels of oppression. In a new and more open tone of personal tolerance towards unbelievers,[214] Lamennais asks that Christians adapt themselves to "the means appropriate to the situation of the minds" about them by "trying to shed light on the vital questions" and by "learning from experience".[215] Catholics who enjoy the "liberty of the children of God" should never fear an open and free discussion with all men. It is the mission of Catholicism to "save mankind a second time"; not, however, through the "triumph of some over others" but rather through the winning of "a common victory" in which all mankind would participate.[216]

It is not to be supposed, however, that the part of the Catholic believer is to be one of merely waiting passively for the results of the workings of eternal logic. In the latter part of the "Seconde Lettre ...", Lamennais makes it abundantly clear that his new grasp of the situation has led him to opt for political activism. The dramatic events of the years immediately following these meditations, with the foundation of "L'Avenir" and of the Agence générale pour la défense de la liberté religieuse, give evidence of his willingness to implement his program with action. Although the laws of Providence direct the evolution of ideas and events to their inevitable conclusions, man is not simply the pawn of time. Much as Ballanche speaks of the "assimilative men" who are capable of synthesizing the opposing forces and, who, for this reason, become the masters of history,[217] Lamennais offers, in his refutation of M. de Frénilly's cautions and conservative approach, the justification for activism.

> When we look for order on earth, the order which could exist there, you send us to *heaven*. When we question religion, reason and history in order to solve the great problems of right and justice here below, you tell us: Patience![218]

One cannot simply accept an unjust state of affairs in the hope that it will work out with time. The demands of justice derive from an absolute source and are not to be fulfilled by fatalistic resignation. Must man accept a life which is always in violation of the laws of a higher justice? Granted, there will always be abuses; but Lamennais

---

[214] G. Weill, *Histoire du catholicisme libéral en France 1828-1908*, Paris, 1909, p. 16.
[215] *Des progrès* ... , p. 69.
[216] Ibid., pp. 66-67.
[217] C. Calippe, *L'attitude sociale des catholiques français au XIXᵉ siècle*, Paris, 1911, T. I, p. 132.
[218] "Seconde lettre ...", p. 410.

refuses to agree with the contention of his noble adversary that Frenchmen must resign themselves to all abuses of power and to leave the final reckoning to the hereafter. The conservative's understanding of Divine intervention is rejected by Lamennais as a mis-interpretation of the nature and function of revolutions and disorder. Revolution and social chaos are not "miraculous" punishments meted out to man by God, but they are "the exterior means employed by God to re-establish order".[219] These means are built into the very nature of the universe; thus, disorder is a function within the legality of the world order which must be accepted as the natural means of rectifying previous disorder. Revolution and resistance to an authority which has ceased to be truly sovereign are justifiable means of directing the historical institutions into the way of justice. The Church, however, is the only judge of consciences in these cases in which the exercise of "the terrible, but necessary right of resistance" is in question.[220] In a resounding conclusion, Lamennais condemns the other-worldly spirituality of his conservative opponents in phrases which are boldly indicative of the spirit of reform and social messianism which will blaze forth in the articles of "L'Avenir". This aspect of Lamennais's thought, that is, the acceptance of the progressive character of history seems to be of crucial importance in understanding the "liberalism" of the mennaisian school.

> ... pivoting on the principle of liberty ... a philosophy of history is developed and the apologetic of Lamennais finds therein its coronation. The master cannot be understood, from the Catholic point of view, except by discerning in his thought what is new in the renaissance of an essentially Christian principle: liberty.[221]

5. *Epistemological Refinements*

One of the most interesting by-products of the publication of the *Essai sur l'indifférence...* was the formation of a school or, rather, an ideological grouping, around the powerful new spokesman of the rising generation of French Catholics which loyally followed him in the years which witnessed the first flowering of mennaisianism at La Chênaie and at Juilly.

[219] Ibid., p. 412.
[220] Ibid., p. 422.
[221] Ch. Denis, "Les contradicteurs de Lamennais", *Annales de Philosophie chré-tienne*, Paris, Août-Septembre 1900, p. 632.

> He is the *master*—and, basically, he will always remain so—of men
> who will become later on the chiefs or the inspiration of the French
> Church: Gerbet, Lacordaire, Montalembert, Charles de Coux, Abbé de
> Salinis, Guéranger, Combalot.[222]

Of all of the above-named, one of the most loyal and brilliant
followers was the retiring Philippe Gerbet, a young priest and author
of several of the most important theological treatises of the
mennaisian current. He established his residence with the oracle of
the new movement and aided him in one of the most touching and
fervent mennaisian enterprises, the foundation of the first seminaries
of the Congregation of St. Peter.

Leaving aside Gerbet's other more personal contributions, we will
concentrate on one slight work which is more germane to our topic
and more proper in the context of a study on Lamennais since it was
included by him as an appendix to *Des Progrès* ... *Sommaire d'un
système des connoissances humaines*, a very important refinement of
the doctrine of knowledge and of the theory of common sense, which
had first been elaborated in the *Essai sur l'indifférence*..., was
achieved during the years of intimate collaboration between
Lamennais and Gerbet as philosophy professors for an unusual
selection of young Christian elite at the center of mennaisian spiritual
and intellectual life, La Chênaie.

> ... the *Sommaire* ..., composed at a time when the cohesion of the
> mennaisian school could not be doubted, reveals the likeness of a
> manifesto which all could approve since the thought of the master
> furnished the essential elements ...[223]

We have already seen how Lamennais had divided human reason
into a dual faculty, the faculty of knowing and that of reasoning.[224] It
should be recalled as well that the problem of human liberty caused
by the granting of absolute priority to the act of faith in the knowing
process was not entirely solved by Lamennais at the earlier stages of
his explicitation of the common sense theory.[225] If the role of the
human intellect is essentially passive, what would become of those
qualities of inventive creativity and spontaneity so often clearly related

---

[222] L. Foucher, *La philosophie catholique en France au XIXe siècle*, Paris, 1955,
p. 52.

[223] J.-R. Derré, *Lamennais, ses amis et le mouvement des idées à l'époque
romantique*, Paris, 1962, p. 306.

[224] See Chapter Three, II 2, "A Social Theory of Certitude".

[225] See Chapter Three, III 1 b, "Christian Liberty"; 2, "Political Implications of
Common Consent".

to the idea of liberty? Due to the literary struggle between classicism and romanticism which was then in full eruption, many otherwise sympathetic young writers and artists were somewhat put off by the authoritarian aspects of the mennaisian doctrine. Although creativity in literary activity is attained through an act of choice, therefore, an act of the will, this same will was rigidly subordinated to the intellect in Lamennais's original concept of the rapport between the will and the intellect. In this sense, *Sommaire* ... was an attempt to free the doctrine of common sense, as Lamennais conceived it, from the rigidity of classicism.

A second difficulty centered around the problem of justifying the idea of progress in history, which began to loom so largely in the mennaisian ideological horizon, within the framework of an epistemology based upon the authority of originally revealed truths. It would seem, logically, that Lamennais should have considered any change as simply a further degradation of the original purity of primitive truth; indeed, he had often mentioned that agitation and instability are the very hallmarks of error and moral depravation. How was it possible for him to make the transposition of his basic orientation from what we might call a vector of retrogression pointing towards a point of original and static immobility to one of progression pointing towards a future attainment of truth? L. Le Guillou sums up the difficulty very accurately in the following fashion.

> ... if the eternal truths are thus erected into temporal absolutes, independent of society and of the dispositions of men, is not blessed contemplation of certain reconstructed skeletons and beautiful fossils the only role allotted to human reason?[226]

Sommaire ... furnishes the link connecting the severe doctrine of the *Essai sur l'indifférence* ... with the commitment to progress emerging from *Des progrès* ... Various articles appearing in the "Mémorial Catholique" between 1826 and 1828 show the efforts of the mennaisian group "to conciliate creative liberty with the discipline imposed by dogma".[227] In the background of this conflict can readily be seen not only the struggle between science and religion, but also, the particularly lively literary war between romanticism and classicism which was the sensation of the decade. In *Sommaire* ..., the goal of

[226] L. Le Guillou, *L'évolution de la pensée religieuse de Félicité Lamennais*, Paris, 1966, p. 89.
[227] J.-R. Derré, *Lamennais, ses idées et le mouvement des idées à l'époque romantique*, Paris, 1962, p. 179.

the author is to refine the doctrine of common consent by preserving the essential priority of faith while, at the same time, justifying, epistemologically, the liberty which they had come to defend politically. The solution hinges upon the distinction made between the order of faith and the order of reason.

The order of faith, as the region of the preliminary act of the intellect came to be known among mennaisians, is the universal bond which all men share and which contains that which is "common and invariable in human thoughts".[228] Only by recognizing truth as that to which "the minds of the generality of men adhere everywhere and always",[229] can there be any possibility of communication between men and of stability in life. Actually, as has been remarked, this notion is simply a way of admitting some englobing meaningfulness quite akin to the classical idea of Nature.

> Thus there exists for Lamennais, as for the classical writers, a human nature, that is, a general and permanent base, valid for all men, in all countries, and in every epoch, an ensemble of fundamental, primitive realities outside of which it is impossible for a human to develop himself.[230]

There is an attachment through faith or an unquestioned acceptance of the given in human experience which bears the qualification of certitude. This certitude is founded upon a superior reason and, on this account, is both the guide and the foundation of the work of individual reason. It is, quite basically, the invariability of being human. The truths of this order are absolute, self-evident, and invariable. Gerbet is careful to note that the difference between the act of accepting the truths of this order or faith is not to be confused with the act of supernatural faith.[231]

[228] Lamennais, "Sommaire d'un système des connoissance humaines", Œuvres Complètes, Paris, 1836-1837, T. IX, pp. 302-303. (In subsequent citations, this work will be referred to simply as "Sommaire ...").

[229] Ibid., p. 302.

[230] L. Le Guillou, L'évolution de la pensée religieuse de Félicité Lamennais, Paris, 1966, p. 93.

[231] "Sommaire ...", p. 303. In this writing, Gerbet simply mentions that those who suppose that he is speaking of theological faith when he speaks of the order of faith are doing so "gratuitously". He holds that he is employing the term in its "most general sense" which is "not to conceive of something but to believe it on the testimony of a higher reason". To understand more thoroughly Gerbet's interesting theological interpretation of the mennaisian doctrine a study would be required of his Des doctrines philosophiques de la certitude dans leurs rappports avec les fondements de la théologie. A summary discussion of this work is presented in L. Foucher, La philosophie catholique en France au XIXᵉ siècle, Paris, 1955, pp. 53-56.

But human activity does not cease with the certainty of everyday belief in certain undeniable realities; human reason is also naturally moved to understand, to form a conceptual ordering of that which it believes. This is the realm of fallible, relative, active human thought whose "condition and inviolate law" is liberty. Individual thought is subordinate to faith, which attains universal certitudes, because it must have these certitudes as a starting point and norm.[232]

Such a designation of human reason as, at once, participant and creative, furnishes the basis of genuine progress. Recognizing the fallibility of human reason, the savant is driven to discover broader and broader generalities reaching towards the infinity upon which superior reason is founded.

> From this fact derives this maxim of extreme importance for the advance of the true philosophical spirit: one must challenge all partial explanations . . .[233]

Touching more directly our topic of tolerance, the mennaisians tried to liberate themselves for good from the charges of authoritarianism which had been leveled against them. Instead of hampering individual thought, only the epistemology of the two orders, in their view, can safeguard liberty of thought since "the immediate consequence of the principle of authority is that one owes nothing more than examination to any judgement of individual reason".[234] "Dependence and liberty" are "inseparable" sources of progress because the one, liberty, drives man to achieve his full development and moral perfection while the other, dependence, guarantees that the directional thrust of this development will be positive and in the channels of progressive evolution.[235]

Once the distinction between the order of faith and the order of reason has been acknowledged, it becomes possible to explain the history of human thought and to fashion a complete classification of human knowledge.[236] Faith and reason explain, as well, the relationship between the individual and society.

---

[232] "Sommaire . . .", pp. 304-305.
[233] Ibid., p. 306.
[234] Ibid., p. 308.
[235] Ibid., p. 310.
[236] L. Le Guillou reminds us that a similar division of knowledge into the two realms of faith and reason was proposed by Pascal in his *Fragment d'un traité du vide*. Confer L. Le Guillou, *L'évolution de la pensée religieuse de Félicité Lamennais*, Paris, 1966, p. 95.

Thus society is composed of two orders, one of dependence, the other of liberty; the one which unites and binds together all individual wills, the other which consists in the expansion of each one of them.[237]

Without rejecting the cornerstone of the earlier mennaisian social theory formed, as it was, upon the notions of authority and obedience, Lamennais begins to enlarge the function of liberty. The imposition of foreign restrictions upon the activity of the spirit, outside of those emanating from the order of faith, is now seen as a fundamental disorder.[238] Combining the adaptation of their epistemology to the needs of reconciling, theoretically, the rights of the individual and the requirements of society with a philosophy of history, inspired, at least, in part by the messianism of Maistre,[239] Lamennais accepted joyfully the challenge of the world, its revolutions and its plurality. The *Sommaire* ... ends upon a hopeful note reflecting the newly won confidence of the school of La Chênaie; the horizons are wider and a grand effort to attain a metaphysics of common sense is in the offing. One can readily see how Lamennais and his group were now prepared to embrace the modern political liberties without falling into the contradictions which they unfailingly found in the heart of doctrinaire liberalism.

[237] "Sommaire ...", pp. 315-316.
[238] Ibid., p. 314.
[239] J.-R. Derré, *Lamennais, ses amis et le mouvement des idées à l'époque romantique*, Paris, 1962, p. 326.

CHAPTER FIVE

THE MENNAISIAN CATHOLIC-LIBERAL SYNTHESIS

I. LEGITIMACY AND REVOLUTION

1. *The Creation of "L'Avenir"*

After the parliamentary failure of the government of Martignac in August, 1829, the Prince de Polignac was brought to power by the king, Charles X, in an effort by the monarch and the conservative elements to restore a more authoritarian and aristocratic rule in the nation. The uneasiness of the electorate with the coloration of the new regime was manifested throughout the months of liberal and republican agitation which preceded the liberal triumph at the polls in July, 1830. The unpopular decrees issued by the king in face of the electoral setback ignited the militant activity of the last days of July which ended in the abdication of Charles X and in the liberals' strategic selection of Louis-Philippe as the new "citizen-King" of the French nation. For the republican and populist elements which had initiated and actually forced the change of dynasties, a revolution had taken place; for the parliamentary liberals and bourgeois interests, there had been simply a change of heads of state in which they saw the triumph of their own class interests.[1]

Lamennais' evaluation of the events of July was definitely akin to that of the radical forces at work within the body-politic. A revolution, such as he had been predicting,[2] had finally removed the decadent Bourbons from the leadership of the French nation. For one who had held that "the nation is weary and disillusioned with ... royalism",[3] the fall of Charles X seemed to be an empirical verification of his own social and political tenets and theories. Events, which rapidly pushed the ancient dynasty from the center of power and disrupted the

[1] J. Droz, *Restauration et Révolution (1815-1871)*, Paris, 1953, pp. 88-90.
[2] For a good résumé of the numerous references in Lamennais's correspondence concerning the imminent fall of the monarchy confer J.-R. Derré, *Lamennais, ses amis et le mouvement des idées à l'époque romantique (1824-1834)*, Paris, 1962, pp. 404-405.
[3] Letter from Lamennais to Countess Senfft, 10 février 1830, reproduced in E. D. Forgues, *Œuvres Posthumes de F. Lamennais*, Paris, 1859, T. II, p. 116.

conservative coalition, seemed to be following the pattern of disintegration which he had prophetically outlined to his disciples and to the reading public during the final years of the previous decade. Enhanced by this seemingly correct fulfillment of his prognostications, Lamennais did not hesitate to welcome the turn of events nor was he lacking a program of action for the new circumstances. While the bourgeois liberals were in a state of doubt, welcoming Louis-Philippe on the one hand and fearing the republican insurgents on the other, and the legitimists in a state of outraged indignation, Lamennais and his followers threw themselves with a buoyant optimism into the thick of the political disputes with the foundation of a newspaper whose purpose was to announce to the French nation their program for national reconciliation under the motto, "Dieu et la liberté".[4] "L'Avenir", as the new journal of opinion was to be named, represents the fulfillment and final synthesis of the mennaisian movement as a cohesive ideological position within the spectrum of Catholicism.

The history of the establishment of "L'Avenir" under the impetus of Gerbet and a now forgotten layman, Harel Tancred, who had first proposed the idea, has been adequately studied elsewhere.[5] Although not officially the editor of the newspaper for which a prospectus or statement of policy appeared on August 20th, 1830, and which was to have a short but brilliant life until the suspension of publication on November 15th, 1831, Lamennais was decidedly the soul and the inspiration of this most renowned and impressive of mennaisian projects.

> "L'Avenir" is Lamennais; Gerbet, Lacordaire, Montalembert, did no more than develop his thought ... it is in his own articles that one must search for an exposé of liberal Catholicism.[6]

Our purpose in this first part of the final chapter of the study is to expose the political theory beneath the conclusions stated by Lamennais in his articles published in "L'Avenir". This political

---

[4] The formula "Dieu et la liberté" was originally used by the first group of liberally tending Catholics in the newspaper "Correspondant". It reportedly comes from the notion expressed by the British minister, Channing, in the phrase, "civil and religious liberty for all". Confer C. Constantin, "Libéralisme Catholique", *Dictionnaire de Théologie Catholique*, Tome IX, 1ère Partie, Paris, 1926, col. 507.

[5] A. Trannoy, *Le romantisme politique de Montalembert avant 1834*, Paris, 1942, pp. 135-139.

[6] G. Weill, *Histoire du catholicisme libéral en France 1828-1908*, Paris, 1909, p. 31.

theory might be described as the mature response of the mennaisian school to the long-discussed problematic posed by the social situation created in the wake of the Revolution of 1789. The civil theology of Gallicanism died its first death on the scaffold with Louis XVI in 1793; an attempted resuscitation of the defunct absolutism was finally abandoned in the three famous days of July, 1830. Historical reality had made it quite obvious to Lamennais that the social bond uniting the French nation could emanate neither from common religious beliefs not from a divinization of political authority.

"L'Avenir", as will be seen, made eminently practical proposals, many of which have since become incorporated in the common law of most European nations, but, in setting forth the practical conclusions arrived at by Lamennais, at this conjuncture of historical happenings, it is interesting to keep in mind that the program of "L'Avenir" is logically deducible from the metaphysical and theological insights which had been developed in and from his writings of the previous decades. To avoid the confusion which arises from the somewhat artificial distinction between "tactical" and "doctrinal" reasoning used in discussions concerning the validity of mennaisian liberalism, it is well to remember, while studying the somewhat precocious and apparently radical proposals of "L'Avenir", that, in the thought of Lamennais, "praxis" and "theoria" are indissolubly wedded. Any attempt to understand the exact position of "L'Avenir" would be misdirected if the inquiry were to dwell solely upon these well-known propositions without unearthing the political philosophy supporting them.

One of the most important advances in Lamennais's thought which blossomed with the appearance of "L'Avenir" is the attainment of a more mature philosophy of rights and law out of which he attempted to fashion a new social pact for the divergent factions of his nation which would reconcile the fundamental need of the nation for a basic social unity and order with the exigencies of an ideological pluralism. It is at this point that Lamennais deals most directly with the problem of tolerance as a political problem, that is, in describing the nature of a viable, yet theoretically acceptable, social bond and in proposing certain recognizable limits for the elasticity of this social order. Our proposal, as previously mentioned, is to describe the political theory of Lamennais as expressed in "L'Avenir". This will be done in four sections which will deal, respectively, with the social reality, the nature of the social compact, the requirements of legitimacy, and, finally, the theory of liberty. A second major division will treat of the role of the Church in this liberally conceived social union, specifically, the separation of Church and State, tolerance, and the relationship of the Church to modern liberties. In the final part of the chapter, we will attempt to show the metaphysical justification of this political doctrine such as it can be gleaned from "L'Avenir" and from other sources, particularly, the philosophical conferences given at the College of Juilly during the same epoch. These sources will provide us with a view of the thought-pattern within which the mennaisian group was shaping its program of Catholic liberalism. We will include in the last section a critique of the philosophical soundness of the principles upon which Lamennais's political theory was constructed.

Historically, Lamennais and his co-workers on "L'Avenir" followed a small group of young Catholic aristocrats—of which Montalembert was a member—which had published the "Correspondant" as the organ of an incipient progressive movement among young Christian laymen. Mennaisian in inspiration, the "Correspondant" was based upon the idea of political activism in defense of the religious liberty of the Church. Lamennais's influence among the young editors, the most notable of whom was Louis de Carné, was indirect. Nonetheless, they worked within the limits of the religious problematic which Lamennais had brought so sharply into focus in *De la religion . . .* and *Des progrès . . .*[7] This rather select and highly motivated circle was the first group to be dubbed with the title of "Catholic liberal", a nomenclature reportedly originating with the liberals of the "Globe" with whom Carné and his companions had considerable contact.[8] The policy of the "Correspondant", however open and progressive it might have been, was still quite timid and without the logical cohesiveness that was to become the hallmark of "L'Avenir". The first doctrinal formulation of Catholic liberalism awaited the foundation of "L'Avenir".

Prior to the publication of the prospectus for the new newspaper, Lamennais, writing to Gerbet concerning the position to be taken in reference to the events of July, declared in his habitually affirmative fashion that "what is done, is done and well-done, it is no longer a

[7] J.-R. Derré, *Lamennais, ses amis et le mouvement des idées à l'époque romantique (1824-1834)*, Paris, 1962, pp. 217-225.
[8] G. Weill, *Histoire du catholicisme libéral en France 1828-1908*, Paris, 1909, pp. 21-25.

question of the past, only the future counts".[9] To seize correctly the significance of the historical moment, Catholics "must understand their position" which is to accept the demise of the Restoration monarchy and "to enter with heart and resolve into liberty".[10] The revolution was, as he explained to Baron Vitrolles, the expression of "a universal reaction of the people against arbitrary power".[11]

Given the principles of Lamennais's common sense epistemology and his unflinching confidence in the power of truth, it is not surprising that he heartily endorsed the journalistic approach as the most appropriate pedagogical medium of his movement. Lamennais saw truth as the public patrimony passing, while clarifying itself, from age to age in an oral tradition. What could be more suitable to effect the transmission of truth than to enter into the market-place of ideas through the newspaper media? He sensed the rising importance of public opinion as a creative principle in public life and as the necessary adjunct of any successful political movement. He recognized, as it will be seen, that the people, the masses of society, had assumed a role of major importance in history and that, if correctly informed, they would create a society of liberty and order. The journalistic venture associated with the launching of "L'Avenir" is markedly representative of the modernity of Lamennais.

2. The Political Philosophy of "L'Avenir"

a) Social Reality and Its Interpretation

"We are going to publish a newspaper", writes Lamennais, " ... it will appear on October 15th; its title is "L'Avenir" and its purpose is to unite men of all opinions and attached to order on the basis of liberty".[12] Lamennais proposed nothing less than to offer a tenable and acceptable solution to what he believed to be the most difficult problem of political philosophy, the relationship between right and force. His resolving of this problem, at least as it was presented in his historical milieu, required a re-thinking of the basic social covenant or social pact upon which the French nation depended for its existence

---

[9] Letter from Lamennais to Gerbet, 3 août 1830, quoted in A. Trannoy, *Le romantisme politique de Montalembert avant 1843*, Paris, 1942, p. 136.

[10] Ibid.

[11] Letter from Lamennais to Baron Vitrolles, 27 août 1830, reproduced in E. D. Forgues, *Œuvres Posthumes de F. Lamennais*, Paris, 1859, T. II, p. 162.

[12] Letter from Lamennais to Countess Senfft, 29 septembre 1830, reproduced in E. D. Forgues, *Œuvres Posthumes de F. Lamennais*, Paris, 1859, T. II, p. 170.

as a political union. In grasping the problem of politics at this level, Lamennais penetrated the core of political reality such as it had been visualized with such original perceptivity by Plato and with such persistent study by Hobbes and the whole 18th century.[13] Whether or not Lamennais's political analysis reaches the depth or the degree of philosophical cohesiveness as that attained by the classical political theorists is not, for the moment, the question. The first point to be made is that, as we hope to demonstrate, Lamennais placed his finger on the raw nerve of political reality when he probed into the regions of essential justice and social coexistence. Secondly, it is our contention that, in so doing, Lamennais abandoned in some measure the purely historical approach to natural rights and natural law, which had been so much in vogue in the early stages of the romantic reaction, for a more classical position, not unlike that of Rousseau and the contractualist theorists, while remaining firmly within the spirit of Romanticism. Upholding the antiquity of the exercise of a right as a criterion for its legitimacy, the earlier traditionalists tended to regard the study of history as a means of discerning these rights. Consequently, a certain static view of justice results; only those rights which have always been in use may be considered as constitutional, that is, as belonging to the body of ancient laws and recognized limitations on power which form the unwritten law of the land. Lamennais, on the other hand, reverses the optic from which he regards history. He no longer casts his glance behind him in order to establish the admissibility of this or that right but rather reads the historical situation in the light of a law of higher reason which, in manifesting itself in the events themselves, reveals the manner in which rights, which have their origin in a non-historical, spiritual source, are to be expressed and implemented. In this newer view, the organization of power and rights in a society becomes a creative project in which the fundamental aim is the fulfillment of the exigencies of justice, which evolve with the development of peoples, and not simply the conserving task assigned to politics in traditionalist thought.

Lamennais, no less than such a renowned student of politics as Hobbes,[14] undertook his political theorizing under the pressure of and

[13] E. Cassirer, *La philosophie des lumières*, Paris, 1966, p. 240.

[14] For an excellent treatment of the pragmatic character of Hobbes' political philosophy consult E. Voegelin, *The New Science of Politics*, Chicago, 1952, particularly, "The End of Modernity", pp. 178-184.

as a result of a menacing political actuality. The empirical data was that of the day to day situation and it provides the point of departure for his remedial quest. It is precisely his diagnosis of this reality exposed in tangible events which must be understood in order to grasp the real significance of the cure which he prescribed. Lamennais gives methodological preference to making a proper assessement of revolutionary political movements, that is, correctly appreciating the data of the lived experience of the French nation. What has happened? Why has it happened? Knowing the answers to these two questions, one is equipped with a knowledge which is indispensable to a social thinker. Tentative explanations of the historical genesis of revolutions, the cause and effect sequence leading up to the events of July, weigh heavily in his correspondence of this epoch and serve as introductory states of the question to several of his early articles. This decidedly empirical approach lends some support to C. Carcopino's placement of Lamennais among the primitive sociologists.[15]

"In less than half a century", states Lamennais in one of his typical introductions to a discussion of the political problem, "we have seen vanish the absolute monarchy of Louis XIV, the republic of the Convention, the Directory, the Consuls, the Empire, and the monarchy of the Charter".[16] Instability of political institutions then is the overwhelming reality of the era. No matter what judgment one might dare to make concerning the rapid succession of governments and the violent transfers of power "one fact remains, human society, stirred to its very depths, is rejecting the old institutions ... and is searching to re-establish itself under new forms".[17] France has become a battleground of interests, the eye of a hurricane of opinions, which results in the division of the population into opposing factions.

Once apprised of the reality and of the depth of division within society, it was necessary to push the analysis beyond observation to the level of explanation. The interpretative activity of the sociologists seems inevitably to lead them beyond the simply positive or data-furnishing aspect of social study into the realm of the philosophy

---

[15] The principal thesis of C. Carcopino is stated by the author in the following statement: "... there is a unity in the thought of Lamennais ... and this unity was sociology". Consult C. Carcopino, Les doctrines sociales de Lamennais, Paris, 1942, p. 68.

[16] Lamennais, "Considérations sur l'époque actuelle", Articles de L'Avenir, Louvain, 1830-1831, T. I, p. 1. (Most of the references to the articles published in "L'Avenir" will be taken from the above collection and will simply be referred to as "A.A.").

[17] Lamennais, "De l'avenir de la société", A.A., T. V, p. 169.

of history.[18] Lamennais, whose sociology was but embryonically empirical and whose essentially metaphysical concern was overpowering, moved with rapidity into this other sphere once he had focused the attention of his readers on the observable phenomena. In one of the most profoundly philosophical articles of the series which he published in the course of the short history of "L'Avenir", "De l'avenir de la société", he invites his readers to consider the revolution of July on a level superior to that of party strife and political passion, that is, on an essentially ontological level at which one can discern the rationality behind the apparently chaotic succession of events.

> If laws emanating from an infinite wisdom preside over the physical world, directing and ruling its movements, and in spite of the sometimes apparent disorder of phenomena, conduct it to its ends with an irresistible force and an immutable regularity, one ought not to believe that the moral world, alone forsaken by Providence, floats hazardously on the immense, dark, stormy sea of the ages, or that it does not have equally its laws which, without altering the nature of free agents, lead them also, following a regular and harmonious order of development, to their particular ends and to the general end of creation.[19]

Admitted then the legal character of the "moral world" to which he often refers, it becomes possible to bypass the purely descriptive and to perceive the laws which are found beyond political passions and the sudden eruptions which disrupt the habitual rhythm of social life. Although the existence of such laws is assumed, since he had abundantly discussed in his earlier writings his concept of the orderly moral universe, he assures his readers that such laws become manifest in history which is itself simply "a more and more clear and precise expression" of these laws which are "dependent upon the passing of the centuries".[20] The fundamental rationality of the moral world becomes, strangely enough, particularly evident at the moment of social transition such as that which was contemporary to the generation of "L'Avenir". One risks, however, not recognizing or even opposing the legal structure of history if one does not see the role of religion, particularly, that of the perfected religion, Christianity as the generative principle behind movement in historical time. Realizing that the moral teachings of the Christian revelation, which describe

---

[18] G. Del Vecchio, *Philosophy of Law*, Washington, 1953, pp. 10-13.
[19] Lamennais, "De l'avenir de la Société", A.A., T. V, pp. 160-161.
[20] Ibid., p. 161.

the essential character of the social bond uniting men, are clarified in an over-expanding moral universe, it is possible to see in the happenings of July "a popular reaction against absolutism" and, more profoundly, "an inevitable effect of an already ancient impulsion, the continuation of a great movement which, having projected itself from the regions of thought into the political world in 1789, announced to the sleeping nations of a corrupt civilization and an outdated order the fall of that order and the birth of a new order".[21]

The ultimate source of this general movement is out of the reach of man and is to be found in the "first and fundamental law" of history, a law of progress through which "humanity tends to free itself progressively from the limitations of its infancy while, as the intellect is being liberated by an evolving and developing Christianity, the people attain, so to speak, the age of man".[22] Attempting to wrest the notion of permanent, irreversible progress from the hands of the secular heirs of Condorcet, Lamennais begins to interpret events in the light of New Testament eschatology. His justification for theologizing the optimistic teleology of the later Enlightenment thinkers was, as it will be shown in Part III of this Chapter, basically metaphysical. It has been necessary, however, to introduce this fundamental idea prior to a discussion of the actual political doctrine of "L'Avenir" since it hovers in the background of all the particular questions to be treated. As K. Jürgensen has proposed, the whole controversy of the doctrinal sincerity of Lamennais and his followers can only be understood if his treatment of the idea of progress in history is borne in mind.[23] Indeed, it might even be said with E. Voegelin that any serious political philosophy necessarily implies a philosophy of history.

> The existence of man in political society is historical existence, and a theory of politics, if it penetrates to principles, must at the same time be a theory of history.[24]

b) *The Basis of a New Social Pact*

The concatenation of the multiple variables which constitute the human personality plus the singularity of genius produced in the historical person of Félicité Lamennais an observer of the historical

[21] Lamennais, "De l'avenir de la société", A.A., T. V, pp. 161-162.

[22] Ibid., p. 162.

[23] K. Jürgensen, *Lamennais und die Gestaltung des Belgischen Staates*, Wiesbaden, 1963, p. 54.

[24] E. Voegelin, *The New Science of Politics*, Chicago, 1952, p. 1.

scene gifted with a genuinely rare insight. This awareness of what was actually happening in the society about him forced him to seek a way out of an intolerably closed system of political responsiveness which he described as "politics of habit" or the "politics of fear".[25] In conjunction with the world-view which resulted from his understanding of the historical process, he came to the important conclusion that revolutionary fervor was, in reality, "an immense effort to return to a normal state".[26] Having once accepted the positive character of social ferment as symptomatic of a fundamental disorder in the basic political structures, he was forced to take up again a preliminary analysis of the essential elements of political union and, following upon this analysis, to propose a solution which would be both theoretically acceptable and practically attainable.

Justice has been aptly defined as "a principle of coordination between subjective beings".[27] The very notion of coordination inevitably evokes the ideas of proportionality and of harmony, the establishment of relationships in which the parts find their proper place and make an adjustment to the whole. Relationships imply the existence of terms to be joined and of a certain affinity between the terms which call for such a relationship. For Lamennais, the evident sociability of man indicates that a social bond should exist but, in fact, what he saw about him was a juxtaposition in the same geo-political space of unrelated and, seemingly, irrelative parts. Thus, in the articles of "L'Avenir", he seems to revert to a methodology closer to the "computative" approach of Hobbes than to the organic, historical approach of his traditionalist forebearers, Bonald and Maistre. Hobbes, it has been noted, "takes individual wills and makes use of them as a coin of exchange, as purely abstract unities".[28] Lamennais does something similar, not from an à priori choice, but by following the dictates of the empirically given. Man is not by nature this anti-social, demi-savage who must be forced into the "Leviathan-State" as a measure of self-protection and of mutual self-defense; but, he has become, in the eyes of Lamennais, reduced to a primitive autonomy in which only the minimal social unities have survived. In effect, all types of government have fallen. "What", he asks, "is stable? . . . what

[25] Lamennais, "Nécessité de s'unir pour le maintien de l'ordre et la conservation des droits communs", A.A., T. I, p. 221.

[26] Lamennais, "Le Pape", A.A., T. I, p. 476.

[27] G. Del Vecchio, *Justice*, Edinburgh, 1952, p. 2.

[28] E. Cassirer, *La philosophie des lumières*, Paris, 1966, p. 257.

remains? ... what survives in the depths of the human heart? Two things", he concludes, "God and liberty".[29] These are the two irreducible realities. God is the one, the source of existence, unity and the true social order, the object and the substance of the eternal order of faith. Liberty describes the ceaseless efforts of the autonomous personal conscience to achieve the final harmony of that spiritual union which alone is true society. In the struggle to attain a true society, or the union of God and humanity, mankind necessarily rejects any domination which does not have its source in the laws of the moral universe which are both the source and the goal of historical dynamism. As long as there is no harmony in the moral order, no unity between God and liberty, or, in epistemological terms, between the order of faith and the order of reason, "the trouble begins and continues to grow until they are again re-united".[30] The basic reason for the division and even antipathy between religion and liberty is to be found in theological error and in the spiritual betrayal of the people by a clergy engrossed in this error and, consequently, subservient to political power interests. In an even harsher fashion, Abbé Gerbet, writing in the *Prospectus* to "L'Avenir", attacks the "bastard theology" of the Gallican advocates of royal absolutism as the basic cause of the alienation of the cause of liberty from its authentic origin, the Christian religion.[31]

No matter what the cause, Lamennais and his followers beheld before them a situation of alienation and desocialization which was, for them, the existential social reality. Translated into political terms, this alienation means that since

> ... the revolution has destroyed the ancient social hierarchy, the corporations, and, in general, all species of political aggregations established on special rights and legally circumscribed common interests, there are but individuals in France ...[32]

Since this is the political reality, it is imperative to grasp it as it is and to accept the fact that France is and can only be a democratic republic. One is consequently forced to accept the mobility of institutions, governments and constitutions.[33] Is this to be considered as an

---

[29] Lamennais, "Considérations sur l'époque actuelle", A.A., T. I, p. 1.

[30] Ibid.

[31] "Prospectus", A.A., T. I, p. 1 (This first statement of principles is generally attributed to Gerbet.)

[32] Lamennais, "Nécessité de s'unir pour le maintien de l'ordre et la conservation des droits communs", A.A., T. I, p. 151.

[33] Ibid.

un-natural state to be resisted or subverted by a politics of intransigence. A definite "no" is the response of "L'Avenir". The democratization of a political society is one of the options open to the people in search of liberty and the true social order and, as a consequence, Lamennais does not hesitate to speak of the "natural order of democracy".[34] Again, binding the political actuality to the rationality of the historical process, he affirms that the "political homogeneity"[35] to which society has been reduced provides a genuine opportunity for creative political thinking. The originality of Lamennais among his co-religionists becomes clearly manifest in the manner in which he intellectually grasped the panorama unfolding before the spectators and participants of the revolution of July, 1830.

> Lamennais more than anyone else understood the march of events; he saw that ancient law, as respectable as it might have been, had no longer any possible application, and that it represented a static conception of social, political and religious life.[36]

Accepted then the reality of this "vast democracy",[37] how does the nation avoid anarchy and ceaseless agitation? The political theorist could do no less than ask as did Lamennais, "... where then is ... the common security in the milieu of chaotic interests and opposing doctrines?"[38] The dangers are obvious as he indicates in the key article, "Nécessité de s'unir pour le maintien de l'ordre et la conservation des droits communs", and it is necessary "to find for all, beyond power, which is necessarily unstable since it varies with opinion, a safeguard against the arbitrary and against persecution no matter what may be their origin".[39] In this same article, which with "Considération sur l'époque actuelle" might be taken as the introductory phases of the new political philosophy, he invites men "who have faith in truth"[40] to consider the possibility of a new social pact upon which to construct, if not a true society, at least the conditions for the eventual attainment of such a society.

[34] Lamennais, "Fausse direction du gouvernement", A.A., T. II, p. 326.

[35] Lamennais, "De la pairie", A.A., T. IV, p. 353.

[36] Ch. Denis, Les contradicteurs de Lamennais", *Annales de philosophie chrétienne*, Paris, Août-Septembre 1900, p. 635.

[37] Lamennais, "Fausse direction du gouvernement", A.A., T. II, p. 327. (Lamennais used this same term in *De la religion* ... but had not yet drawn such positive conclusions from his admission.)

[38] Lamennais, "Nécessité de s'unir pour le maintien de l'ordre et la conservation des droits communs", A.A., T. I, pp. 152-153.

[39] Ibid., p. 153.

[40] Ibid., p. 159.

What are the conditions of this new social pact? Will such a social pact be based upon the principle of justice or upon a pragmatically devised truce? In order to answer these two questions, it will be necessary to clarify Lamennais's methodology which is itself clearly indicative of the evolution of his thought. Concerning the nature of the social covenant which Lamennais offered to his fellow-citizens, it is interesting to notice that, while resting faithful to the traditionalist principle that constitutions and governments cannot be constructed in an a priori fashion, that is, a government "ought to grow, by its own internal forces, from an anterior germ";[41] he, nonetheless, approaches a contractualist position by affirming that the basis for a social accord exists even without the common core of religious beliefs which he had so forcefully defended as indispensable to social organization in the *Essai sur l'indifférence*... and in subsequent writings. How does he bridge the gap between political organicism and political associationism? First, he frees himself from the question of forms insofar as governments are concerned. Forms, monarchical, aristocratic, or democratic, are really indifferent matters since they belong to the order of opinion or human convention, that is, they are totally dependent upon the social realities. The important question is whether or not the form itself is governed by reason or by force, in brief, whether or not justice becomes manifest in the institutional form. In "D'une grave erreur des honnêtes gens" written to convince recalcitrant Catholic legitimists of the reasonability of his acceptance of liberal democracy, he explores in detail the various possibilities of government under reason or justice. In the state which is founded upon Divine Reason and in which there is unity through obedience to a commonly recognized divine order, a situation of perfect harmony and perfect liberty would exist. But there can also be a political order founded upon reason alone, that is, the coordination of independent reasons upon the grounds of a mutual acceptance of individual rights and liberties. A third possibility is government under the reason of one man but such is necessarily despotism since it implies a reversion to force.[42] The postulate underlying the analysis is the following:

> ... the reason of each man, considered without rapport to God, being by its essence independent of the reason of every other man, and power, being only a man similar in every way to all other men, without privilege

[41] Lamennais, "Fausse direction du gouvernement", A.A., T. II, p. 322.
[42] Lamennais, "D'une grave erreur des honnêtes gens", A.A., T. I, pp. 218-219.

or superiority of nature, it follows that man in power has no right to impose on other men his own reason as rule and law . . . he is and cannot be, insofar as power, other than brute force.[43]

Obedience alone makes possible a social union but obedience to anyone other than to God is dependence or slavery; thus, when obedience cannot be achieved through a common adherence of naturally independent subjects to a universally recognized supreme reason, the only alternative to brute force as molder of the commonweal is a system in which independence is the fundamental law.[44] The same analysis is stated in quite a succinct fashion in an earlier article.

> When nothing is fixed in the world, neither the idea of law and of power, nor the idea of justice, nor even the idea of truth, we can only escape from a frightening succession of tyrannies by an immense development of individual liberty which becomes the only possible guarantee for the security of everyone until social beliefs are re-affirmed and until the intellects, dispersed, so to speak, in a limitless space, begin again to gravitate to a common center.[45]

In terms quite reminiscent of both Hobbes and Rousseau, Lamennais, while respecting the exigencies of his theological and metaphysical principles, poses the question of political unity by reducing social reality beyond institutional forms to its ultimate atomic unities, the individual and such primitive components as the family. Since nobility, hereditary rights and feudal corporations have been swept away, there remains but "an homogeneous mass of thirty-two million individuals declared equal by the law".[46] Given this raw material of political right, basic equality, it is only logical to conclude that "the democratic element is the only element which subsists in France".[47] As has been previously noted, one of the permanent elements of Lamennais's thought was the acceptance, in principle, of a basic human equality and even of a Rousseau-like appreciation of fundamental human autonomy.[48] It is not difficult, therefore, to rediscover the associationist or contractualist character of his political anthropology reappearing when he found himself

---

[43] Lamennais, "D'une grave erreur des honnêtes gens", A.A., T. I, p. 218.
[44] Ibid.
[45] Lamennais, "Considérations sur l'époque actuelle", A.A., T. I, p. 4.
[46] Lamennais, "Fausse direction du gouvernement", A.A., T. II, p. 325.
[47] Ibid.
[48] See Chapter Three, III 1 b. "Christian Liberty".

confronted with a situation which he interpreted as being empirically that which Hobbes and Rousseau had employed symbolically.

In terms of actual political choice, Lamennais proposed that all Frenchmen desirous of order and a free exercise of their natural liberties unite in a common accord "for the defense of order and of our common rights against anyone who makes an attempt against them".[49] The common recognition of the Charter of August, 1830, represents the tangible affirmation of the new covenant founded on the principle that "from now on, there is no life except in liberty, a liberty equal for all".[50] We will return to a discussion of Lamennais's understanding of these liberties in section d, "Common Liberties: Principles of the Social Pact"; but, before doing so, it is necessary to enter more deeply into the philosophy of law and rights which served as the justification, in theory, for his bold proposals. In reality, Lamennais embraced with absolute sincerity the political system of public law and the social philosophy emanating from the revolution of 1789.[51]

c) Legitimacy and Legality

We have previously asked the question concerning the exact philosophical nature of the reasons behind the social pact proposed by Lamennais, a pact which envisioned the common, unrestricted, adherence to the Charter of all dissident elements and opinions, including the members of a Church which had traditionally affirmed for itself a unique relationship to truth, and, consequently, a unique relationship to the State. The answer is to be found in Lamennais's exposition of the principles of justice and rights which, for him, are indispensable in any social order which would be truly human and consonant with transcendent values. The notion of legitimacy is centric to the discussion and its definition will give the key to a proper grasping of the problem of law and rights as visualized by Lamennais. It might be mentioned, in addition, that the problem of legitimacy or

[49] Lamennais, "Nécessité de s'unir pour le maintien de l'ordre et la conservation des droits communs", A.A., T. I, p. 152.

[50] Ibid., p. 159.

[51] It has been clearly indicated that, if Lamennais accepted the system, his understanding of it was based upon quite distinct principles. K. Jürgensen takes pains to point out the error of the historian, F. Schnabel, and others, who tend to think of Lamennais as a converted Jacobin. Consult K. Jürgensen, *Lamennais und die Gestaltung des Belgischen Staates*, Wiesbaden, 1963, p. 60.

the right to claim sovereignty or jurisdiction within the body-politic was historically, following the substitution of the ruling Bourbons by the Orlean branch of the family through supralegal means, a point of controversy which seriously divided French Catholicism during the uneasy days of anti-clerical efflorescence which accompanied the change of dynasties.[52]

Legitimacy, as it has been noted, was considered by the early traditionalists as an historic right. We have already seen how Lamennais, at the time of the publication of *De la religion* ..., had begun to diverge from this important principle of conservative political theory.[53] At the epoch of "L'Avenir", the separation of Lamennais from the so-called Historical School of Natural Law becomes definitive. His position now becomes closer to that of the classical political theorists of the Enlightenment. The brilliant commentator of the philosophy of the "esprit forts", E. Cassirer, has accurately caught the essence of their political problematic when he described their treatment of the question of rights as being "in no way ... fixed upon the consideration of rights historically acquired", but, he continues, upon "the rights which we have from birth".[54] We hope to show, admitting, of course, important differences and nuances arising from the very experience of Romanticism, that, in his treatment of rights as in his treatment of the social pact, Lamennais returned to the naturalist methodology in an effort to find a way out of the seemingly insoluble conflict between the unitary world-view of the Roman Church and the pluri-dimensional character of the existing political spectrum.

The theoretical defense of the mennaisian position taken in reference to democracy, revolution, and modern liberties is best summed up, from the point of view of political theory, in his important, "Des doctrines de L'Avenir". Introducing his apologetic with an unswerving and unhesitating confession of faith in the Catholic Church and a reaffirmation of his loyalty to the Holy See and to the hierarchy, he reiterates, at the same time, his unequivocal rejection of all modes of political power based upon force or the coercion of consciences. Historically, it was necessary to return to the sources to appreciate the true Christian philosophy of liberty and order. Gallicanism had created a situation of tyranny, largely, as Gerbet

---

[52] A. R. Vidler, *Prophecy and Papacy*, London, 1954, pp. 152-158.
[53] See Chapter Four, I 2 a, "Religion and Law".
[54] E. Cassirer, *La philosophie des lumieres*, Paris, 1966, p. 240.

remarked, through a servile theology which had destroyed "the ancient notion of power and obedience".[55]

What is this ancient notion upon which legitimate power may be erected and recognized? "For us", states Lamennais, "justice is the necessary basis of law and it alone constitutes the legitimacy of power".[56] Lamennais returns thus to an ahistorical, and, as will be seen in Part III of this Chapter, a fundamentally ontological conceptualization of justice and law. Legitimacy belongs with justice to the category of invariables and differs essentially from legality which is simply the historical realization of legitimacy, "determined in its form and mode of transmission by positive human laws".[57] Legality, then, or the actual form of government, is transitory and, "arbitrary in itself, it can vary and does, in fact, vary with time".[58] Essentially an historical phenomenon, legality merely constitutes a "relative and subordinate right" which is dependent, for its continued existence, upon its conformity with "immutable, eternal right from which it derives" or "with justice, which constitutes ... the only true legitimacy".[59] Gone, therefore, are the claims of rulers which are founded only upon the historical factor of duration. Not history but justice "remains always the imperishable root of all that which is ordained among men".[60] If the legality of the present political structure is in question, the people are no longer subjected to its jurisdiction but are subject only to justice or to primitive legitimacy which entails supporting that element or force "which ... guarantees the security of persons and properties and which presents itself as protector of both the acquired rights of all and of common liberties".[61] In practical terms, the only government in the France of 1830 which could be termed legitimate and, consequently, legal, is that which protects and obeys the Charter since the Charter is itself the historical embodiment of values which transcend the historical order. By distinguishing between "things of time" and "eternal things", the citizen is enabled to place institutional and hereditary sovereignties in the proper perspective realizing that political authority is not legitimate through the longevity of its existence but that it becomes legitimate through

---

[55] "Prospectus", A.A., T. I, p. 1.
[56] Lamennais, "Des doctrines de L'Avenir", A.A., T. I, p. 383.
[57] Ibid., pp. 383-384.
[58] Ibid.
[59] Ibid.
[60] Ibid.
[61] Ibid.

its adherence to justice and respect for the rights of all citizens.[62]

Forced, by an acerbic criticism from his conservative co-religionists, to clarify and to defend the orthodoxy of the doctrines of "L'Avenir", Lamennais and his co-workers prepared an important ideological statement of principles in a joint article entitled, "Déclaration présentée au Saint-Siège par les rédacteurs de L'Avenir". On the question of political and civil society, the Catholic liberals defended their distinction between legitimacy and legality as an extension of the epistemological distinction between the order of faith and the order of reason. All legitimate sovereignty exercises power by divine right "since God, Who has created man as a social being, wished all that is necessary for the conservation of society".[63] But the divine right of a just state authority is not the only manifestation of inalienable sovereignty in social reality for "individuals, families, peoples, equally possess divine rights which are not concessions of a prince but which have their source in something anterior and superior to any political power whatsoever".[64] In reality, political power is only necessary to safeguard the functioning of this plurality of sovereignties under the law of justice and any regime which accomplishes this task is of divine right or legitimate. As a result, the loss of power is inevitable when a government violates the fundamental law of justice. This should be accomplished, if possible, without violence by means of a moral act or the transfer of allegiance from the offending governmental regime to that social force which will provide a government founded on justice. In practical terms, this is tantamount to an admission of the principle of popular sovereignty with the adjunctive right to rebel.[65]

Governments, thus, belong to the order of legality and are the result of a human convention which determines the transmission of power and the limits to be imposed upon the exercise of coercive power according to the historical circumstances. The editors of "L'Avenir" use the term "contrat synallagmatique"[66] or, a reciprocal contract, to describe the social pact which actualizes political power. A traditional justification for their contractualist position is sought from such

---

[62] Lamennais, "Considérations sur l'époque actuelle", A.A., T. I, p. 5.

[63] "Déclarations présentées au Saint-Siège par les rédacteurs de L'Avenir", A.A., T. II, p. 464. (This interesting summation of the doctrines of the group around Lamennais was published jointly and signed by the editors. The name of F. de La Mennais heads the list of signatories.)

[64] Ibid.

[65] Ibid., p. 467.

[66] Ibid., p. 469.

sources as St. Thomas, Suarez, and Bellarmine. But is this not simply a new version of the social contract theory of Rousseau? Lamennais and the others maintain that there are two essential differences, namely, the social contract is not itself the law of justice as it is for Rousseau but is dependent upon a divine order of justice and is not created out of the "General Will"; furthermore, the social pact between the governed and the governing is simply a formal, historical manifestation of a temporal character which is based upon a fundamentally ontological sociability or original state of society which is perpetual and indissoluble. Governments may be changed by consent, legal process, or revolt; but the spiritual union of intelligent beings which constitutes the moral cosmos in union with God is itself changeless.[67]

Lamennais further clarifies his position in his vigorous "Réponse à la lettre du P. Ventura". The fears of his Roman friend, the first open sign of growing suspicion in Rome concerning "L'Avenir", were, in the opinion of Lamennais, based upon a misinterpretation of the notion of sovereignty such as it had been conceived by the new liberals. In brief, Lamennais rather testily answered that his notion of sovereignty, which is simply that God communicates the right to govern directly to the people and, through them, to the rulers, was none other than that of a series of theologians and canonists whom he quotes in his defense.[68] This defense of the position of "L'Avenir" vis-à-vis the new democratic order emerging from the French Revolution against charges of unorthodoxy by means of quoting frequently and at length from recognized Catholic authorities from the past is quite typical of the sense of re-discovery which permeates the writings of "L'Avenir". It was necessary to prove to the world of liberalism and progress that there was no basic incompatibility between the traditional religion, properly understood, and the aspirations of mankind towards a free society.

d) *Common Liberties: Principles of the Social Pact*

The sort of political union which the editors of "L'Avenir" had in mind was not simply one of raw necessity but, as is characteristic of all non-coercive organization among subjective beings, was one requiring a certain common agreement on mutually accepted

---

[67] "Déclarations présentées au Saint-Siège par les rédacteurs de L'Avenir", A.A., T. II, p. 468-470.

[68] Lamennais, "Réponse à la lettre du P. Ventura", A.A., T. III, pp. 30-42.

principles. It was truly a political consensus and a political consensus is not merely a truce agreed to by exhausted combatants. Public consensus conceived as "a systematization of experience"[69] points to certain rational presuppositions which are accepted by those who choose to join in the consensus-producing civic dialogue. As J. C. Murray has noted, "only the theory of natural law is able to give account of the public moral experience that is the public consensus".[70] Although employing different terms and inspired by distinct first principles, Lamennais came to speak a language analogous to that of the public consensus which had come to replace the older juridical language as the exchangeable currency of the realm of civic discussion. Public opinion had become, in effect, a regulatory influence in an egalitarian society which was in the process of outgrowing the highly regulated modes of civic intercourse characteristic of hierarchical societies.

Lamennais seized upon the importance of public opinion both as a real political force and, on a more idealistic basis, as the vital expression of an expanding tradition. Opinions, the nemesis of the philosophical ideal of truth, tend to coagulate and to form a layer of nearly universally accepted norms around which the community takes shape. What had become manifestly apparent to Lamennais was that there was widespread agreement among modern Western peoples in their quest for a liberation from the restrictions of political powers and the confinement of older social structures.

> ... liberty is the common desire, the universal wish and the efforts of men of good will ought to tend towards its realization; through this, order will be re-born...[71]

This has been the true insight of liberalism; liberals have seen that liberty ought to be equal for all, the common stuff of the social alliance.

Yet, what the liberals see is "the fact" of liberty. They lack the ability to understand that the liberties which they propose must be established on firmer grounds if they are to endure. Catholicism, Lamennais contends, provides the basis, in right, for a constant liberty which is in reality, the just order.[72] We will take up this question of

[69] J. C. Murray, S.J., *We Hold These Truths*, New York, 1960, p. 107.
[70] Ibid., p. 109.
[71] Lamennais, "De la République", A.A., T. III, p. 227.
[72] Lamennais, "Considérations sur l'époque actuelle", A.A., T. I, pp. 3-4.

the Church and its rapport with the new order in the section immediately following. Our purpose here is to show how Lamennais constructs a theory of liberty which is compatible with both the common rights doctrine of the liberals and his previous position as a defender of the unique Divine sovereignty.

The liberties of the Charter are the bond of union between the believers and non-believers. Men of good will are united not only out of fear of violence and of the arbitrary but also because they accept as the "first basis of public peace, the sacred right of all who touch French soil", liberty of conscience.[73] Does this mean the absence of truth and, consequently, of just authority in the French nation?

> ... On the contrary, it alone assures their rights [those of conscience and honor]. For, on the one hand, liberty of conscience allows each one the right to believe everything which seems to him to be true and to act according to his beliefs insofar as he does not trouble public order; and, on the other hand, by establishing the most perfect civil tolerance, implies in no way dogmatic tolerance which is, in reality, the absence of all belief and even of every opinion ...[74]

How does such a position relate, without contradiction, to what Lamennais had previously said with such emphasis concerning the danger to society presented by indifference? We will discuss the attitude of "L'Avenir" towards tolerance more specifically in Part II; but it might be noted for the present that there is no question of contradiction between the Lamennais of the *Essai sur l'indifférence...* and the Lamennais of the "L'Avenir". There are factors, as it will be seen, already homogeneous to his earlier thought which, when more fully developed, rendered his position more supple. Such important notions as his incorporation of the secular idea of progress and the continuing purification of his primordial principle concerning the spiritual nature of society will be discussed in the final section and will show, we believe, that there was no absolute reversal in Lamennais's thought but an internal evolution fed by external events. For the moment, it would be well to recall that liberty of conscience, as originally viewed by Lamennais, was considered as an inalienable human right at the very source of personality.[75]

As seen in "L'Avenir", this spiritual independence of man from

---

[73] Lamennais, "Nécessité de s'unir pour le maintien de l'ordre et la conservation des droits communs", A.A., T. I, p. 160.
[74] Ibid.
[75] See Chapter Three, III 1 b, "Christian Liberty".

all human authority arises from "this grand and fundamental maxim, that power, by its very nature, has no authority either over the spirit or the conscience".[76] Liberty of conscience, which, due to the oppressive character of modern governments, must be publicly recognized and defended, has its ultimate justification in a theological reality. "No one owes an account of his faith to human power".[77] Why is this? Because only God "has the right to penetrate ... the sanctuary of the soul".[78] Again, he states, that the human intellect and conscience constitute "a region which escapes the empire" of political power.[79]

Such testimonies are multiple in the articles of Lamennais and his companions and may be summed up by the lapidary statement made by him in "De l'avenir de la société", "in general, all that constitutes the spiritual order ... is, by right, independent" of temporal authority.[80] The spiritual is by right independent of the secular arm in the same fashion as the order of faith is prior and superior to the order of reason; thus, the temporal responds to the inspiration of the invariable spiritual realities but can in no way seek to dominate the realm of the spirit without losing its own derived right to direct temporal affairs. But in addition, liberty of conscience is not simply a right to the interior life; it is the right of a person who is a socio-historical reality. Liberty of conscience would mean very little in terms of the practical if there were not allied liberties which are both logically derivatives and necessary supports of the fundamental right of every person to be unmolested in his basic relationship with the Divine. It is quite apparent to Lamennais that liberty of education, of the press and of association are the natural consequences of the most natural and inalienable of all rights and are, thus, themselves, natural and imprescriptible rights which cannot be impinged without impinging at the same time liberty of conscience. What would be the practical significance of a right to form a free opinion were there no possibility to communicate the opinion held? If one keeps in mind the special importance assigned to communication in Lamennais's metaphysic of society, that is, briefly, that language and the oral tradition are the media through which primitive truth is transmitted

---

[76] Lamennais, "De la République", A.A., T. III, p. 229.
[77] Lamennais, "De la séparation de l'église et de l'état", A.A., T. I, p. 24.
[78] Ibid.
[79] Lamennais, "D'une grave erreur des honnêtes gens", A.A., T. I, p. 219.
[80] Lamennais, "De l'avenir de la société", A.A., T. V, p. 164.

through history, it is not difficult to appreciate the priority given to the liberties of communication such as education and the press in his theory of liberty.[81]

Both liberty of education and liberty of the press imply the right of people to associate among themselves to advance their ideas and to defend their interests through political action. This is necessary because "there is always, even in the most just and moderate power, a tendency to invade" the domain of the private and the spiritual.[82] In a shrewd analysis which antedates the studies of modern political scientists on the nature and importance of pressure groups, Lamennais, in the light of the importance of public opinion, realized that such opinion must have the means of taking a definite shape and of exercising real influence and such is possible only through a protected liberty of association.[83] It is strange that such a sympathetic observer as Abbé Ch. Denis could hold that Lamennais's "concept of modern man", at the time of the "L'Avenir", "is totally individualistic".[84] Such a judgement seems to miss the nuances of Lamennais's thinking on liberty which, if allowing for the essential and absolute character of the liberty of the autonomous personal conscience, did not for that disregard the social aspects of liberty. The ontological principles which are in the background of the mennaisian political doctrine would seem to verify the idea that, while Lamennais employs the vocabulary of liberalism, his basic point of departure remains eminently social. On the ontological level,

---

[81] The best statement of this argument is to be found in Lamennais's "Des doctrines de L'Avenir", A.A., T. I, pp. 386-387. He repeats the thesis of the close relationship between the three derivative liberties, education, press, and association, with considerable clarity in his "Fausse direction du gouvernement", A.A., T. II, p. 326. The inseparability of liberty of education from religious liberty receives more detailed attention in his "Oppression des catholiques", A.A., T. I, pp. 315-319. An extremely interesting definition of the specific sense in which the mennaisians were speaking of liberty at this time was given by Abbé Gerbet in a petition written by him to various Deputies concerning the rights of Catholic schools. "This word liberty", states Gerbet, "does not have for us the vague sense attributed to it either in dreams of inexperience or in passionate desires. By it, we understand well-determined rights, clearly defined by the public conscience and, moreover, consecrated by our new social pact. Among these rights, we place, in the first rank, liberty of education". This hand-written manuscript was published by Abbé Kerbiriou, "Les problèmes de l'école de la Chênaie", La Revue de l'Ouest, Brest, 1935. The citation made above is from an extract of the Kerbiriou article, No. 456, F.I.C. Archives, Highlands, Jersey, C.I., p. 11.

[82] Lamennais, "Des doctrines de L'Avenir", A.A., T. I, p. 387.

[83] Ibid.

[84] Ch. Denis, "Les contradicteurs de Lamennais", Annales de philosophie chrétienne, Paris, Août-Septembre 1900, p. 637.

which we will treat in Part III, individuality is equivalent to matter or to limitation. Lamennais is not seeking to define and defend the rights of the individual as an individual but rather the rights of the person who is defined by his original sociability and universality. The political struggle is not as the liberals see it, that is, the individual versus society, but more exactly society, the primitive bond of spiritual beings, versus collectivity or the mere organization, through force, of individuals.

What Lamennais seems to be pointing to is a plurality of derived sovereignties under the unique sovereignty of God. Not only individuals but also natural unities such as families, communes, and nations possess sovereignty, or, what amounts to the same for Lamennais, a natural liberty or right to administer for oneself.[85] How does this agglomeration of sovereign unities attain a harmony or a viable social accord? When each "natural" unity is allowed to function freely and is not subjected to an a priori organization, a natural compatibility will result.

> The variety which would result from this would only make the political unity of the State stronger for absolute similarity, contrary to liberty because it is contrary to nature, creates a merely apparent and material unity and destroys the true vital unity which results from the intimate, energetic and particular life of each part of the social body . . .[86]

Thus, Lamennais exposes the basis for a "powerful confederation founded on immutable rights" which will "momentarily substitute for the stability of governments and institutions".[87] Such an alliance does not create a true society but it will accomplish the task of saving the nation from anarchy and of opening the only possible route to the final attainment of a perfect social solidarity.

After having seen the mennaisian doctrines of the social contract, legitimacy, and liberty as they were expressed in "L'Avenir" as the program of Catholic liberalism, our task now becomes one of exposing the way in which he united these theories, so similar to the 18th century doctrines of natural rights yet, as we shall see, quite other in inspiration, with the principle of authority which, for him, is embodied in the Catholic Church.

---

[85] Lamennais, "De l'avenir de la société", A.A., T. V, pp. 165-166.
[86] Lamennais, "Des doctrines de L'Avenir", A.A., T. I, p. 388.
[87] Lamennais, "Nécessité de s'unir pour le maintien de l'ordre et la conservation des droits communs", A.A., T. I, p. 161.

II. The Church in a Liberal Society

1. *The separation of Church and State*

a) *The Mennaisian Theory of Separation*

The ultramontane ecclesiology which Félicité Lamennais had embraced as early as 1814 with the publication of *Tradition* ... was, without doubt, a prime mover in driving the early Restoration apostle of the principle of authority into the ranks of liberalism. It has been noted several times that his anguished concern for the spiritual freedom of the Church, which alone would permit an authentic renewal of social faith, was the most constant preoccupation of his earlier writings.[88] Separation of Church and State had been broached by him, as a means to obtain this end, prior to the publication of "L'Avenir" in *Des progrès* ... and, especially, in his two letters to the Archbishop of Paris. By 1830, the issue was no longer academic. Separation of Church and State had become a legal reality in the new constitution, at least insofar as Catholicism was no longer recognized as the religion of the French State. This separation, however, was not really complete since the attendant religious legislation generally followed the pattern molded by the Gallicans and the anti-clerical liberals during the second half of the previous decade. The tendency towards an administered Church remained although the Church was now only legally recognized as being the religion of the majority of the nation.[89] Instead of registering shock and outrage when faced with the new provisions of the Charter, Lamennais openly accepted them, particularly, the notion of separation, and set out to justify the new legal situation to his co-religionists as well as to oppose those in government who would make a sham of separation by using it to perpetuate the abusive practices of previous regimes. It soon became obvious that "the principal and truly revolutionary point" of the program of "L'Avenir", "was religious liberty and its corollary, separation of Church and State".[90]

The first strong public position taken by Lamennais on the question was pronounced in an article dedicated to the very problem under the title, "De la séparation de l'église et de l'état". He had already made

[88] See Chapter Three, I b, "An early discussion of the nature of Spiritual Sovereignty"; also, III 1 c, "Towards a Free Church".

[89] A. R. Vidler, *Prophecy and Papacy*, London, 1954, pp. 155-156.

[90] A. Dansette, "La Mennais contre son temps", *Revue de Paris*, Paris, Novembre 1947, p. 121.

his position abundantly clear in his correspondence even before the revolution of July.[91] In fact, with the advent of "L'Avenir", Lamennais brought into public view a program of principles and action which had been "nearly totally elaborated a year earlier".[92] The time had come, however, to rally popular support, for the good of the Church, to the idea of liberty through separation. The argument employed in this leading article takes into account the well-known thesis of Chapters X and IX of Tome I of the *Essai sur l'indifférence*... concerning the rapport between religion and society. A decade later, he maintained essentially the same principles. The unity of peoples is founded on a law which is superior to that of material interests; it is the "bond of the spirits", the mennaisian synonym for religion or "that law which, through ruling thoughts and wills, leads the individual to social unity".[93] Religion is not restricted to the domain of passive religious experience, an idea which Lamennais never accepted, but, is, and will remain in his thought the source from which the exterior relations within the city are constructed. The civil bond can never be more than "the extension or the complement of the primitive society of the spirit".[94]

This liaison is so basic that it is necessary to admit that religious and civic society are "naturally inseparable";[95] from their very union order is defined and achieved. Order is almost mechanically gauged to the degree of communion in belief. Nevertheless, situations may arise in which the original unity of faith no longer exists; beliefs divide and sects multiply. "In one and the same State ... several spiritual societies are formed".[96] The State is no longer able to identify with any particular spiritual society without oppressing the others; in fact, the State becomes riven with divisions since spiritual societies tend to exteriorize and to create states within the State. Historically, what has happened is that various sects have had political power and have used it to repress the other religious groups thus producing not unity but

---

[91] Letter from Lamennais to Marquis Coriolis, 9 mai 1830, reproduced in E. D. Forgues, *Œuvres Posthumes de F. Lamennais*, Paris, 1859, T. II, p. 136. A similar clear statement of the position of "L'Avenir", even before its birth is contained in the letter of Lamennais to Baron Vitrolles, 30 mai 1830, reproduced in Eugène Forgues, *Correspondance inédite entre Lamennais et le baron de Vitrolles*, Paris, 1886, pp. 202-204.

[92] J. Poisson, *Le romantisme social de Lamennais*, Paris, 1931, p. 95.

[93] Lamennais, "De la séparation de l'église et de l'état", A.A., T. I, p. 24.

[94] Ibid.

[95] Ibid.

[96] Ibid.

"a permanent political and civil war".[97] When a nation is brought to such a condition, "the only remedy ... is to allow this spiritual war to continue and to terminate by means of purely spiritual weapons".[98] At first sight, this sort of argument seems to resemble that of the "Politiques"; but, as will be seen, Lamennais's conclusion is founded upon entirely distinct principles which are ideologically closer to those of the Ana-baptists than to those of the publicists.[99]

The fundamental cause for the ceaseless civic strife emanating from religious differences is that the nature of religious unity has been misunderstood and the means to attain it have been inappropriate. The use of "material force ... the very appearance of constraint ... brutal violence"[100] in matters of conscience not only fails to bring about the triumph of religious truth but, in actuality, prevents the free acquiescence of men to a common faith. The region of the human conscience is sacred and beyond the reach of the police power of the State. The contrary view, holds Lamennais, is contrary to and destructive of Catholicism. Whenever force has been applied to resolve religious disputes in favor of one sect and even in favor of the true Church "bloody divisions, calamities and crimes without number"[101] have been the result. The fundamental argument used by Lamennais to support his plea for a total separation of Church and State issues from his recognition of the absolute and inalienable character of liberty of conscience. The succession of events and the unfailing instinct of the people have forced men to realize that "the time of violence is no more; there are rights which can no longer be attacked with impunity".[102]

Once the condition of religious diversity is the historical reality, Church-State relations, if maintained on the traditional juridical basis, that is, the establishment structure, degenerate to a governmental policy of protection. The price of protection, however, is paid in the coin of alienation, for the Church becomes a shield for the State against opposition, an instrument of power groups which might be currently responsible for the employment of the coercive force of the State.

---

[97] Lamennais, "De la séparation de l'église et de l'état", A.A., T. I, p. 24.
[98] Ibid.
[99] See Chapter Two, II, "Tolerance: A Modern Problem".
[100] Lamennais, "De la séparation de l'église et de l'état", A.A., T. I, p. 24.
[101] Ibid., p. 25.
[102] Ibid., pp. 26-27.

In the false position in which her relations with the temporal power place her, [the Church] is presented to men under an human appearance which alienates them from her; while hobbled and weighed down by a thousand obligations which deprive her of that movement which is her own, she languishes within herself, suppressed under the weight of an abject servitude.[103]

The reason advanced for the thesis of separation, after the initial argument had been grounded on the transcendent character of liberty of conscience, was based upon a keen historical insight, such as mentioned above, into the character of the national State such as it had evolved from the absolutism of the 17th century and the radicalism of the Revolution. Lamennais realized more clearly than his fellow Catholics, especially those who professed Gallican preferences, that the new idea of national sovereignty rendered the union of Church and State a hazardous risk for the Church rather than a privilege enjoyed by legal and historical right. Governments, following the elemental democratization effected by the Revolution, became identified with political parties which, being divested of all sacral pretensions, were simply representative of secular interests and opinion. A government's protection of the Church was taken inevitably by the opponents of the government as a political alliance of the Church with the party in power.[104] The experience of the immediate past made it quite apparent to Lamennais that, if the Church accepts the protection of the government, she is really submitting herself to a thinly veiled oppression. Not only does the Church become the object of suspicion and of hatred, such as was manifest in the popular reaction against the Church in the July Revolution, but she will not dare "to resist power ... even if her conscience strictly obliges her to do so and if the maxims of the Gospels and the canons of the Church require it as a rigorous duty".[105]

Is there any alternative to the administrative oppression accepted as the price to be paid for the ambivalent privilege of protection? For Lamennais, there is no need for second thoughts "we must save our faith and we will save it through liberty".[106] The Charter offers the possibility of loosening the chains of history which have stultified

[103] Lamennais, "De la séparation de l'église et de l'état," A.A., T. I, p. 26.
[104] C. Constantin, "Libéralisme Catholique", Dictionnaire de Théologie Catholique, T. IX, Partie 1ère, Paris, 1926, cols. 511-521.
[105] Lamennais, "De la séparation de l'église et de l'état", A.A., T. I, p. 27.
[106] Ibid.

Catholics with a false sense of security. If the Church accepts the liberties of the Charter and the principle of separation contained therein and if Catholics demand that governments adhere without exception to the system of common liberties proposed by the Charter, the Church will enter honestly and completely into the common accord which alone binds all Frenchmen.

> All the French, no matter what may be the diversity of their opinions, have the same interest in maintaining the frank and complete execution [of the Charter]; and, moreover, we are concerned with the first of all liberties, religious liberty, and with a consequence of this liberty willed not only by Catholics but by the whole of France.[107]

Liberty of conscience and historical progress provide the rationale for the new politics of national reconciliation and the new Christian apologetic of action and modernity. This double line of argumentation runs throughout the articles which followed "De la séparation de l'église et de l'état", with, as it will be noted in the section immediately following, important refinements.

b) *Lamennais and the Theory of Thesis-Hypothesis*

L. Le Guillou, with his habitual perspicacity, has noted a certain similarity between the position of Lamennais in "De la séparation de l'église et de l'état" and that taken by Bishop Dupanloup three decades later in his efforts to explain the *Syllabus* and the encyclical "Quanta Cura" of Pius IX.[108] There is certainly a basis for comparing the terminology and the intentions of those who utilized the famous thesis/hypothesis distinction with the reasoning which Lamennais employed in speaking of the natural character of the union between religion and civil society and the historical, situational character of their separation. Indeed, there would be an even greater similarity between some of the modern interpretations of the much discussed distinction, such as that of Canon Leclercq,[109] and the mennaisian understanding of the rapport between the ideal and the real. There is, nonetheless, a broad, if not unbridgeable, gap between the thinking of Lamennais and that of the "Civilta cattolica" editors who first made use of the thesis/hypothesis theme. Writing in reaction to the famous

---

[107] Lamennais, "De la séparation de l'église et de l'état", A.A., T. I, p. 28.
[108] L. Le Guillou, *L'évolution de la pensée religieuse de Félicité Lamennais*, Paris, 1966, p. 120.
[109] J. Leclercq, *La liberté d'opinion et les catholiques*, Paris, 1963, pp. 238-246.

discourse of Montalembert at the Congress of Malines, the Roman journalist, while not totally critical of the liberal tendencies of the famous disciple of Lamennais, was quick to note that such modern liberties as liberty of conscience, with its correlative, the idea of Church-State separation, while admissible in special or hypothetical conditions as not only concessions but also as genuinely defensible, are, if taken as universal principles, inadmissible.[110] Nothing could be more alien to the doctrine and the spirit of "L'Avenir" than a dichotomy of this sort.

There are phrases in the earlier articles of "L'Avenir" which tend to recall the tactical emphasis which Lamennais gave to the idea of separation in his conclusions to the second part of *De la religion* ... and which carried over into *Des progrès* ... The timidity and theoretical uncertainty begins to vanish, however, as the doctrine is purified through a repetition of the theme and defensive argumentation. In the "Déclaration présentée au Saint-Siège par les rédacteurs de L'Avenir", the editors of the new journal do not fail to mention that they do not mean by separation an independence of isolation between the two spheres nor do they wish to deny the "inherent right" of spiritual sovereignty, which, for them, as ultramontanes, is to be found in the Papacy. Similarly, in this somewhat apologetical article, they emphasized the circumstantial character of the political situation which had brought them to their choice and even conclude with the statement that "we know that in a Catholic social order Church and State ought to be united".[111]

Even if one takes into account the fact that the line of argument followed in "Déclaration présentée au Saint-Siège par les rédacteurs de L'Avenir" is somewhat hedged by the very fact that it was both a joint declaration and an attempt to save the appearances of orthodoxy in the face of a mounting conservative opposition, does it not, in effect, bear a definite resemblance to the thesis/hypothesis distinction? Our answer is that the resemblance is more apparent than real, more an exterior similarity of conclusions than an interior identification of arguments.

---

[110] R. Aubert, *Le pontificat de Pie IX, (1846-1878)*, Paris, 1963, pp. 250-252. A brief, interesting account of the origin of the thesis/hypothesis distinction by the conservative editors of "Civilta cattolica" and its use by the liberal Catholics is given in R.-C. Gerest, "La liberté religieuse dans la conscience de l'église", *Lumière et Vie*, Paris, Juillet-Octobre 1964, pp. 5-35.

[111] "Déclaration présenté au Saint-Siège par les rédacteurs de L'Avenir", A.A., T. II, p. 477.

First, it is necessary to understand what Lamennais meant when he spoke about the natural inseparability of religion and the political order while upholding, as justifiable, the necessity of their separation. The union of the Church and State or the impregnation of the temporal by the spiritual is not conceptualized by Lamennais in juridical terms. The Church is not, for him, the external, quasi-state of the canonists but the primitive society of intelligent beings or "the living expression of social intelligence".[112] It is not in the area of concordats and legal structures that one must search for the true rapport which exists between matter and spirit or between force and reason, expressions which are used interchangeably by Lamennais to explain the relationship of religion to the prime matter from which societies are made. The institutional accoutrements of a society often obscure the real situation in the society of the spirits. Separation or non-separation, as a merely legal affair, it would seem, is relatively unimportant since the institutional does not create the real. On the contrary, if juridical structures do not represent actually existing order of beliefs, they become burdensome and unjust. This is an important point for Lamennais and he takes pains to mention that this failure to view the deeper reality behind institutions by his contemporaries is one of the reasons why he is misunderstood.

> They have always looked for salvation, not in the invariable laws through which God governs intelligent beings, but in the form, almost arbitrary in itself, of institutions, in a man, in a race, in all that which is nothing...[113]

If there was any hesitation in the earlier articles, all doubt was left behind by the time Lamennais wrote his two famous articles, "De l'avenir de la société" and "Ce que sera le catholicisme dans la société nouvelle", in the final months of the comet-like existence of "L'Avenir". The all-pervading idea is that of a continuing progress directed and motivated by a spiritual Christianity. Separation of the Church from the protection of the State is not in any way seen as a sad necessity occasioned by the unfortunate dispersion of religious beliefs. There is, in his mind, a divine work taking place in "the idea of right ... being separated in a more and more complete manner from the idea of force".[114] It is an uneven progression towards a

---

[112] Lamennais, "De la position de l'église en France", A.A., T. II, p. 155.
[113] Lamennais, "D'une grave erreur des honnêtes gens", A.A., T. I, p. 220.
[114] Lamennais, "De l'avenir de la société, A.A., T. V, p. 163.

spiritualization of society in which France has a privileged role. There is a providential tendency "to realize a social order based upon the most absolute spiritual independence" and, with this liberation of the spirit, that is, the Church in the purest sense, Governments will become "simple regulatory agents placed by national delegation at the head of a system of free administration".[115]

It is false to harken back to the Middle Ages as the ideal for Church-State relations. A certain mixture of the spiritual and the temporal was necessary in the epoch of "royal paternity" but such was an "imperfect mode of society".[116] In fact, far from being ideal, the interference of the Emperors in the spiritual order created conflict and violation of superior rights; the "accord of the priest and the empire" never enjoyed more than a fictional existence.[117] Useless, then, are all efforts to reconstruct "one of the most magnificent ruins of history".[118] It is certain that Christ has dominion over all and that His Vicar has received from Christ the fullness of this spiritual right; nevertheless, a temporal power does exist, according to the constant tradition of the Church, which is independent and autonomous.[119] The point which he is striving to make above all else is that a Catholic social order requires only a believing people and liberty. Given the liberty to do so, the people will accomplish a Christianization of society which does not imply a sacralization of the State. The old royal powers which were a mixture of the spiritual and the temporal must be sharply cut back leaving spiritual power to the Pope.

The spiritual power of the Papacy or the Church does reach the domain of conscience but the coercive power of the Church is always spiritual and never physical. In the concluding paragraphs of "De l'avenir de la société", Lamennais begins to give more importance to the proper density of the temporal sphere which, since he had been concentrating on the freedom of the Church, had been somewhat neglected. Unfortunately, the exact delineation of the respective rights of the two spheres, particularly the temporal sphere, is somewhat schematically and simplistically stated. The people should be free to choose their own system of temporal administration which will be maintained in political check by its subordination to the Charter and

[115] Lamennais, "De la l'avenir de la société, A.A., T V, p. 163.
[116] Ibid., p. 175.
[117] Ibid., p. 176.
[118] Ibid.
[119] Ibid., p. 177.

the political activities of the citizens. In a not too clear reference to matters over which the Church would exercise no authority, he mentions that such material interests as "the properties of the families, the communes and the province" are beyond her jurisdiction for her mission should be simply to "regulate customs by precepts and beliefs by revealed dogmas".[120] Apparently, the experience of condemnation and "Mirari vos" helped Lamennais to focus his thought more sharply on the complexity of the grey areas which are not so easily placed in one jurisdiction or the other. There is a basic weakness in the somewhat utopian and unrealistic politics of "L'Avenir" and the concept of pure liberty. We will return to this point in Part III of the present chapter.

Returning to our original problem, the obvious conclusion to be drawn is that there is no thesis/hypothesis distinction for Lamennais. The thesis, if one wishes to call it by such an appellation, is eschatological; all that is historical and temporal is, and always has been, hypothesis. The really important fact is the universal tendency to free the spiritual from its enervating alliance with the temporal, a tendency which is an "immense progress in the true notion and public sentiment of right".[121] The separation of the Church from the police function of political society is a positive gain. Far from being alarmed, Christians should realize that the independence of peoples, liberty of conscience and its necessary consequence, the separation of the two orders, are simply signs of the goal to which "Christian peoples are tending", that is, "a unique and grand society".[122] The thesis of separation assumes, thus, a very specific and major function in the mennaisian edifice, and, rightfully so, since "it appears as a new act of faith in the temporal government of Providence and the rigorous consequence of the theory of society" which he had previously developed.[123]

---

[120] Lamennais, "De l'avenir de la société", A.A., T. V, p. 178. In a short but revealing article, "Du serment politique", A.A., T. IV, pp. 96-99, Lamennais discusses the moral implications of the promises made to a secular State. In his thought, the sacral character of the oath should not carry over to the limited type of promise which is to be made to a neutral authority. The contractualist implications of his thought are quite evident.

[121] Ibid., p. 165.

[122] Ibid., pp. 178-179.

[123] J.-R. Derré, *Lamennais, ses amis amis et le mouvement des idées à l'époque romantique*, Paris, 1962, p. 437.

2. Tolerance

The tolerance of religions other than the Catholic religion is not directly treated by Lamennais in the articles which he wrote for "L'Avenir". His great and almost obsessive preoccupation was the total liberty of the Catholic Church to conduct her own affairs unhampered by governmental restriction. It was this concern which brought him to see the inviolable character of liberty of conscience and to reappraise the entire problematic of tolerance. One could interpret cynically Laski's comment that Lamennais's appeal to liberty arises from the fact that "men who are persecuted always appeal to the principles of freedom".[124] There is, however, more than a grain of truth in what the learned English liberal has to say. E. Faguet has seen a similar strategic element in mennaisian liberalism since, he notes, Lamennais saw clearly that the position of Catholicism had been reversed in France and that, although possessing the illusion of being a majority, Catholics were, in fact, fast becoming a minority.[125] Yet, as even Faguet admits, there was much more than a tactical manoeuvre in the new and startling championing of religious liberty by a formerly uncompromising advocate of the rights of the Church who had once labeled Rousseau's instructions on the moral excellence of tolerance to the young Emile as "absurd".[126]

Quite obviously, once Lamennais had felt the pressure of governmental coercion and had seen the apathy of a Church encumbered by the restrictive embrace of official recognition, he had second thoughts about the real sense of religious liberty as viewed in the context of the modern world. In accepting the political implications of religious liberty, such as the liberals understood them, Lamennais placed the Church on an equal footing in civil law with all other sects and was perfectly consequent in the conclusions which he drew from his endorsement of the liberal position. If "he asked for and wished liberties which were favorable to his Church", he accepted as well, "those which are unfavorable to her".[127] The experience of history,

[124] H. J. Laski, *Authority in the Modern State*, New Haven, 1919, p. 231.

[125] E. Faguet, *Politiques et Moralistes du XIXe siècle*, Paris, 1898, T. II, pp. 110-111.

[126] F. Duine, "Notes de La Mennais sur un exemplaire de Rousseau", *L'Hermine*, Rennes, 20 mai 1907, p. 118. Reviewing the books of Lamennais's library, Abbé F. Duine, a devoted mennaisian student, discovered, among the comments in Lamennais's handwriting on a copy of *Émile* from a 1793 edition of Rousseau, the epithet "absurde" next to the phrase of Rousseau, "but that it please God, I never teach them the cruel dogma of intolerance".

[127] E. Faguet, *Politiques et Moralistes du XIXe siècle*, Paris, 1898, T. II, p. 116.

which he never fails to evoke, has taught Catholics that evil is not in liberty itself; on the contrary, the failure of the paternalistic attitudes upon which regimes of the past have been constructed has forced men, particularly Catholics, to realize that liberty is "the first need of the people, the true and the only condition of order in the absence of the divine principle . . ."[128]

The toleration of all opinions and religious views is part and parcel of the doctrine of religious liberty which Lamennais devised. As has been shown, he based his demands for the freedom of the Church to teach and to administer her own affairs on an appeal to the principle of liberty of conscience. Approaching the question on these grounds, Lamennais placed himself squarely within the tradition of liberalism. He avoided basing his appeal for the liberty of the Church on the argument that, because the Church is the true Church, and, since only truth has a right to propagate itself in the public domain, the Church ought to enjoy full liberty of action. It is interesting that this sort of argumentation, with its exclusivist basis and implications, did not appear in the columns of "L'Avenir".

Liberty itself and a liberty equal for all are sufficient to establish an accord in the midst of discord which is nothing less than the acceptance, without restrictions, of civic tolerance. This peaceful coexistence is in no way gained through the sacrifice of belief or the homogenization of dogmas through indifference. Liberty of conscience, guaranteed for all, does not imply, for Catholics, dogmatic indifference.

> . . . the Catholic renounces no point of his doctrine; he preaches it; he defends it; he propagates it through reason and persuasion, recognizing the same right for Protestants, Jews, or any sect whatsoever as long as submitted to the laws of the country.[129]

The error of the past is that "we have not wished to be free together and, for this reason, we have all been slaves".[130]

Although Lamennais dwelt upon the abuses suffered by the Church at the hands of the ministries and dedicated himself almost exclusively to the cause of liberty for his co-religionists, he did not intend to restrict the benefits of his efforts to the Church.

---

[128] Lamennais, "D'une grave erreur des honnêtes gens", A.A., T. I, p. 220.
[129] Lamennais, "Nécessité de s'unir pour le maintien de l'ordre et la conservation des droits communs", A.A., T. I, p. 160.
[130] Ibid., p. 162.

> ... In defending their rights so scandalously violated, Catholics are not
> fighting only for themselves; they form, if one would permit the
> expression, the avant-garde of humanity marching towards the conquest
> of the future ... they are erecting the altar upon which the peoples
> liberated and once again become brothers through the union of order and
> liberty extend to one another a hand ...[131]

In even more clear but less lyrical terms he reaffirms the utter sincerity
of the commitment of Catholics to the system of common liberty,
which was succinctly expressed as "liberty in all for all",[132] in his
"Réponse à un article du Moniteur". "We do not demand it for
ourselves alone", he assures his opponents, "we wish it for all of our
brothers, no matter what may be their beliefs; we wish it completely
for all, equally for all".[133] In fact, so vigorous is Lamennais's adoption
of the notion of common liberty and mutual toleration that he
recognizes as the only limit which may be imposed upon individual
liberty the well-known liberal dictum that the liberty of one is only
restricted by the liberty of another. Lamennais feels free to admit this
position because he believes that the authority of truth, an authority
emanating from the intrinsic validity of a true statement, will impose
itself when men are free to recognize it. Liberty is the necessary
condition for a social harmony founded on truth; coercion or the
application of force hampers its attainment. The ambiguous nature of
this solution to the problem stemming from a collision of rights will
be discussed in the critique.

A final point to be made concerning Lamennais's treatment of
tolerance is that not only did he accept the system of civil toleration
as it has come into existence in modern Western nations, without, of
course, the philosophical presuppositions in which, for some, it is
necessarily founded, but he also alluded to the moral requirements of
the new order. A civic life in common accord participated in by men
of opposing beliefs requires the exercise and the perfection of certain
virtues which can alone make of the constitutional accord a viable
practicality. The sentiments of "mutual love and delicate compassion"
will bring men together in spite of ideological differences; "an altar ...
to pity" should be elevated by common effort in order that men might

---

[131] Lamennais, "De la liberté religieuse", A.A., T. VI, p. 111.
[132] "Suspension de L'Avenir", A.A., T. VII, p. 147. This final declaration of the editors
of "L'Avenir" before their departure for Rome to receive Papal approbation was also a
joint article signed by all.
[133] Lamennais, "Réponse à un article du Moniteur", A.A., T. VI, p. 222.

have compassion for one another.[134] In the eloquent final phrases of "De l'avenir de la société", he begs his readers to realize that liberty, which tends to divide while liberating, will fail without love. An order to be based in liberty requires for its survival and success "an immense charity" which only Catholicism can bring to the society a-building.[135]

Actually, the clearest statement on tolerance in "L'Avenir" came not from Lamennais but from his most loyal collaborator, Gerbet, who wrote a brilliant exposé of the position of the Catholic liberals on the question of tolerance. The content of this remarkably clear article could not be better expressed than by quoting the summation of the argument which, given by the author himself, is truly in itself an extraordinarily precise recapitulation of the mennaisian doctrine of tolerance.

> In résumé, we believe that it has been established that the restrictive regime of liberty of conscience which entered into the constitution of the Middle Ages, had for its base a transitional state of society; so much for the past; furthermore, that wherever a new social order is established, and becomes, by the very force of the real situation, the expression of the state of the spirits, divided as they are in their beliefs, every attempt against liberty of conscience attacks the basic conditions and very foundations of this new social order, so much for the present, and, in particular for the actual situation in France. It is also clear that if the faith prevails by means of liberty, liberty itself, far from being buried by the triumph which it has prepared, will participate henceforth in the very immortality of religion whose destinies will be inseparably united to those of liberty, so much for the future. In conclusion, it has also been established that the progress of truth in the whole world depends upon the universal abolition of constraint.[136]

There are three elements which run through Gerbet's development of the theme, namely, the evolution of history, the inviolability of the individual conscience, and the confidence of the Catholic in his own faith or in the simple power of truth independent of all material supports. Since man is an embodied spirit, he must manifest exteriorly the dictates of his conscience, or, the truth as he finds it in his relations with others and with God in the spiritual society of which he

---

[134] Lamennais, "Considérations sur l'époque actuelle", A.A., T. I, pp. 5-6.
[135] Lamennais, "De l'avenir de la société", A.A., T. V, pp. 178-179.
[136] G., "Eclaircissemens sur la liberté de conscience", A.A., T. V, p. 212. (Although this article is simply signed "G." it is clearly by Gerbet. The practice of signing simply by use of the first initial of the family name was quite common in "L'Avenir").

is, consciously or unconsciously, a member. Tolerance is necessary to protect this exteriorization of the life of the spirit. These are principal mennaisian themes which, having been developed in a halting and probing fashion during the restless years which marked the publication of the *Essai sur l'indifférence* ..., *De la religion* ..., *Des progrès*, and the many other articles and letters of the solitary of La Chênaie, finally were synthesized by him and by his followers at the advent of "L'Avenir". By avoiding both the skeptical implications of a libertarian tolerance and the narrow, restrictive character of the traditional Catholic approach to civic toleration, "L'Avenir" provided French Catholics with a basis, acceptable to both the demands of their faith and to the requirements of pluralism, for entering loyally and sincerely into modern society. Their concept of tolerance was not one founded upon the notion of concession but upon their religious beliefs. Their approach can be compared to that of a recent writer on the subject of tolerance who holds the following principle as crucial to the Catholic position in relation to toleration.

> The consideration of the transcendence of faith, far from being superficial or useless, alone permits us to establish perfectly the grounds for tolerance. It would be an illusion to wish to establish toleration solely or principally on social and political considerations.[137]

3. *The Liberating Role of the Church*

The ultramontanism of Lamennais reaches far beyond the canonical questions of jurisdictions and even of infallibility. The Church is the transcendent order, the law of collectivities, which enters into or becomes a creative cause in human history giving purpose, meaning, and value to events, movements, and human ideals. We have discussed previously the initial attempts of Lamennais to describe the role of the Church as mediator and source of the dynamism of history.[138] With "L'Avenir", the bold but somewhat shrouded directives of *Des progrès* ... become the axioms of mennaisian ecclesiology. The defense of the legal separation of Church and State and the espousal of modern liberties and democracy must be placed against the

[137] A. Léonard, O.P., "Liberté de la Foi et Tolérance civile", in *Tolérance et communauté humaine*, Tournai, 1952, p. 135.
[138] See Chapter Three. III 3, "History and Truth"; also, Chapter Four, II 3 b, "The Church and Liberalism", and II, 4, "The Inner Dynamics of Providence".

background of this ultramontane ecclesiology in order that they might be seen and understood in their proper context. What then is Lamennais's understanding of the Church and of her role in history and in political life which undergirds the ideology of Catholic Liberalism?

Père Lecanuet, the biographer of Montalembert, has identified the dream of "L'Avenir" as that of men envisioning "a great Christian republic of which the Pope would be not the dominating ruler but the moderator and the arbiter...".[139] Lamennais, in fact, had often expressed his admiration for Leibnitz and for his conception of the function which the Papacy could fulfill in the establishment of an international order in Europe.[140] We have already mentioned the importance of the return to the Middle Ages for the first generation of Romantics. "Clearly", remarks H. Schenk, "the Romantic hankering after the Middle Ages was bound up with the deep desire for political stability".[141] An alliance of Roman Catholicism and the romantic spirit produced a wave of conversions, a sentimental theology, a variety of ecumenical schemes, and a vague desire for the Respublica Christiana of other times.[142] "The Catholic Church", in the opinion of C. Schmitt, "seemed to offer them what they were looking for, a large irrational community, a universal historical tradition, and the personal God of the ancient metaphysics".[143] By 1830, the fascination of the romantic spirit with political reaction, which has been described as "one of the numerous paradoxes which belong to the essence of Romanticism",[144] had vanished and the romantic élan was once again revolutionary.

From the point of view of the history of Romanticism, "L'Avenir" is something of a point of passage through which the orthodox Catholic mennaisians passed from one romantic generation into another. Lamennais's ultramontanism, as we have indicated,[145] had already begun to show the impact of the vagaries to which concepts

---

[139] Lecanuet, *Montalembert d'après son journal et sa correspondance*, 3 Vols., Paris, 1895, T. I, p. 203.

[140] *Tradition* ..., pp. LXXII-LXXIII; *De la religion* ..., pp. 109-112.

[141] H. Schenk, *The Mind of the European Romantics*, London, 1966, p. 37.

[142] For these extremely interesting tendencies of the Romantic Period consult ibid., especially, "The Return to Catholicism", pp. 93-101, and "Oecumenical Trends", pp. 102-109.

[143] C. Schmitt, *Romantisme Politique*, Paris, 1928, p. 72.

[144] Ibid., p. 43.

[145] See Chapter Three, III 1 c, "Towards a Free Church".

are subject when under the spell of the romantic imagination. There is a tendency on the part of the romantic mind, arising from the priority given to imagination and sensibility in art and literature, to subjectivize the content of experience.[146] In a like fashion, the Absolute of a transcendental metaphysics is immanentized in such creations of the imagination, with, of course, a certain 'fundamentum in re', as Society, People, Community, Humanity, or History.[147] The various cults of Romanticism embraced quite often the word itself, usually expressive of an emotion, and not the definable content of the word or the concept behind it. In this sense, the ultramontanism of Lamennais was more of an ideal, an ultimate generalization or, even, a conceptualized hope, than a way of defining the jurisdictions or describing the political structure of the Roman Church. In a similar way, the epistemological justification for the apparent softening of a previously hard-line taken in questions of authority was accomplished by attributing a wider scope to the free activity of the intellect in the order of reason and through a certain spiritualization, or, almost, a certain relativizing of the elements within the order of faith. It will be necessary to return to this point. For the moment, in order to seize the romantic intent behind the mennaisian ultramontane doctrine as it evolved at the epoch of "L'Avenir", it will be useful to see just how he visualizes the role of the Church in history. Once this is done, one can understand how the fusion of liberalism and Catholicism was, for him, but a step towards a higher synthesis or a wider generalization which would hasten the irreversible movement of history towards the infinite.

The two realities, liberty and order, are represented by liberalism and Catholicism. They ought, naturally, to be united; liberalism, itself, is Christian in its origins and aspirations. The great tragedy of modern times has been the separation of the two columns upon which society is based. Liberalism, if left alone, will devolve into anarchy. Such ideas already familiar to those who had read *Des progrès . . .* and, especially, the two letters to the Archbishop of Paris, are taken up with new vigor in "L'Avenir". As Lamennais saw it, the goal of the Catholic was not to become a liberal but to "render liberalism Christian" and, by so doing, to create "the social

---

[146] For a discussion of the problem of Romanticism as a literary and philosophical question consult, R. Duhamel, *Aux sources du romantisme français*, Ottawa, 1964, particularly, Chapitre Premier, "Il y a une querelle romantique!", pp. 9-20.

[147] C. Schmitt, *Romantisme Politique*, Paris, 1928, pp. 63-64.

party".[148] Catholicism, then, had a definite socio-political mission upon the fulfillment of which depends the society of the future.

Does such a mission run counter to the very nature of a Church which has always appeared, at least, to most as an authoritarian, hierarchical structure? To hold that there exists a basic opposition between the drive towards liberty and the Church is to misunderstand the natures of both the Church and the revolution. The Church, as the original society of the spirit, is the source of the revolutionary élan as well as the guardian of the eternal principles of truth and justice. How is this so? Revolutions, as Lamennais viewed them, at least those taking their inspiration from the Revolution of 1789, were the reaction of reason against force or of spiritual Christianity against material power. History must be seen as a progressive "intellectual and moral development" which requires "a proportional development in liberty because man, as in the case of the child, ought to grow in liberty as he grows in intellect".[149] The origin of this aspiration of man towards greater and greater progress is Christianity which "by sowing the first seeds of the true and the good ... abolished slavery and created that which is called by us, the People".[150]

> That which is happening now is the prolongation of this liberating action which will extend itself into the coming centuries until man, having completed the entire circle of his possible perfection here below, is transformed through the laws of his immortal nature in order to enter into a new order of development which will never cease because it will be that of the infinite cycle of eternity.[151]

Lamennais was extremely fond of this reading of history, which bears a close resemblance to certain secular messianic ideas, and repeated this analysis of the origin of the revolutionary fervor even more apodictically towards the final issues of "L'Avenir". The movement, which burst upon the world with such fury in 1789, "comes from higher" sources for "it comes from God Who has willed that society advance perpetually towards an end which it cannot attain

[148] Lamennais uses the term "parti social" with considerable frequency in his correspondence in reference to the fusion of liberalism and Catholicism. Confer the letter from Lamennais to Benoît D'Azy, 11 mai 1830, reproduced in A. Laveille, *Un Lamennais inconnu*, Paris, 1898, p. 252. The same term appears with a more detailed explanation in his letter to Baron Vitrolles, 30 mai 1830, in Eugène Forgues, *Correspondance inédite entre Lamennais et le baron de Vitrolles*, Paris, 1886, p. 203.

[149] Lamennais, "Le Pape", A.A., T. I, p. 477.

[150] Ibid.

[151] Ibid., p. 478.

on earth but which it should approach ever more closely . . ."[152] Not only must the Church join the movement of liberty "which no one can stop because God has placed the germ of it in his creatures";[153] but she must recognize her fundamental identification with it. The Church is the "principal motor"[154] of the liberal movements sweeping the Continent; the examples of Ireland, Belgium, and Poland are empirical evidence of the religious source of the widespread desire of the peoples to liberate themselves from force and unreason.[155] The anti-religious outbursts which have accompanied some of the revolutions do not contradict his principal thesis since these are often but the manifestation of a just anger not against the true Church but against a clergy identified with tyranny. Where liberalism has ignored its religious origins, as in Spain, Portugal, and Italy, the revolutions have failed to produce either religious or political freedoms.[156]

Since liberalism cannot be understood outside of Catholicism nor can its true ends be gained without the cooperation of the true principle of order, Catholicism has an immediate task which Lamennais ascribes to the new Pontiff whose election is awaited following the death of Pius VIII.

> The task of the Papacy in the present crisis will be to re-establish the equilibrium between human nature and the indestructible laws which has been broken by renewing the intimate union of faith and science, of force and law, and of power and liberty.[157]

Before, however, undertaking this mission, the Church must accept its liberation from concordats and the binding legal relationships of an official establishment. "God is breaking these chains with the hands of the people".[158]

Christianity and the People actually become fused in Lamennais's eschatological vision of history. Before judging both the values and the weaknesses of this somewhat remarkable combination forged within the fires of a romantic soul, it is imperative to be aware of the fact that Lamennais was not simply the visionary of fervid imagination, as he is sometimes described,[159] but he was as well a man with a

[152] Lamennais, "De l'avenir de la société", A.A., T. V, p. 162.
[153] Ibid., p. 169.
[154] Ibid., p. 170.
[155] Ibid., pp. 170-171.
[156] Lamennais, "De la liberté religieuses", A.A., T. VI, p. 109.
[157] Lamennais, "Le Pape", A.A., T. I, p. 476.
[158] Ibid., p. 477.
[159] A. Dansette, "La Mennais contre son temps", Revue de Paris, Paris, Novembre 1947, p. 127.

philosophical vocation. In order to demonstrate that a more nuanced approach is necessary in the study of Lamennais's Catholic Liberalism, an effort must be made to uncover the metaphysical sources of the doctrines of "L'Avenir".

III. METAPHYSICAL JUSTIFICATION

1. *The Idea of a Catholic Philosophy*

Lamennais's desire to formulate a general philosophical synthesis, so often expressed in his correspondence and exhortations to his friends, has already been the subject of discussion.[160] While engaged with Gerbet and the associates of "L'Avenir" in the publication of the newspaper, Lamennais did not cease his functions as professor for the seminarians who had gathered around him to form the Congregation of St. Peter at La Chênaie. A combination of fortuitous circumstances, plus the necessity of being closer to Paris and the center of the activities undertaken by his followers, caused Lamennais to transfer his student body to the ancient College at Juilly. During the academic year 1830-31, Lamennais and Gerbet continued the series of philosophical conferences which had originated as courses for seminarians. At Juilly, however, in addition to the seminarians, such notable figures of the Romantic generation as Victor Hugo, Lamartine, and Sainte-Beuve were to be seen among those attending the lectures.[161]

As mentioned previously, two versions of these conferences of Lamennais have been published.[162] Since a technical comparative study of these two versions — a badly needed study — is beyond the scope of our dissertation, we will use material from both texts as it might be suitable to our limited need for depicting the background of ideas which will complete the ideological setting within which "L'Avenir" took form.

In addition to the many letters which refer to a Christian or

[160] See Chapter One, II, "Lamennais as a Philosopher".

[161] Chr. Maréchal, Introduction, *Essai d'un système de philosophie catholique*, Paris, 1906, pp. XVI-XXII.

[162] See Chapter One, I, "Life and Works of Félicité Lamennais", Footnote 45. In our review of the ideas of Lamennais in the conferences of Juilly, we will use principally the later text of *Essai d'un système de philosophie catholique* published by Y. Le Hir, Rennes, 1954. This text has been more easily accessible to the writer. The text prepared by Chr. Maréchal from the notes of students will be used for material from those conferences which are missing from the manuscript studied by Y. Le Hir.

Catholic philosophy or even to the "philosophy of Christianity" which would be "the great work, the point of confluence at which all the divergent forces of humanity will join in unity",[163] there is clear indication of the scope of Lamennais's philosophical intention in his interesting article, "Ce que sera le catholicisme dans la société nouvelle". "Catholic science", he maintains, "is yet to be created".[164]

> Sooner or later ... a general system of explanation, a true philosophy in conformity with the needs of the times will develop from the certain notions of faith ... and, once established on the constitutive laws of the intellect, will lead the diverse orders of knowledge to unity by showing that the lesser orders, animated, in some way, by the same life, dependent upon the same principles, have their reason and their foundation in the higher and by uniting more closely again that which the nature of things has united eternally, belief and conception, God and the universe.[165]

What is the ultimate reason for the present disarray in the human spirit which shows itself in the oppositions between science and faith and, in the social order, between the individual and society, or between liberty and authority? At bottom, the problem has its basis in the dualistic character of human knowledge which stems from the distinct approaches required of man in his relations with the infinite and the finite. It is not that creation itself is ultimately dualistic nor that the infinite and the finite are unbridgeably divided for both are contained in the idea of being. Indeed, every proposition constructed by man contains the dual elements. There is no intelligible order without the word "is" which in itself "supposes the pure, universal, infinite idea of being".[166] In order, however, to render the infinite intelligible, accessible to the finite intellect, it must be determined. Thus, "these two elements, the finite and the infinite, join simultaneously to actually form the intellect and are to be found in all knowledge".[167] The mode of grasping the infinite is faith, an act, essentially passive, through which the subject is cognizant of the limitlessness of being without being able to seize it in its entirety. What can be grasped and understood is the determined, definable

---

[163] Letter from Lamennais probably written to a certain Janvier, Juilly, 18 février 1831, reproduced by F. Duine, "Documents mennaisiens", Extract from *Annales de Bretagne*, Rennes-Paris, 1919, p. 11.

[164] Lamennais, "Ce que sera le catholicisme dans la société nouvelle", A.A., T. V, p. 185.

[165] Ibid.

[166] Ibid., p. 183.

[167] Ibid.

elements of the proposition and this knowledge constitutes the domain of science.

While distinct as modes of knowledge, science and faith are indissolubly united. "There is no conception without faith; no faith without the beginning of conception or science".[168] To justify scientific theories or the universal validity of the principles of science, it is necessary to go beyond the stage of observation to the "dogmas of faith" by which Lamennais means "the notions which faith gives to" science "of the infinite Being, its necessary properties, its modes of existence and its laws".[169] No valid science can be constructed, in the opinion of Lamennais, without an ontological base which is provided by the original grasp of universal being through an act of faith which is connatural to the human intellect.

Why is this science to be a "Catholic science"? Primarily, because it is based upon an experience which is the very basis of Christian theology, the existence of an infinite God. As Lamennais sees it, the Church is the "type and the means"[170] of that sort of final unity which is implied in the definition of religion which is, as always for the author of the *Essai sur l'indifférence* ..., "the perfect law of justice and truth".[171] The Catholic Church, although historical, represents the ideal of the indissoluble union of the finite and the infinite, the source of the moral law of love which alone can harmonize liberty and knowledge in a perfect society.

Given the very nature of journalistic writing, "Ce que sera le catholicisme dans la société nouvelle" is necessarily sketchy and unsatisfactory from the point of view of philosophy. The reader must go to the conferences of Juilly to have a clearer notion of what Lamennais is thinking as he speculates on the future harmony of all in the One. Although L. Le Guillou has justly remarked that the current notions which we have of the *Essai d'un système de philosophie catholique*, as the conferences of Juilly have been called, are not sufficient to enable the student of Lamennais to establish with complete scientific rigor the exact significance and complexity of Lamennais's philosophical thought at this period,[172] we are forced,

---

[168] Lamennais, "Ce que sera le catholicisme dans la société nouvelle", A.A., T. V, p. 183.

[169] Ibid., p. 184.

[170] Ibid., p. 187.

[171] Ibid., p. 182.

[172] L. Le Guillou, *L'évolution de la pensée religieuse de Félicité Lamennais*, Paris, 1966, p. 286.

given the genetic character of this study, to return to the conferences of Juilly such as we have them in an attempt to ferret out the key ideas which lend structural support to the theories of "L'Avenir". To be sure, *Esquisse d'une philosophie* is a much more accomplished synthesis. Nevertheless, it would be unhistorical to exegete the doctrines of "L'Avenir" by means of a systematization achieved at a later date under widely differing circumstances and inspired by such definitive theological mutations.

2. *Progress and the Doctrine of Rights*

Our contention throughout the section of Chapter Five dedicated to the exposition of the political doctrines of "L'Avenir" has been that the mennaisian adaptation to the realities of modern society was doctrinal rather than tactical. This remains to be demonstrated and we shall attempt in this final expository section of the dissertation to show that there is a fundamental relation between the metaphysical doctrine expostulated by Lamennais in the conferences of Juilly and the political notion of liberty and rights developed in "L'Avenir". We will return, therefore, to the more purely speculative elements of his thought in the realm of ontology only insofar as they are related to his social and political thought. First, however, we might ask ourselves whether or not Lamennais saw any relation between his ontology and his social theory. When introducing a number of talks which he gave concerning man, after having spoken in a series of lectures about God, the universe, the organic and the inorganic levels of creation, he states his principle in the following fashion.

> The particular science of man depends upon the general science of the universe and of God, because, in the totality of things where nothing is isolated, no part can be properly conceived unless the relations which it has with the whole and the diverse parts of the whole are understood.
> ... The science of man, therefore, supposes the science of God, that is, an order of prior, fundamental principles.[173]

In a similar fashion, when discussing the temporal organization of society, he repeats with emphasis the unitary character of his approach to all of the sciences, including the science of politics.

---

[173] Chr. Maréchal, *Essai d'un système de philosophie catholique*, Paris, 1906, pp. 217-218. (This conference entitled "De l'homme" is not found in the Le Hir edition.)

> All of the laws of intelligent creatures, all of the laws of humanity and, consequently, all of the laws of society, are included in those which we have just exposed ... and free, human conventions, which, in temporal society, are given the name of laws, do not have this character and cannot be considered under this notion unless they are ruled by the essential and immutable laws of superior order.[174]

There are two key notions which ought to be retained from the conferences of Juilly, namely, the triadic structure of reality and the perpetual evolution of the finite towards the infinite. Both of these notions were inspired, respectively, by the Christian dogmas of the Trinity and Creation, dogmas which are taken by Lamennais as universal facts and which become the axioms from which he deduces the laws governing the inferior orders of being.

The Trinity provides the philosopher with an indication of the type of structure governing reality and thus, with a means of understanding the order of the universe and the nature of society. God is identified as the infinite source or substance of all that is; but God is not simply indistinct Being or Substance. There are three necessary properties which flow from the idea of infinite Being which are the capacity for being, the form assumed in being, and the term which unites Force and Form, or Intellect, which is Love.[175] This triadic notion of the infinite becomes in turn the archetype of creation. All that is is in some way a part of the infinite which leads Lamennais to formulate a theory of participation along the line of an exemplar causality; the reason for the existence of any creature is to be found in the idea of that which is originally in the Divine Intellect. The three modalities of creation, inorganic, organic, and intellectual, participate in varying degrees in the infinite substance from which they have somehow been projected beyond into the finite which is itself conceived as limit. Thus, creatures, indivisibly one as being, have a dual character; they are finite because they are specified through an idea, and, infinite, because this idea is an eternal type in the Divine Intellect.[176]

Since creation is for Lamennais a communication of being,[177] the very idea of society, as a first reality, is rooted in the rapport which is

---

[174] Y. Le Hir, *Essai d'un système de philosophie catholique*, Rennes, 1954, p. 313. (In subsequent citations, this work will be referred to simply as *Essai d'un système...*).

[175] *Essai d'un système...*, particularly, Chapitre IV, "Dieu", pp. 19-21.

[176] Ibid., particularly, Chapitre V, "De l'intelligence dans l'univers", pp. 24-28.

[177] Ibid., pp. 52-55; 69-72.

established in this original communication between Creator and creature.[178] What is communicated? The properties of Force, Intellect, and Love, which being found in the Divinity and in the three orders of creation, determine the relations existing vertically between the Creator and the orders of creation and horizontally among the individuals within each modality of creation.[179] Creation itself is "an immense communion"[180] in which the lower levels participate in the higher levels of creation and in which all are submitted to the unique law of order which is the expression of form or the presence of the Divine Word in creation. Whatever is common to all individuals of a species or an order is their nature, form or truth.[181] With man, however, creation progresses beyond the "blind society"[182] of the organic world towards true sociability which results from the introduction of the element of freedom into the relations existing in the interaction of creative force, reason or the intelligible word, and love. The study of this relationship forms the basis for the "science of man".[183] Reality in this conceptualization, which Chr. Maréchal calls a "social representation of the universe",[184] is seen as basically one but the one manifests itself in a multiplicity of dynamic relations all modeled upon the triadic structure of the Trinity.[185]

Lamennais's meditations upon the Trinity and his understanding of creation as an exteriorization of Divine Ideas through "a free act" of the Creator's omnipotence "which produces them beyond in such a way that at the very moment in which they begin to be they are essentially separated from Him",[186] also provide him with a means of

---

[178] Lamennais employs a striking phrase to emphasize this idea, "... qui dit communication dit société", in *Essai du système...*, p. 280.

[179] This idea is repeated frequently. Consult, for example, Chapitre VII, "Du concours des trois personnes divines dans la création", in Ibid., pp. 69-72.

[180] Ibid., p. 262.

[181] Ibid., pp. 120-122.

[182] Ibid., p. 158.

[183] Ibid., pp. 169-170.

[184] Chr. Maréchal, Introduction, *Essai d'un système de philosophie catholique*, Paris, 1906, p. XXVI.

[185] J. Poisson, in his excellent study on the mennaisian metaphysics of society, traces the origin of the idea to Augustinian sources. "Unity in triplicity, such is the rhythm of this synthesis which was first called *Essai d'un système de philosophie catholique*, later, *Esquisse d'une philosophie*, and which Lamennais sounded out when, after having enumerated the divine properties, he said, "everything is deduced from this very clearly ..." For a discussion of Poisson's thesis concerning the Augustinian influence consult, *Le romantisme social de Lamennais*, Paris, 1931, pp. 156-162.

[186] *Essai d'un système ...*, p. 44.

grasping the phenomenon of change. It should be remembered that time and again in the articles of "L'Avenir" Lamennais appealed to the fact of change, a phenomenon which had deeply impressed his generation, as an essential, if not the most essential, reason for his radical departure from traditional political positions. Decidedly convinced of the presence of an all-pervading Providence in human history, he elaborated this theme, which is one of the most essential elements of his thought, into a sort of "Christian evolutionism".[187]

Change is not ultimately irrational but rather the manifestation of the constitutive laws of the universe and of society at work in the temporal order. He considers it fundamental that creation be "represented as the progressive manifestation of all that which is in God and in the same order as is found in God".[188] The necessary and eternal properties of infinite Being, Force, Intellect and Love, are communicated to creatures and become the properties of production, conservation and development in the temporal order. Production is the prevailing tendency of existence towards total existence; conservation is the formal or legal principle governing the evolutionary force; and, development is the harmonizing principle uniting force and legality. The universe is subject to successive transformations in which individuality or limit is destroyed and a more perfect communication of the divine properties achieved.[189] "In effect", he notes, "one recognizes a possible development without limit in the being of every creature and in its properties".[190]

Having thus briefly sketched the elemental ideas of the mennaisian metaphysics which will help to shed some light upon his political thought, it will now be necessary to establish the rapport between these notions, that is, the ontological origins of society and the evolutionary tendency of all creation, and the doctrine of social coexistence enunciated in "L'Avenir". We had mentioned that although Lamennais approaches Hobbes and Rousseau, at least methodologically, in his exposé of political theory in "L'Avenir", his basic metaphysical options place him entirely within another tradition. What do we mean by this? First, society and human sociability are for Lamennais both ontological and eschatological

---

[187] J.-R. Derré, *Lamennais, ses amis et le mouvement des idées à l'époque romantique*, Paris, 1962, p. 341.
[188] *Essai d'un système* ..., pp. 50-51.
[189] Ibid., pp. 137-139.
[190] Ibid., p. 65.

realities. Man as truly man remains, in the *Essai d'un système de philosophie catholique* as in the *Essai sur l'indifférence* ..., dependent for his very being upon society. Man is not born as a fully developed person but as an individual endowed with the capacity of hearing the word which enlightens and through which he becomes a person. In sharing the two worlds, organic and intellectual, man is subject to the laws of each. His individual unity is the result of his subjection to the physical order but "the superior world ... in revealing the Absolute to him, engenders in him both intelligence and liberty, and makes of him a true person".[191] The constant mennaisian theme concerning the interdependence of man and society is thereby re-enforced by his incorporation of the traditionalist theory of language into a metaphysics of Revelation.

Taking his fundamental description of reality into consideration, the political discussions of "L'Avenir" may be seen as more than a simple re-statement of liberalism. The individual as individual, for Lamennais, belongs to the order of temporality, that is, a passing phase of limitation or restriction restraining the full development of the person. The person, on the other hand, is the universal type, an incarnated divine idea, which originates in the perfect sociability of the Trinity and which is in the process of making manifest this sociability in history. Man has rights, it would seem, not as an isolated individual but as a creature whose dignity and claim to respect and just treatment arise from the very fact of creation which is itself that social bond by definition uniting creature and Creator and creatures among themselves in a society of the spirit which already exists in the Divine model but which becomes manifest in the finite order as the whole of creation approaches, in the historical process, the infinite. Although the terms which Lamennais uses in the articles of "L'Avenir" are quite similar to those which had been developed in the vocabulary of Liberalism, the individual about whom he speaks is not the individual of the associationist's imagination who, in possession of anterior rights, attempts to adjust these rights to the social fact. This libertarian idea of the individual represents for Lamennais the very extreme of degradation.[192] Thus, the basic political problematic is conceived of not

---

[191] Chr. Maréchal, *Essai d'un système de philosophie catholique*, Paris, 1906, p. 219. (This second conference, entitled "L'homme", belongs to the second group of conferences which are not among the manuscripts found by Le Hir.)

[192] In the interesting "Entretien philosophique" published by Maréchal, Lamennais, in discussing with his students the history of man, underlines the relationship which he sees between isolation from society or individualism and moral disorder in the

in terms of protecting the individual against the intrusions of the social but rather in terms of establishing the necessary conditions for the greater development of that spiritual society, which is the only real society, by means of liberating the truth from institutional distortion or from official repression. Liberty, it should be recalled, is defined by Lamennais as "the absence of obstacles which prevent a being from attaining its end".[193] In its most profound sense, original human liberty emanates from the harmony between the creature and the Creator or the whole of creation; thus, Lamennais adheres quite strictly to his original ideas concerning liberty as a relationship of the obedience of man to eternal truth which obedience liberates man from subjugation to the particular or the non-spiritual. Although lost through an act of common sinfulness or disobedience, this essential liberty has been restored through the redemptive act of Christ, an act which is universal in its effects. Once this original liberty has been restored, free will or liberty of action in the order of the finite or the realm of particular reason is restored as well.[194]

Lamennais's conceptualization of rights in the political order must be viewed against this basically theological definition of liberty. Realizing this, we are led to ask that, if all men, in varying degrees, participate in truth and in the society of the spirit, which is the very source of their liberty, what is the relationship between this society and political society? In Lamennais's thought, there is no real society among men except this "spiritual society";[195] this is the "natural society"[196] which is held together by the universal laws of creation. Political society, on the other hand, is called "exterior society" or "an organism . . . the body of mankind".[197]

> As long as mankind is spiritually one, its organism is essentially one. And, if, in different ways, this unity is broken, it is because the spiritual society itself has been broken to the same degree.[198]

universe. As a result of sin, man becomes separated from the whole and lives in an anti-natural state of alienation from God and from his fellow-man. Confer, *Essai d'un système de philosophie catholique*, Paris, 1906, pp. 278-289.

[193] Chr. Maréchal, *Essai d'un système de philosophie catholique*, Paris, 1906, p. 248. (It is interesting to note the consistency in Lamennais's retention of this notion of liberty which he had earlier given in his essay, "De la liberté". See Chapter Four, II 1, "Christian Liberty in a Secularized World".)

[194] Ibid., pp. 248-249.

[195] *Essai d'un système . . .*, p. 313.

[196] Ibid., p. 315.

[197] Ibid., p. 313.

[198] Ibid.

If mankind had remained in a state of original innocence, there would have been an exteriorization of interior harmony and "human society would have been simply an order of relations founded on justice, equity, charity, that is, on right itself".[199] But the history of man can only be understood if man accepts the notion of original sin or its equivalent.[200] As a consequence of this degradation, force has become the determining factor in the organization of power but this is not an irremediable situation because the principle of Christianity, incorporating the primitive revelation upon which the society of the spirit is founded and the renewal of this revelation in Christ is unalterably directed towards a goal which is the full liberation of mankind from the individuality of the organic world and the complete realization of the spiritual society.

From this evolutionary vantage point, it is possible to survey the political actuality, the ferment of revolution and change, as an uneven, yet, progressive, actualization of "an interior, instinctive work within humanity ... which is pushing in new and less imperfect directions".[201] The new social body or political exteriorization will not result from the intervention of force, but "it will form itself from itself, as all organisms, in virtue of an internal force of development inherent in all beings".[202] And what is particularly characteristic of this new transformation? A quantitative growth in liberty and, consequently, a real progression since "the perfect society is perfect liberty".[203]

Viewed against this ideological backdrop, the political platform of "L'Avenir" can be logically placed within Lamennais's theologico-philosophical world-view. His demands for wider liberties are entirely compatible with, indeed, are inspired by this evolutionary view of humanity and of history. A major thesis of "L'Avenir" is the contention that the progress of mankind has rendered necessary new expressions, in the form of modern liberties, of the fundamental

---

[199] *Essai d'un système...*, p. 317.

[200] In two very enlightening fragments reproduced by Maréchal, the notion of original sin and its importance to obtaining an understanding of human history are strongly emphasized by Lamennais. Consult, Chr. Maréchal, *Essai d'un système de philosophie catholique*, Paris, 1906, particularly, "Conversation: Influence de la Philosophie sur les sociétés, ou: Influence de la philosophie sociale", pp. 197-214; also, "Du péché originel", pp. 229-231.

[201] *Essai d'un système ...*, p. 316.

[202] Ibid.

[203] Ibid.

spiritual right born of man's inalienable relationship to the society of the spirit. In this sense, he speaks of liberty as the driving force behind the efforts of human society to reform or substitute the old institutions or organisms which hinder the progress of the spirit. As a result of this progression, a way must be found to secure the "rights emanating from this new state of society".[204] It is quite evident in his long article "De l'avenir de la société" that he conceives of the history of mankind's striving for liberty as a gradual becoming aware of rights and liberties, implicit in the nature of man as a spiritual being, but rendered explicit in conjunction with the progress of the intellect, the famous growth of man from the infancy of the Middle Ages to the "Age of Man" which Lamennais equates with the modern era.[205] Such a doctrine is fundamentally a political application of the mennaisian metaphysics which was being simultaneously developed in the conferences of Juilly.

In the over-all picture, Church-State relations are seen in a new optic. The relations between the religious order and the temporal order may be conceived of as the rapport between the interior, universal society of the spirit and a political exteriorization which will be compatible with the evolutionary phase through which the spiritual society is passing. Man is in a continual process of liberation from his limitations or his individuality, a process which is common to the whole as well as to the single subject. It is the presence of the Word, the Divine Intellect or universal reason which preserves unity and order in the midst of change and the symbol or sign of this presence is Christianity. Although retaining the common sense notion of social verification and the idea of an incarnate principle of authority in the Papacy,[206] the Church, as he notes in "Les derniers temps",[207] is subject to the universal law of progression which, through a greater communication of the general properties, destroys barriers which hinder this communication or this greater manifestation of God in creation. When institutional structures, which are by nature temporary, stand in the way of the movement towards universal fraternity, they will be changed even if they are ecclesiastical. He is not clear as to how these changes will be brought about but simply affirms

---

[204] Lamennais, "Fausse direction du gouvernement", A.A., T. II, p. 323.
[205] Lamennais, "De l'avenir de la société", A.A., T. V, p. 162.
[206] Chr. Maréchal, *Essai d'un système de philosophie catholique*, Paris, p. 211.
[207] *Essai d'un système* ..., pp. 307-309.

that, if necessary, they will occur. The only rule possible when aware of the uncertainty of institutions is "to be submitted to the established order of God as long as God conserves it".[208]

The emphasis is decidedly placed upon a sort of spiritual Christianity or Catholicism which is both the hidden truth in the universe not yet fully manifested and "the basis of selection which allows for the retention of only that which is true and useful in each doctrine".[209] All that is exterior, institutional and restrictive belongs to the organic level of creation which is subject to disappear as the spiritual unity of mankind progresses beyond these older protective shells. The new is built upon the ruins of the old; such is the nature of mennaisian progress. As one author has remarked, "in this system, the social phenomenon retains no proper specificity: it is but the particular application of supernatural dispositions which transcend it".[210]

The fact of change had driven Lamennais to seek a rationality for change as well as for diversity and the sources to which he fled were the Christian dogmas of Creation, the Fall and the Redemption. There is finally, for him, one philosophy which explains the one and the many in creation and the presence of diversity among men. This is the Catholic philosophy which he defines as an open philosophy since it is basically the reflection of the finite reason on the infinite and, as result, will never be complete. A total reflection will only be achieved after a process of selecting and synthesizing of all that is universal and durable in the temporal. In affirming his philosophical thought in this fashion, Lamennais comes really to affirm all philosophy. All is in a state of partial manifestation; thus, all should be tolerated because the inevitable forces of a providential evolution will purify and separate the universal from the particular.

By means of this evolutionary optic, Lamennais approaches in a certain way, the position of Lessing, who, it will be recalled, came to justify tolerance as an attitude of respect for the partial truth to be found in the very plurality of religions and subjects.[211] P. Ricœur has well recaptured the reasonableness of such thinking and has shown

---

[208] *Essai d'un système* . . . , p. 309.

[209] L. Le Guillou, *L'évolution de la pensée religieuse de Félicité Lamennais*, Paris, 1966, p. 115.

[210] J.-R. Derré, *Lamennais, ses amis et le mouvement des idées à l'époque romantique*, Paris, 1962, p. 389.

[211] See Chapter Two, III b, "Defense of the New".

that a true spirit of tolerance requires a recognition of both the exigency for unity and the acceptance of the limited truthfulness of the multiple.[212]

[212] P. Ricœur, *Histoire et Vérité*, (2nd ed.) Paris, 1955, particularly, "Note sur le vœu et la tâche de l'unité", pp. 193-197.

CHAPTER SIX

CONCLUSIONS AND CRITICAL REMARKS

I. RECAPITULATION

Everyone has heard of Félicité Lamennais. Most are acquainted with the drama of "L'Avenir" and with the strongly worded Papal condemnation of the first program of Catholic liberalism formulated by Lamennais and his followers. The spiritual crisis of Lamennais, his hesitation and, finally, his separation from the Church which he had so ardently defended have all become elements of a type of confrontation between the Church and modern thought quite similar in scope and in tragedy to that which took place two centuries earlier between Rome and Galileo. In the case of Lamennais, the figure of the prophet has been immortalized while Lamennais the thinker, the philosopher of La Chênaie, has paled into obscurity. In our study, we have sought to recapture, not so much the prophetic Lamennais and the impact of his prognostications as the philosophical Lamennais and the inner realm of his thought, that hidden work of the spirit which gave birth to a movement of reconciliation between the Church and the modern world. Our attempt to discover, in the measure in which such a discovery is possible, the logical trajectory followed by Lamennais in the years leading up to "L'Avenir" has been an attempt to see from within. After having made this effort, our task, in these concluding paragraphs, is to summarize the result of our research and to judge philosophically the validity or tenability of this thought considered in itself.

The theme of tolerance, seen in its historical origins and political implications, has given us the problematic and has provided both the point of departure and the point of reference for the various subjects which have been scrutinized. It seems quite clear that tolerance is itself a label, a useful nomenclature for an aggregate of problems reaching into the domains of theology, metaphysics, politics and ethics. Although our research has been restricted to the political aspect of tolerance, that is, to the question of civil tolerance seen, especially, in the context of the relations between the civil order and religion and the institutions of the religious body, which, in this case, concerns particularly the Catholic Church, it has not been possible either due to the nature of the problem itself or out of fidelity to the thought of Lamennais to avoid touching upon a rather wide range of topics which hinge upon or are implied in the original question.

Lamennais early seized upon the relevance of the problem of tolerance to the elemental ethico-political questions which had been forced upon his generation by historical events and anterior ideological developments. It had become imperative, as is always the case when men have experienced tyranny or the threat of anarchy, to ask anew the fundamental questions concerning the very stuff of society. How is it possible for men to live together in harmony? If it is possible, what type of order must men seek to establish? What price must be paid for order and peace, the essential conditions for the expansion and development of human existence?

The original mennaisian intuition is that men are intended to live together not merely through coercion and force but through a deeper communion which would reflect the ultimate metaphysical reality of oneness in God. Whereas post-Cartesian thought had done much to deepen the philosophy of subjectivity, politically enshrined in such constitutional monuments as the Declaration of the Rights of Man and the Bill of Rights, there had not been a concomitant realization of a philosophy of community. The traditionalist reaction, of which Lamennais was to become the last spokesman, was an attempt to fill the social vacuum created by the rise of libertarian creeds. In the face of social disintegration, Lamennais reasserted the belief that the life of men together in society was more than a balance of interests or a physical juxtaposition of atomic particles.

This society of which Lamennais speaks is the arena of responsible human action, an area, therefore, subject to moral law or, at least, pointing to an ethical dimension. In the early writings of Lamennais, particularly, *Réflexions sur l'état . . .*, this moral preoccupation with the state of civilization, which was to become for him a moral mission, is sharply apparent. Out of this moral concern he was led to ask how is it possible to distinguish between right and wrong, to establish an ethic with a claim to universality, if such does not rest upon an ultimate world-view or a metaphysics? Consequently, in evaluating Lamennais's thought, it is vitally important to be aware of this metaphysical concern and to see clearly the relationship of the initial ontological position which he assumed and maintained with the notional development which followed thoughout his career.

Man is, in his ultimate definition, social and, if this is so, the realization of this sociability ought to be subject to an ultimate rationality emanating from the laws of being. For this reason, these laws or the truth of society could never be a matter of indifference. Thus, Lamennais's early anguish over the system of tolerance, such as he saw it evolving around him, was expressly the concern of a moral philosopher for the spiritual well-being and harmony of the city which, he realized, was, in the long run, more important to the life of the city and for man than the material refinements of a civilization. In the *Essai sur l'indifférence* . . . , tolerance is seen as a truce or a final concession to moral exhaustion, a willingness to share some sort of life in common out of material or utilitarian interest. Could such an arrangement establish the basis for a community? How could order be founded upon justice if men could not agree upon the definition of justice? The ethical question implies, in turn, an epistemological question and, for this reason, Lamennais's attention is turned to the problem of certitude and its relationship to the nature of power and authority in the pages of the *Essai sur l'indifférence* . . . It is not tolerance as an attitude of patience or respect but tolerance accepted as the only basis for social coexistence and rationally justified through philosophical skepticism and moral lassitude which brought forth from Lamennais the strong criticism of the concept of tolerance such as it had evolved in his own era.

Society, in the mennaisian vision, is founded upon more solid grounds; it is, in fact, rooted in the very unity of God and, consequently, is indistinguishable from religion understood in the primitive sense of bond or union between the Creator and creation. His philosophy of community looks to a universal communication in truth, a society of the spirit, as both the cause and the norm governing human relations. The original society is the source of values and, thus, liberty itself is indefinable outside of the context of religion. The model or the historical embodiment of this original and transcendent society is the Church. Lamennais thus attempted to fashion out of the Christian Church, its Revelation and Tradition, a social philosophy incorporating a metaphysics of society, a social theory of knowledge and an ethic. We have discussed the ramifications of this attempt, particularly as structured in the *Essai sur l'indifférence* . . . in Chapter Three. Combining a fascinating assortment of influences, he equipped himself with a large vision of reality which he had hoped would become a philosophy of spiritual restoration, a decidedly apologetical but, nonetheless, vigorous attempt to address himself to his contemporaries and to recall to their attention truths which he believed they had overlooked.

The mennaisian vision, so sensitive to social realities, was not a closed fixation upon a galaxy of changeless dogmas. There is in the methodology employed by Lamennais and inherited from Bonald and Maistre a genuine attachment to the real. We need only to be reminded of his reliance upon history and his treatment of religious beliefs as universal facts, empirical data which can be verified through the criterion of common consent. Following the *Essai sur l'indifférence* . . . in which he did not develop fully the political implications of his social and epistemological thought, he turned more attentively to the political realities using his first principles as criteria for evaluating the state of society. At the moment of the writing of *De la religion* . . ., we discover a Lamennais caught in the seemingly irreconciliable opposition between the political reality which he so accurately describes and his own philosophy of spiritual restoration. Nevertheless, two important results begin to emerge from the harsh polemics of the mid-1820's. First he realized, perhaps somewhat begrudgingly at the beginning, that the restoration of man to society and of true community to man could not be a matter of return to older institutional patterns. The phenomena of secularization, tolerance, and liberalism could not be ignored; the social and political realities contained a message which he courageously began to read. Secondly, while retaining his ideal of unity and his belief in the spiritual community as the basis for the organization of political life, he began to adapt his principles through a process of generalization and synthesis in order to absorb those elements of liberalism which began to appear to him as correlates of his own spiritual values. The process of transposing the doctrine of rights and liberty, such as it had evolved under the catch-all label of liberalism, into a larger world-view built upon an ontologistic concept of reality was the task undertaken by Lamennais between *De la religion* . . . and "L'Avenir".

The medieval society, which provided Lamennais with an historical point of reference or a model, much as the Greek city-state had served Rousseau, was studied anew by Lamennais not simply as an historian but as a political theorist. Out of these reflections Lamennais drew important conclusions concerning the nature of sovereignty and the non-historical, absolute character of a higher law of justice which were

actually to become the points of fusion between liberalism and
mennaisian social philosophy. This law, although, in principle,
transcendent, is known through the authority of tradition or the
teachings of the Church. At times, Lamennais relates this authority
very closely to the authority of the people or the common consent of
mankind and this identification grows stronger as his confidence in
Rome weakens and as his understanding of the democratic
implications embedded in his notion of original equality begins to
broaden. In *Des progrès ...*, he came to see with startling clarity that
the notion of justice and of sovereignty which he had discovered in
what he conceived to be the ultramontane political theory of the
medieval Popes was quite similar to the theory of sovereignty and
public power defended by the liberals. In recognizing a basic identity
between his own notion of divine law and the liberal doctrine of
natural law, he saw at the same time a parallel between the theory of
natural rights and his own notions concerning the spiritual sources of
liberty. These twin discoveries made possible the political program of
"L'Avenir" which Lamennais looked upon as a reincorporation of the
valid intuitions of liberalism into a broader social philosophy or
into a Catholic world-view. Although starting at opposite points of
departure, Lamennais and the liberals, at least in Lamennais's
opinion, had come to a common agreement on the organization of
power and, thus, had formed the basis for a social pact founded
upon an elementary ethical consensus. In effect, Lamennais had
accepted the system of tolerance without acccepting the ideological
basis upon which such a system of social coexistence had formerly
been constructed.

How had such a mutation taken place between the *Essai sur
l'indifférence ...* and "L'Avenir"? We have held the position that the
movement of Lamennais's thought, taking into consideration the
peculiarities of the psychology of the Romanticists, shows a pattern of
consistency and of considerable adaptability. It would seem that *De la
religion ...* represents, ideologically, the breaking through by
Lamennais of the restrictions of his early traditionalism and the
beginning of the tendency towards the liberal synthesis. The definitive
rupture with the conservative political theory of legitimacy, which is
the principal political innovation of *De la religion ...*, is of critical
importance in the initiation of this tendency. In effect, Lamennais
accepts, with his refusal to admit the historical argument as the unique
justification for the legitimate exercise of sovereignty, the

238

de-sacralization of temporal institutions. The State is de-absolutized and becomes for him an institution among other institutions in a plurality of social realities. Simultaneously, he began to see the truly universal implications of his theory of an original spiritual society and, as a consequence, his notion of the Church became more and more general and universal. Not the institutional character of the Church but the idea of a spiritual Church, unrestricted by a merely temporal or legal definition, begins to loom large in his writings. As a consequence of these two developments, the whole problem of Church-State relations was seen in a new context. Separation becomes not only a tactical advantage for the Church but a proper reflection of the nature of the relationship between the spiritual order and the temporal order. With the State desacralized, insofar as Lamennais reduces the State to a purely administrative and functional role which should be the physical reflection of the state of the spiritual society, and the Church defined as a spiritual society which renounces all use of force, tolerance becomes not only acceptable but necessary to safeguard harmony in the temporal and liberty in the spiritual.

Such a position requires an evolutionary view of history since the spiritual society is considered as both goal and movement but not as a fully realized condition in the temporal order. This eschatological understanding of the rapport between the finite and the infinite, which begins to dominate in Lamennais's view of history after 1826, provided him with a justification for his abandonment of the more static concepts of order, which had been held by the earlier reactionary thinkers, in favor of a philosophy of progress. Once such an attitude is adopted—not unsimilar to that of Lessing—truth becomes known in a progressive fashion through the free activity of the spirit. Tolerance or a system of liberty is again shown to be reasonable not out of indifference but out of respect for the truth which is to be found to be partially or opaquely present in all opinions. In Lamennais's mind, this position does not represent a return to individualism nor a rejection of his epistemological principle of authority since the criterion of certitude remains the common consent of mankind seen, however, no longer as the conservative guardian of revealed dogmas which are handed down from generation to generation but as the source of seminal truths which require the activity of the human spirit in communion with the universal sentiments of mankind to attain their full explicitation. It seems, therefore, quite evident that the mennaisian concept of history gave his philosophy a suppleness which

239

allowed him to overcome the contradiction which might otherwise have remained between his initial authoritarianism and his later liberalism.

II. The Philosophical Character of the Mennaisian System

Before judging specifically the value of Lamennais's approach to the problem of tolerance and social coexistence, it would be useful to make a few particular comments concerning the purely philosophical character of the mennaisian undertaking. His political doctrine, as our study has indicated, is a part of a larger quest for a total grasp of reality.

We have already discussed at some length in Part II, "Lamennais as a Philosopher", (Chapter One), the peculiarities of the rapport between traditionalism and philosophy considered as a rational science. Traditionalism has a place in the history of thought but there are particular problems which are posed, chiefly, concerning the role of reason within traditionalist thought. Our answer to the question concerning the validity of treating Lamennais as a philosopher was that he certainly did share, at least, in a broad sense, in the philosophical vocation and that his historical importance justifies a philosophical study of his thought. There are, however, certain basic weaknesses in mennaisianism considered as a system or as a total view of reality which, indeed, its author intended it to be. Our intention, in the following paragraphs, is to point out these philosophical difficulties which tend to carry over into the mennaisian political theory.

1. *Concerning Common Consent as a Criterion of Certitude*

Is the theory of common consent a proper basis for a philosophical inquiry? Taking the psychology of belief or the common sense, habitual, certitude proper to the pre-philosophical mind as a basis for his epistemology, Lamennais seems to have oversimplified the properly reflective character of the philosophical task. Is it valid to substitute the authority of tradition for the certitude of evidence as a criterion for recognizing absolute or metaphysical truth?

Although our study has not been directly concerned with the problem of Lamennais's epistemology, the question does enter into the over-all consideration of Lamennais's philosophy. Lamennais requires a prior assent to certain universal beliefs as preliminary to the activity of the reason. This is not the same as the simple acceptance of the "doxa" which is considered as a prerequisite for the philosophical reflection by many modern philosophers. The mennaisian approach requires an assent to all of these opinions which may be considered as universal and the fact that they are universal is the sign of their truthfulness. But who is to say which opinions or beliefs are really universal? Even if one were to accept a teaching authority such as the Papacy, one must still, on the level of reflection, judge before making assent. Men do live by an initial, primitive assent but it becomes the philosopher's task to question this initial assent or natural faith. As E. Faguet has noted in his critique of Lamennais, "the consideration of universal consent does not lead to a genuine conquest of truth; it is not a philosophical method but an expedient".[1]

At base, Lamennais's reliance on natural faith in universal beliefs seems to be an appeal to sentiment. The infallibility which Lamennais attributes to tradition does not correspond to experience. How many universal beliefs of mankind have been proven false with the advance of science! The arbitrary character of Lamennais's choice of universal consent as a criterion for certitude is particularly demonstrated when one considers his treatment of the natural sciences within the framework of his epistemology. This particular weakness of mennaisianism has been constantly pointed out in the criticisms of his thought.[2]

2. The Problem of Lamennais's Catholic Philosophy

One of the strongest criticisms directed against the ontologistic position of Lamennais has been summed up in the following manner:

[1] E. Faguet, *Politiques et Moralistes du XIXᵉ siècle*, Paris, 1898, T. II, p. 103.
[2] A. Fonck, "Le Ménaisianisme", *Dictionnaire de Théologie Catholique*, T. XVIII, 2ième Partie, Paris, 1925, col. 2513. R. P. Quilty, in his interesting thesis on the epistemological sources of Lamennais's political theory, has proposed that the theory of common sense actually undermines Lamennais's later efforts to establish a workable system of democracy. Through relying upon an authority other than that of the free, individual reason, he would seem necessarily to drift into either an "extreme authoritarianism or to latent anarchy". Confer R. P. Quilty, "The Influence of Hugues Félicité de Lamennais' Epistemology on his Theory of Democracy", Abstract of a Dissertation, *The Catholic University of America Studies in Politics, Governmental and International Law*, Vol. 4, Abstract Series, pp. 1-14.

> ... the chief objection which could be made against the mennaisian
> system ... [is] ... the insufficient distinction of the two levels, the human
> and the divine, the minimizing, through a certain conceptualization of
> the general reason, of the role of Revelation ...[3]

The tendency to confuse the natural and the supernatural, which we
have noted previously,[4] extends throughout the mennaisian system. He
seems to have failed to have recognized the radical difference between
the authority of tradition and the act of natural faith in this authority
and the authority of God revealing and the act of supernatural faith
through which this revelation is received.[5] There is a confusion of the
two domains which leads to naturalizing the supernatural or
supernaturalizing the natural. The result is the same.

Lamennais's willingness to use the content of Revelation as an
object for philosophical reflection would seem to be perfectly valid.
The religious experience of mankind is justly within the scope of the
philosophical quest but a serious question arises when the dogmas of
this Revelation are uncritically accepted as philosophical first
principles. One might admit with Lamennais that the given in
religious experience is part of the totality which is the source and the
stuff of philosophical reflection but it is quite another matter to
identify the dogmas of Revelation with the order of pre-reflected
experience. At the base of this confusion is to be found the a priori
acceptance by the traditionalists of a primitive revelation viewed as a
total revelation of a universal law of nature and society. Although the
idea fits well with the monistic ontology fashioned by Lamennais, it
is an unproved assumption upon which his whole philosophical
thought is based. This, of course, is the crux of the problem. Can an
argument from an extrinsic authority rather than a principle of
evidence provide the basis for philosophical investigation?

3. The Problem of Method

One is struck primarily by the logical difficulties which are

---

[3] L. Le Guillou, *L'évolution de la pensée religieuse de Félicité Lamennais*, Paris,
1966, p. 204.

[4] See Chapter Three, III 2, "Political Implications of Common Consent", Footnote
271; also Chapter Four, I 2 a, "Religion and Law", Footnote 41.

[5] The Jesuit, Father Rozaven, one of Lamennais's earliest and strongest theological
critics had made this point a central element in his study of mennaisian philosophy.
Confer L. Le Guillou, *L'évolution de la pensée religieuse de Félicité Lamennais*, Paris,
1966, pp. 199-208.

presented in Lamennais's tendency to employ generalizations. If his thought were reducible to a syllogistic organization, the result would likely indicate a wide use of "latius hos". Since, however, we are dealing with inductive thought proceeding by way of synthesis, it would be more correct to say that Lamennais—in a fashion quite similar to that of other Romanticists—[6] went beyond the restricted content of the given to predicate unjustifiably universal or general conclusions. As a consequence of this tendency to disregard the exigencies of logic and the limitations of the real, we discover a series of remarkable but questionable generalizations. The phenomenon of language becomes identified with Revelation; sociability becomes the synonym for religion; the similarities arising from a comparative study of religions are all too quickly transposed into a universal Christianity; and the practical certitude which is justly attributed to common sense and to tradition is elevated beyond its pragmatic function to become the very criterion of all certitude.

III. The Validity of Mennaisian Insights

1. *Unity and Plurality*

Keeping in mind the weaknesses to be found in Lamennais's first principles and in his methodology, it will be necessary to evaluate the political doctrine—the principal object of this study—which resulted from these speculative efforts. Before descending to particular matters, the obvious remark to be made concerning the over-all mennaisian effort is that history has revealed the value of many of the particular insights attributed to Lamennais and "L'Avenir". The mere fact that history has followed his prognostications and has vindicated his honor as a prophet is a tribute to his vision. Moreover, since the mennaisian prophecies were not pronouncements emitted from a void, we must ask ourselves anew whether or not there is not more to Lamennais than the prophet. What is there in his thought which retains a perennial value and interest?

---

[6] In his classical study on Romantic political theory, C. Schmitt has pointedly remarked that the study of the Romanticists ought always be undertaken with a certain caution since there would seem to be a fundamental indetermination in the language of the Romanticists which leads to vast, but not always justifiable, generalizations. "In terms of grammar and of logic", maintains Schmitt, "this sort of literature means that the romantic idea always gives the predicate and never the subject of an explicative proposition. Such is quite simply the key to the romantic labyrinth". Confer, C. Schmitt, *Romantisme Politique*, Paris, 1928, p. 16.

Much is to be said for the superior vision which Lamennais had of human society and of religion. By returning to the ontological sources of unity, sociability and justice, he reached beyond the limited horizons which restrained his contemporaries to recapture the essence of an important truth, namely, that the ordering of a society, the political mission of mankind, cannot prescind from the ethical and spiritual realities or norms against which the particular laws or political organization of the city are to be judged. There is a high ethical value, for example, in the distinction which Lamennais made between legitimacy and legality and a sense of modernity in his ability to recognize the weakness of the conservative argument in favor of hereditary rights. Similarly, his recognition of the similarities between his own theologically inspired notion of divine law and the liberal notion of natural law shows keen insight.

If Lamennais's efforts to attain a unified view of the whole of reality and a reduction of the whole to a certain legal transparency enabled him to go beyond traditionalism and to re-evaluate the insights of the liberal thinkers within the context of a Christian philosophy, it must also be admitted that his final synthesis is open to the same criticisms as classical liberalism itself. The plurality and density of the real, which had been vigorously defended by the earlier traditionalists, and Lamennais himself, as well as by the followers of the whole Historical School of Law against the mechanistic and natural views of reality, seem to be lost again in Lamennais's social cosmos. Through his synthetic method of reducing the pluralistic character of historical and institutional reality to spiritual entities grouped in a non-historical, ideal order of relationships, Lamennais manages to attain an idealistic or eschatological fusion of conflicting elements existing in the temporal order but, in the process, loses the touch with reality which is the hallmark of the traditionalist critique. At the time of "L'Avenir", there was a certain lack of empirical rigor or even of that respect for the nature of things and of social organisms which is so evident in the social and political thought of Aristotle.[7] For Lamennais, the "esse proprium" of the State and of the Church, considered as humanly organized institutional entities, vanishes and one is left with a series of abstractions. The legal and juridical character of institutional

---

[7] The fundamental differences between the Aristotelian tradition in political theory, especially concerning the organization of power or sovereignty, and the other traditions are briefly and lucidly summarized by J. Darbellay in his Introduction to the French translation of Kant's *Vers la paix perpétuelle*, Paris, 1958, pp. 9-45.

relationships is lost and replaced through reducing the spiritual and the temporal to two orders of being whose rapport is seen as that which exists on the metaphysical level between the infinite and the finite. All is seen in view of a final eschatological unity, which, while being an inspiring vision, does not provide a fully realistic and adequate approach to the concrete problems of power and the complexity of historical, temporal realities.

Even in the quest for solutions to the most real problems of the practical order, it is important to maintain Lamennais's vision of unity and of a final social solidarity in truth and in justice.[8] But an end to be sought and worked for is a project for which the real, taken as it is, provides the matter and establishes the limits.

> That reality is through and through and in its concreteness an absolute unity is, for man, a metaphysical postulate and a hope. But this unity is not some magnitude which he can control. Only in God is everything one. In the realm of the creaturely and the finite, however, the pluralism and antagonism of reality cannot be synthesized away.[9]

In a similar fashion, the immanentization of the idea of a providentially directed progress results in just that redivinization of the political order which Lamennais had wished to avoid. Lamennais's frequent allusions at the epoch of "L'Avenir" to the "last times"[10] and his belief in the new society of harmony between liberty and order without taking into account the depths of the irrational in the human and without grasping realistically the necessity of the coercive power of the State would seem to indicate that he had fallen victim to what E. Voegelin has aptly phrased the "Gnostic temptation".[11] Transposed from the high theological plane on which Lamennais fashioned his

---

[8] An interesting comment on the importance of giving ideological priority to the "ontological oneness of human nature" in constructing a theory of international order may be found in T. Westow, "The Argument about Pacifism: A Critical Survey of Studies in English", *Concilium*, London, May 1966, pp. 56-63.

[9] This is the summary of an idea taken from J. Splett, "Ideologie und Toleranz" and reproduced in H. Fries, "Theological Reflections on Pluralism", *Theological Studies*, Woodstock, March 1967, p. 18.

[10] This type of apocalyptic language is particularly evident in his later articles. He states, for example, "...we are but entering in the period in which the last great promises made by the Redeemer to man will be accomplished". Confer, Lamennais, "Ce que sera le catholicisme dans la société nouvelle", A.A., T. V, p. 187.

[11] In his interesting study of political theory, E. Voegelin describes political Gnosticism as a permanent "counter-existential" tendency in Western political thought which has appeared in various forms of political utopianism and progressivism. Consult E. Voegelin, *The New Science of Politics*, Chicago, 1952, pp. 117-121.

concept of eschatological progress to that of a secular messianism, the quasi-religious idea of progress brings with it a certain unrealistic and abstract approach to such concrete problems as social unity and tolerance. It is interesting to note that the trend of Lamennais's thought following his rupture with the Church "is characterized by a turn towards purely immanentist evolution".[12]

2. *Mennaisian Liberalism*

Although, as we have just pointed out, there are basic weaknesses indigenous to liberalism and to the secular notion of progress which remain even after Lamenais's baptism of both, there are also elements of positive enrichment to be recognized in the synthesis which he fashioned between liberalism and Christianity. He saw a basic compatibility between the liberal doctrine concerning the priority in nature of certain rights which must be retained and recognized in any society and the Christian notion of the priority of spiritual values. Instead of the state of nature as seen by Locke, Lamennais returns to the dogma of creation and recognizes therein the source of spiritual liberty which, as an original, inviolable right, is the source of contingent rights which are positively developed and recognized in conjunction with the evolution of society. It is to the enduring credit of Lamennais that he opened the eyes of his co-religionists to the "truth" of liberalism, that is, the claim of the individual to personal liberties is founded upon a right which is something more than contingent or merely hereditary.

Similarly, Lamennais's emphatic defense of an original human sociability counters the individualistic tendency to be found in the liberal doctrine. By trying to ground his notion of rights in a theoretical premise of social relationship and not in an individualistic concept of primitive autonomy, Lamennais avoids the anti-social characteristics of liberalism such as became all too manifest in economic liberalism. In the mennaisian view, personal liberty loses the taint of egoism and becomes the condition for human fraternity and solidarity. Liberty is always seen within the context of a spiritual society and, as a consequence, can never be considered as a claim to act freely without a concomitant recognition of the social

---

[12] W. Gurian, "Lamennais", *Review of Politics*, Notre Dame, Indiana, April 1947, p. 227.

responsibility which parallels its use. On account of this theological socialization of the liberal anthropology, Lamennais's political activity, following the publication of *Paroles d'un croyant*, bears a marked inclination towards a primitive socialism[13] and his influence among future generations has been more as a social democrat than as a liberal pure and simple.[14]

3. Religious Liberty and Tolerance

Considering, however, the original question of tolerance, it remains to be seen whether or not Lamennais provided a viable solution to the problem of diversity and unity within the body-politic. Very much on the positive side of the ledger is to be found the mennaisian idea of religious liberty. Having purified his concept of religious liberty, first conceived in *Tradition ...* and in *De la religion ...* as simply liberty for the Church, and, later, in "L'Avenir", seen more as an original right of theological origin belonging to every person, he came close to the modern notion of subjective rights. In a sense, he retained something of the older objectivistic notion of religious liberty, that is, that only truth has rights, but the difference is to be found in the underlying metaphysical idea of what this truth is. Total truth is not known, for truth is in the process of becoming manifest. The bearers of this truth in the historical, temporal, order are persons and not institutions considered in their legal dimensions. By incorporating the idea of progress with his first insights into the anteriority and the non-contingent character of the spiritual order, Lamennais came to the conclusion that the recognition of equal liberty for all would alone make possible the full revelation of truth. It is, finally, no longer a question of whether or not truth or error have rights but one of whether or not the life of the spirit, the realm of ideas, is left free to attain its full development.

One is forced to question not so much the theological presuppositions of Lamennais's doctrine of religious liberty — which is

---

[13] L. Le Guillou, *L'évolution de la pensée religieuse de Félicité Lamennais*, Paris, 1966, particularly, "Le socialisme de Lamennais", pp. 388-401.

[14] Commenting on posterior Catholic social and political movements in France, A. Dansette has noted that "... From L'Avenir to Catholic Action movements and the M.R.P., in passing through Lacordaire and the 'New Era' in 1848, Cardinal Lavigerie and 'Le Sillon' of the beginning of the twentieth century, the same mennaisian inspiration, under diverse political and social forms, may be found". Confer, A. Dansette, "La Mennais contre son temps", *Revue de Paris*, Novembre 1947, p. 128.

really quite close to more modern notions — [15] but rather his conceptualization of the relationship between the temporal and the spiritual which is at the root of the whole problematic of tolerance considered in its political aspects. There seems to be an oversimplification of the problem in the mind of Lamennais which arises from the dualistic sort of separation which he seeks between the spiritual society and the temporal sphere. There is a deep strain of cartesianism in Lamennais, in spite of his protests against "social Manicheanism"[16] which returns to falsify the rapport which he establishes between the temporal and spiritual likening this relationship, as he does, to one of body to soul. We have seen how he had spoken of the State as a function or reflection of the spiritual society.[17] Is it really possible for the spiritual society or the Church to live the somewhat disembodied existence which Lamennais seems to attribute to it? What happens to those grey areas of conflict which necessarily exist precisely because the Church and the believer are social, historical, and political entities? A charter of recognized liberties is not itself sufficient to solve the problems posed by the use of these liberties and by the necessity of rendering the use of these liberties compatible with the common good or unified purpose of the community. Lamennais fails to view the problem of tolerance from the point of view of the State just as he fails to fully appreciate the institutional and juridical density which defines both Church and State in their temporal roles.

The utopian coloring of Lamennais's thought at the time of "L'Avenir", due to his tendency to immanentize the eschatological order, is plainly apparent in the unrealistic manner in which he treats the problem of power. Society itself is composed of a plurality of sovereignties or entities, both individual and aggregate, which possess

---

[15] A comparison of Lamennais's concept of religious liberty with the document produced by the Second Vatican Council on this subject would reveal some interesting points of similarity. Such notions as the moral source of the exigency for religious liberty, the incompetency of the political arm in matters of religion and conscience, and the recognition of the essential need of the Church for a complete freedom to exercise her mission, have all become, through a process of refinement and debate, essential elements of Catholic thought. Confer, for a brief but lucid treatment of the conciliar document, J. C. Murray, "Vers une intelligence du développement de la doctrine de l'Église sur la liberté religieuse", published in *La liberté religieuse: Déclaration "Dignitatis humanae personae"*, Paris, 1967, pp. 116-117.

[16] See Chapter Four, II 3 a, "Church and State", Footnote 171.

[17] See Chapter Four, II 3 a, "Church and State", Footnote 172; also Chapter Five, II 1 b, "Lamennais and the Theory of Thesis-Hypothesis".

a power which is immanent to their structures or which emanates from the organic and objective nature of these entities. The State, however, possesses the power of coercion over this plurality of sovereignties for the conservation of order in society or in order to limit the use of liberties for the common good. By the same token, the State is a restricted sovereignty but it is not clear in the thought of Lamennais as to just how this relationship of sovereignties is to be worked out. The community which is visualized by "L'Avenir" was a community for men of good will but, unfortunately, even men of good will often find themselves in situations in which there is an inevitable collision of interests. While a system of liberties or tolerance should allow for a certain working out of conflicts without the intervention of the State, experience would seem to indicate that a legal structure defining the limits of elasticity within the social fabric and supported by the police power of the State is also necessary for the attainment and the protection of the common good. In this sense, Lamennais's political treatment of the problem of tolerance was somewhat primitive and not fully realistic.

IV. GENERAL CONCLUSION

The work which has been undertaken in the preceding pages has been essentially an essay in the history of ideas. We have considered a particular problem and the treatment of this problem by a remarkable historical figure whose name has become associated with the quest for modern liberties and, above all, in the history of the Church, with the vast mission of adaptation and understanding which has become the principal task of the Church since the Revolution of 1789. Lamennais is remembered, and, justly so, because he was the great pioneer, the prophetic voice, among Catholic thinkers in the area of religious reassessment of the political and social forces and ideas which erupted with the processes of secularization. What he had initiated with the synthesis of "L'Avenir" was the beginning of a long and painful effort by religious men to understand this revolution in values and in the basic relationship between the sacral and the temporal.

After having exposed and analyzed his doctrines and after having submitted them to a certain critical evaluation, we find, quite frankly, evidence of basic weaknesses which lead the philosophical critic to question seriously the system as a system. The mixing of theology

249

and metaphysics, the under-estimation of individual reason, the imprecision of language, and the tendency to rely upon the power of the imagination rather than upon the concreteness of the real, are all elements which tend to devaluate mennaisianism as a systematic philosophy. The same characteristics are sources as well of the soft points or inadequacies of his political theory.

It is not difficult, of course, to seize upon the failures of Lamennais as a philosopher when the philosophy which he constructed is considered apart in an abstract fashion, that is, removed from its historical and cultural setting. If, however, we consider mennaisianism within the order of the history of ideas, as a part of a wider development of thought, we cannot fail to see in it not only the courage but also the spiritual grandeur of its founder.

We have attempted to show the rapport which exists between mennaisianism and the epoch of its formulation. It is a type of transitional thought such as may be found among some, although certainly not all, of the figures of the Romantic movement. One can readily recognize in the efforts made to close the gaps between intuition and reason, between aspiration and reality, the workings of the romantic imagination. The old certainties had been destroyed; the future certainties not yet discovered. The human spirit, which resists such instabilities, must search for a new order or a new classicism to give sense and discipline to life. Lacking both the proper formation and even the proper historical conditions in which to erect a tenable rational system, the Romanticist, such as Lamennais, bridges the chasm between the limits of reason and the vision of the ideal by means of imaginative inventiveness.

Lamennais was an innovator, a bold thinker, and a vigorous spirit. He served as the spiritual catalyst through whom a fusion between the old and the new was at first, awkwardly, yet sincerely, achieved. It was he who reminded his co-religionists of theological and evangelical truths which they had all too frequently left out of their "politics of habit". Perhaps, in the long-run, Lamennais must be seen as primarily a spiritual figure, a discoverer of values. He could not always justify his visions nor render his insights acceptable to naked reason but the validity of what he saw before others even dared to look has been authenticated by time.

BIBLIOGRAPHY

A complete bibliography of the works of Félicité Lamennais and of the many writings published about Lamennais and the mennaisian movement will not be attempted in the bibliography presented here. Three important bibliographical collections concerning Lamennais have been published over the course of the years and these will be indicated at the outset.

The bibliography proper commences with a chronological listing of the works of Lamennais which have been employed in this dissertation. In presenting the titles of these works, the original spelling will be maintained. A second section dealing with primary mennaisian sources will include those various collections of unedited materials, particularly, correspondence, which have been utilized or consulted. These collections will be listed under the name of the author responsible for the presentation.

A third major division of the bibliography refers to those works which treat directly of Lamennais or of such allied topics as Romanticism and the Restoration. A final division will be necessary to present those secondary sources which have been cited or consulted in the preparation of this thesis as well as other references.

I. BIBLIOGRAPHICAL SOURCES

Duine, F. *Essai de bibliographie de Félicité Robert de La Mennais, comprenant plus de 1300 articles*, Paris, Garnier 1923, 133 pp.

Quérard, J.-M. *Notice bibliographique des ouvrages de H. de La Mennais, de leurs réfutations, de leur apologies et des biographies de cet écrivain*, Paris, 1849, 149 pp.

Talvart, H. and Place, J. *Bibliographie des auteurs modernes de langue française*, Tome XI, Paris, 1952, under "Lamennais (Félicité de)", pp. 167-229.

II. WORKS OF FÉLICITÉ LAMENNAIS

A. Chronological Listing

(1809) *Réflexions sur l'état de l'église en France pendant le dix-huitième siècle et sur sa situation actuelle, suivie de mélanges religieux et philosophiques par F. De La Mennais*, (édition 1819), Paris, Tournachon-Molin et H. Sequin, MDCCCXIX.

(1814) (Without the names of the authors) *Tradition de l'église sur l'institution des évêques*, 3 Vols., Liège, 1814.

— — *Oeuvres Complètes de F. De La Mennais*, 12 Vols., Paris, Daubrée et Cailleux, 1836-1837.

(1817-1823) I-IV. *Essai sur l'indifférence en matière de religion.*

(1821) V. *Défense de l'essai sur l'indifférence en matière de religion.*

— — VI. *Réflexions sur l'état de l'église en France pendant le XVIIIe siècle et sur sa situation actuelle, suivies de mélanges religieux et philosophiques.*

(1826) VII. *De la religion considérée dans ses rapports avec l'ordre politique et civil.*

— — VIII. *Mélanges religieux et philosophiques.*

(1829) IX. *Des progrès de la révolution et de la guerre contre l'église suivis de deux lettres à Monseigneur l'Archevêque de Paris.*

(1830-1831) X. *Journaux, ou articles publiés dans le Mémorial Catholique et L'Avenir.*

— —*Essai d'un système de philosophie catholique par M. l'abbé F. de La Mennais.* (Ed. Y. Le Hir), Rennes, J. Plihon, 1954, XL, 342 pp.

— — *Essai d'un système de philosophie catholique (1830-1831) par F. De La Mennais,* (Ed. Chr. Maréchal), Paris, Bloud, 1906, XXXIX, 429 pp.

B. *Correspondence and other unedited sources*

BARTHOU, L. "I. Lettres à Saint-Victor", *Revue des Deux Mondes,* Paris, 1er novembre 1923, pp. 169-200.

— —. "II. Lettres à Saint-Victor", *Revue des Deux Mondes,* Paris, 15 novembre 1923, pp. 395-420.

BLAIZE, A. *Œuvres inédites de F. Lamennais,* 2 Vols, Paris, 1866, E. Dentu, XVI, 455 pp.; 390 pp.

DE COURCY, H. *Lettres inédites de J.-M. et F. de La Mennais adressés à Mgr. Bruté,* Introduction by E. de la Gournerie, Nantes, V. Forest et E. Grimaud, 1862, (2nd Ed.), LXI, 178 pp.

D'HAUSSONVILLE. *Lettres inédites de Lamennais à la baronne Cottu (1818-1854)* Paris, Perrin, 1910, LXII, 338 pp.

— —. "Lettres inédites publiées par le comte D'Haussonville", in *La Revue Hebdomadaire,* Paris, (16), 17 avril 1909, pp. 281-294. (These were letters written by Lamennais to Baron Cottu.)

DUBOIS DE LA VILLERABEL, A. *Confidence de La Mennais: lettres inédites de 1821-1848,* Paris, Perrin, 1886, 327 pp.

DUDON, P. "Fragment inédit d'un mémoire de Lamennais à Léon XII", in *Recherches de Sciences Religieuses* T. I, Paris, 1910, pp. 476-485.

— —. "Lamennais en Italie", in *Études,* Paris, 20 février 1933, pp. 422-442.

— —. "Lettres de Lamennais", in *Documents d'Histoïre,* Paris, (1), mars 1911, pp. 146-155.

— —. "Lettres de Lamennais", in *Documents d'Histoire,* Paris, (2), juin 1911, pp. 316-319.

— —. "Lettres de Lamennais à de Coux', in *Études,* Paris, 5 avril 1911, pp. 83-88.

— —. "Lettres inédites de Lamennais au Chanoine Buzzetti" in *Études,* Paris, 20 janvier 1910, pp. 206-221.

— —. "Lettres inédites de Lamennais à Ventura (1826)", in *Études,* Paris, 5 mars 1910, pp. 602-618.

— —. "Lettres inédites de Lamennais à Ventura (1827-1829)", in *Études,* Paris, 20 avril 1910, pp. 239-254.

— —. "Lettres inédites de Lamennais à Ventura (1830-1833)", in *Études,* Paris, 5 juin 1910, pp. 621-643.

DUDON, P. "Trois lettres inédites de Lamennais", in *Document d'Histoire*, Paris, (2-4), mars-décembre 1913, pp. 481-489.

— —. "Trois lettres inédites de Lamennais au P. Godinet, Jésuite", in *Études*, Paris, 1909, pp. 206-223.

DUINE, F. "Documents ménaisiens", in *Annales de Bretagne*, Rennes-Paris, (1), 1919, pp. 15-50.

— —. "Lettres inédites de La Mennais", in *L'Hermine*, Rennes, 20 mai 1907, pp. 33-41.

— —. "Lettres inédites de La Mennais et documents nouveaux", in *Annales de Bretagne*, Rennes, (2), janvier 1913, pp. 178-202.

FORGUES, E. D. *Œuvres posthumes de F. Lamennais*, 2 Vols., Paris, Paulin et Le Chevalier, 1859, CXXII, 424 pp.; 504 pp.

FORGUES, Eugène. *Lettres inédites de Lamennais à Montalembert*, Paris, Perrin, 1898, 402 pp.

— —. *Correspondance inédite entre Lamennais et le baron de Vitrolles*, Paris, Charpentier, 1886, 487 pp.

GIRAUD, V. "Lettres inédites de Lamennais", in *La Revue Latine*, Paris, (9), 25 septembre 1904, pp. 542-550. (This article includes an important preface by the author concerning the importance and the extension of Lamennais's correspondence.)

— —. "Une correspondance inédite de Lamennais", in *Revue des Deux Mondes*, Paris, 15 octobre 1905, pp. 765-799.

LAVEILLE, A. *Un Lamennais inconnu; lettres inédites de Lamennais à Benoît d'Azy*, Paris, Perrin, 1898, LXV, 357 pp.

ROUSSEL, A. *Lamennais et ses correspondants inconnus*, Paris, Téqui, 1912, VIII, 455 pp.

— —. *Lamennais intime d'après une correspondance inédite*, Paris, Lethielleux, 1897, XVI, 455 pp.

III. WORKS TREATING OF LAMENNAIS, THE RESTORATION OR ROMANTICISM

Articles de L'Avenir, 7 Vols., Louvain, Vanlinthout et Vandenzande, 1830-1831.

AUBERT, R. *Le pontificat de Pie IX*, Vol. 21 in A. Fliche and V. Martin: *Histoire de l'Église*, Paris, Bloud & Gay, (New Ed.), 1963, 592 pp.

— —. *Le problème de l'acte de foi, données traditionnelles et résultats des controverses récentes*, Louvain, E. Warny, (3rd Ed.), 1958, pp. 102-112.

— —. "Religious Liberty from 'Mirari vos' to the Syllabus", in *Concilium*, London, (7) September 1965, pp. 49-57.

BAGGE, D. *Les idées politiques en France sous la Restauration*, Paris, Presses Universitaires de France, 1952, XIV, 462 pp.

BINAUT, L. "I. Lamennais et sa philosophie", in *Revue des Deux Mondes*, Paris, 15 août 1860.

— —. "II. Joseph de Maistre et Lamennais", in *Revue des Deux Mondes*, Paris, 1er février 1861.

BLAIZE, A. *Essai Biographique sur M. F. De La Mennais*, Paris, Garnier, 1858, XIX, 279 pp.

BLONDEL, M. "Une note inédite de La Mennais contre la Religion naturelle et le

'Semi-déisme'", in *Annales de Philosophie Chrétienne*, Paris, avril-septembre 1912, pp. 166-180.

BOUDES, R. "I. Lamennais: Le catholicisme libéral", in *Revue de l'Université d'Ottawa*, Ottawa, avril-juin 1959, pp. 166-180.

— —. "II. Lamennais: le drame intérieur", in *Revue de l'Université d'Ottawa*, Ottawa, juillet-septembre 1959, pp. 298-321.

BOUTARD, C. *Lamennais, sa vie et ses doctrines*, 3 Vols., Paris, Perrin, 1905-1913.

BOVARD, R. *Drame de conscience: le caractère et l'évolution religieuse de Lamennais*, Paris, Scorpion, 1961, 188 pp.

BREMOND, H. "Lamennais et la critique contemporaine", in *Le Correspondant*, Paris, 10 mars 1908, pp. 954-977.

— —. *Pour le romantisme*, Paris, Bloud & Gay, 1924, XV, 250 pp.

BROUSSE, F. *Lamennais et le christianisme universel*, Paris, Scorpion, 1963, 158 pp.

CALIPPE, C. *L'attitude sociale des catholiques français au XIXe siècle*, 3 Vols., Paris, Bloud, 1911-1912.

— —. "Les relations d'Auguste Comte et de Lamennais", in *Revue du clergé français*, Paris, 1er octobre 1918, pp. 17-28.

CAPURSO, M. "Un momento nella vita di La Mennais: La lettura dei 'Promessi sposi'", in *Nuova Antologia*, Rome, novembre 1950, pp. 278-296.

CARCOPINO, C. *Les doctrines sociales de Lamennais*, Paris, Presses Universitaires de France, 1942, 219 pp.

Catalogue de Livres rares et précieux provenant de la Bibliothèque de M. F. de La Mennais, Paris, Daubrée et Cailleux, 1836, 160 pp.

CITOLEUX, M. "Alfred de Vigny et La Mennais", in *Annales de Bretagne*, Rennes-Paris, juillet 1916, pp. 301-322.

CONSTANTIN, C. "Libéralisme Catholique", in *Dictionnaire de Théologie Catholique*, Tome IX, 1ière Partie, Paris, 1926, cols. 506-630.

DANSETTE, A. "La Mennais contre son temps", in *Revue de Paris*, Paris, (11), novembre 1947, pp. 110-128.

DE BERTIER DE SAUVIGNY, G. *La Restauration*, Paris, Flammarion (New Edition), 1955, 490 pp.

DENIS, C. "Les contradicteurs de Lamennais", in *Annales de Philosophie Chrétienne*, Paris, avril-septembre, 1900, pp. 221-238; 631-643.

DERRE, J.-R. *Lamennais ses amis et le mouvement des idées à l'époque romantique (1824-1834)*, Paris, C. Klincksieck, 1962, 763 pp.

DESCHAMPS. "Souvenirs Universitaires: 1. L'Université et Lamennais", in *Mémoires de l'Académie des Sciences, Inscriptions et Belles-Lettres de Toulouse*, Toulouse, 9ième Série, 1893, pp. 32-51.

DROZ, J.; GENET, L.; VIDALENC, J. *Restaurations et Révolutions (1815-1871)* Vol. I. *L'époque contemporaine*, Paris, Clio: P.U.F., 657 pp.

DUDON, P. "La Bibliothèque de Lamennais", in *Étude*, Paris, 20 avril 1912, pp. 230-248.

— —. "Lamennais fondateur d'ordre", in *Études*, Paris, Novembre 1910, pp. 449-473.

— —. "Le romantisme social de Lamennais", in *Études*, Paris, 5 juillet 1932, pp. 77-87.

DUHAMEL, R. *Aux sources du romantisme français*, Ottawa, Éditions de l'Université d'Ottawa, 1964, 230 pp.

DUINE, F. "Influence de La Harpe sur La Mennais", in *Annales de Bretagne*, Rennes-Paris, janvier 1913, pp. 198-202.

DUINE, F. "Lamennais à Juilly", in *Revue de Bretagne*, Vannes, decembre 1904.

— —. "La Mennais et Pascal", in *Annales de Bretagne*, Rennes-Paris, T. XXXV, (4), 1923, pp. 568-577.

— —. *La Mennais, sa vie, ses idées, ses ouvrages d'après les sources imprimées et les documents inédits*, Paris, Bibliothèque d'histoire littéraire et de critique, 1922, 389 pp.

— —. "Notes de La Mennais sur un exemplaire de J.-J. Rousseau", in *L'Hermine*, Rennes, 20 janvier 1907, pp. 113-124.

— —. "Notes pour l'étude de La Mennais", in *Annales de Bretagne*, Rennes-Paris, janvier 1914, pp. 189-220.

DUROSELLE, J.-B. *Les débuts du catholicisme social en France (1822-1870)*, Paris, Presses Universitaires de France, 1951, 787 pp.

EVANS, D. *Social Romanticism in France 1830-1848*, Oxford, Clarendon Press, 1951, 149 pp.

FAGUET, E. *Politiques et Moralistes du XIXe siècle*, 3 Vols., Paris, Nouvelle Bibliothèque littéraire, 1891-1900.

FEUGÈRE, A. *Lamennais avant l'Essai sur l'indifférence d'après des documents inédits (1782-1817)*, Paris, Bloud, 1906, 460 pp. (There is an excellent chronological listing of Lamennais's correspondence in this work with references to the place of its publication.)

FONCK, A. "Lamennais (Félicité de)" in *Dictionnaire de Théologie Catholique, T. XVIII, 2ième Partie, Paris, 1925, cols. 2473-2526*.

FOUCHER, L. *La philosophie catholique en France au XIXe siècle avant la renaissance thomiste et dans son rapport avec elle (1800-1880)*, Paris, J. Vrin, 1955, 280 pp.

G. "Eclaircissements sur la liberté de conscience", in *Articles de L'Avenir*, T. V, Louvain, Vanlinthout et Vandenzande, 1831, pp. 205-212.

GAULMIER, J. "Note sur l'apologétique mennaisienne et l'Orientalisme", in *Mélanges Louis Massignon*, T. II, Damas, 1957, pp. 251-258.

GIBSON, W. *The Abbé de La Mennais and the liberal catholic movement in France*, London, Longmans, 1896, 346 pp.

GOYAU, G. *Autour du catholicisme social*, Paris, Perrin, 1924, 305 pp.

— —. *Le portefeuille de Lamennais (1818-1836)*, Paris, Nouvelle Bibliothèque Romantique, 1930.

GURIAN, W. *Die politischen und sozialen Ideen des französischen Katholizismus*, Münster, Gladbach, 1929, 418 pp.

— —. "Lamennais" in *The Review of Politics*, Notre Dame, Indiana, (9) April 1947, pp. 205-229.

HAAG, H. *Les origines du catholicisme libéral en Belgique (1789-1839)*, Louvain, E. Nauwelaerts, 1950, 300 pp.

HOCEDEZ, E. *Histoire de la Théologie au XIXe siècle*, 3 Vols., Paris, Desclée de Brouwer, 1947-1952.

JANET, P. *La philosophie de Lamennais*, Paris, Alcan, 1890, 157 pp.

JÜRGENSEN, K. *Lamennais und die Gestaltung des Belgischen Staates; Der liberale Katholizismus in der Verfassungsbewegung des 19. Jahrhunderts*, Wiesbaden, Franz Steiner Verlag GMBH, 1963, 433 pp.

KERBIRIOU. "Les problèmes de l'école de la Chênaie", in *Revue de l'Ouest*, Brest, 1935. (An extract from this article has been used from the Archives des Frères de l'Instruction Chrétienne, No. 456, Highlands, Jersey.)

LASKI, H. J. *Authority in the Modern State*, New Haven, Yale University Press, 1919, 398 pp.

LAVEDAN, P. "La Mennais et Jean-Jacques Rousseau", in *Mercure de France*, Paris, 16 mars 1914, pp. 296-316.

LECANUET. *Montalembert d'après son journal et sa correspondance*, 3Vols., Paris, Ch. Poussielgue, 1895-1902.

LEFLON, J. *La crise révolutionnaire (1789-1846)* Vol. 20, in A. Fliche and V. Martin: *Histoire de l'Église*, Paris, Bloud & Gay, 1951, 524 pp.

LE GUILLOU, L. *Les Discussions Critiques Journal de la Crise mennaisienne*, Paris, Armand Colin, 1967, 111 pp.

— —. *L'évolution de la pensée religieuse de Félicité Lamennais*, Paris, Armand Colin, 1966, 498 pp.

LE HIR, Y. *"Les paroles d'un croyant", de Lamennais. Texte publié sur le manuscrit autographe avec des variantes, une introduction et un commentaire*, Paris, Paris Univ. Faculté des Lettres, 1949, 292 pp.

LICHTENBERGER, H. "Qu'est-ce que le Romantisme?" in *Cahiers du Sud*, Marseilles, mai-juin 1937, pp. 349-358.

MARECHAL, C. "L'abbé de La Mennais, le comte de Montlosier et le baron d'Eckstein: un problème d'influence", in *Revue d'Histoire littéraire de la France*, Paris, janvier-mars 1950, pp. 16-26.

— —. *La famille de La Mennais sous l'ancien régime et la révolution*. Paris, Perrin, 1913, 345 pp.

— —. *La jeunesse de La Mennais. Contribution à l'étude des origines du romantisme religieux en France au XIXe siècle*, Paris, Perrin, 1913, 719 pp.

— —. "La Mennais, Descartes et St. Thomas", in *Revue Philosophique*, Paris, 1947, pp. 443-451.

— —. *La Mennais: la dispute de l'Essai sur l'indifférence*, Paris, Ed. Champion, 1925, 450 pp.

— —. "La vraie doctrine philosophique de La Mennais. Le retour à la raison", in *Revue Philosophique*, Paris, 1949, pp. 319-330.

— —. "Note critique sur les conférences de philosophie catholique de l'abbé de La Mennais", in *Revue d'Histoire Littéraire de la France*, Paris, 1939, pp. 175-178.

MELLON, S. *The Political Uses of History: A study of Historians in the French Restoration*, Stanford, California, Stanford University Press, 1958, 226 pp.

MERCIER, *Lamennais d'après sa correspondance et les travaux les plus récents*, Paris, Lecoffre, 1895.

NEDONCELLE, M. (Ed.) *L'ecclésiologie au XIXe siècle*, Paris, Éditions du Cerf, 1960, 392 pp.

OECHSLIN, J.-J. *Le mouvement ultra-royaliste sous la Restauration. Son idéologie et son action politique (1814-1830)*, Paris, 1960, 218 pp.

PEARSON, C. "The Politico-Social Ideas of Hugues Félicité Robert de Lamennais (1830-1854)", abridgment of a thesis, New York, Graduate School of New York University, 1936, 24 pp.

PLAMENATZ, J. *The Revolutionary Movement in France 1815-1871*, London, Longmans, Green and Co., 1952, 184 pp.

POISSON, J. *Le romantisme et la souveraineté. Enquête bibliographique sur la philosophie du pouvoir pendant la Restauration et la Monarchie de Juillet (1815-1848)*, Paris, J. Vrin, 1932, 189 pp.

POISSON, J. *Le romantisme social de Lamennais. Essai sur la métaphysique des deux sociétés*, Paris, J. Vrin, 1931, 472 pp.

QUILTY, R. "The influence of Hugues Félicité de Lamennais' epistemology on his theory of democracy", abridgment of a thesis, Washington, 1954, 14 pp.

RAVAISSON, F. *La philosophie en France au XIXᵉ siècle*, Paris, Hachette, (2nd Ed.) 1889, 325 pp.

REMOND, R. *La Mennais et la démocratie*, Paris, Presses Universitaires de France, 1948, 76 pp.

RENAN, E. "Lamennais et ses écrits", in *Revue des Deux Mondes*, Paris, 15 août 1857, pp. 765-795.

ROE, W. G. *Lamennais and England. The Reception of Lamennais' religious Ideas in the Nineteenth Century*, London, Oxford University Press, 1966, 229 pp.

ROUSSEL, A. *Lamennais à la chênaie. Supérieur général de la Congrégation de Saint-Pierre (1828-1833)*, Paris, Téqui, 1909, 300 pp.

— —. *Lamennais d'après-des-documents inédits*, 2 Vols., Rennes, Hyacinthe Caillière, 1892, 282 pp.; 470 pp.

SCHENK, H. G. "I. Lamennais 1782-1854", in *The Month*, March 1954, pp. 153-160.

— —. "II. Lamennais 1782-1854", in *The Month*, June 1954, pp. 332-338.

— —. *The Mind of the European Romantics, An essay in cultural history*, London, Constable, 1966, XXIV, 303 pp.

SCHMITT, C. *Romantisme Politique*, (Translation of *Politische Romantik* by P. Linn), Paris, Bibliothèque française de philosophie, 1928, 165 pp.

SPULLER, E. *Lamennais: étude d'histoire politique et religieuse*, Paris, Hachette, 1892, XX, 361 pp.

TRANNOY, A. *Le romantisme politique de Montalembert avant 1843*, Paris, Bloud, 1942, 624 pp.

VERSLUYS, J. *Essai sur le caractère de Lamennais*, Amsterdam, 1929, 158 pp.

VIATTE, A. *Les interprétations du catholicisme chez les romantiques*, Paris, E. De Boccard, 1922, 387 pp.

VIDLER, A. R. *Prophecy and Papacy. A study of Lamennais, the Church, and the Revolution*, London, SCM Press, 1954, 300 pp.

WEILL, G. *Histoire du Catholicisme libéral en France 1828-1908*, Paris, Alcan, 1909, 312 pp.

IV. SECONDARY SOURCES

ACTON (Lord). *Essays on Freedom and Power*, (ed. G. Himmelfarb), New York, Meridian Books, 1957, 350 pp.

ARISTOTLE. *Politics* (Translation by B. Jowett), Intro. by M. Lerner, New York, Random House, 1943, 337 pp.

ARNAUD, P. (Ed.) *Rousseau et le philosophie politique, 5. Annales de philosophie politique*, Paris, Presses Universitaires de France, 1965, 255 pp.

AUBERT, R. (et. al) *Tolérance et communauté humaine*, Tournai, Castermann, 1952.

AUGUSTINE. *Obras de San Agustin*, Intro. by V. Capanaga, O.R.S.A., T. I, Madrid, Biblioteca de Autores Cristianos, 1957, 812 pp.

BARNES, H. E. *A History of Historical Writing*, New York, Dover Publications (Second Revised Edition), 1962, 450 pp.

BAUCHER, J. "Liberté", in *Dictionnaire de Théologie Catholique*, T. IX, 1ière Partie, Paris, 1926, cols. 660-705.

BREHIER, E. *Études de Philosophie Moderne*, Paris, Presses Universitaires de France, 1965, 239 pp.

BUTLER, C. *The Vatican Council, 1869-1870*, Westminster, Maryland, The Newman Press, 1962, 510 pp.

CASSIRER, E. *La philosophie des lumières*, (Translation of *Die Philosophie der Aufklärung* by P. Quillet), Paris, Fayard, 1966, 351 pp.

— —. *The Myth of the State*, New Haven, Yale University Press, (Fifth Printing) 1963, 303 pp.

COPLESTON, F. *A History of Philosophy*, Vol. 4, *Modern Philosophy: Descartes to Leibniz*, Garden City, New York, Doubleday (Image Book), 1963, 400 pp.

DAWSON, C. *Progress and Religion*, New York, Sheed & Ward, (Paperback), 1938.

— —. *The Dynamics of World History*, (ed. J. J. Mulloy), New York, Sheed & Ward, 1957.

DE ALBORNOZ, A. F. *The basis of Religious Liberty*, London, SCM Press, 1963.

DE BONALD, L. *Œuvres de M. de Bonald*, 8 Vols., Brussels, Société Nationale, 1845.

DE BROGLIE, G. *Le droit naturel à la liberté religieuse*, Paris, Beauchesne, 1964, 184 pp.

DEL VECCHIO, G. *Justice*, (Translation of *La giustizia*), Edinburgh, University Press, 1952, 236 pp.

— —. *Philosophy of Law*, (Translation of *Lezioni di filosofia del diritto* by T. O. Martin from 8th edition), Washington, The Catholic University of America Press, 1953, 474 pp.

DE MAISTRE, J. *The Works of Joseph de Maistre*, (Translation, selections and introduction by J. Lively), London, George Allen and Unwin, 1965, 303 pp.

DE MAISTRE, R. *Lettres et Opuscules inédits du comte J. De Maistre*, T. II, Paris, (5ième édition) Vaton Frères, 1869, 529 pp.

DESCARTES, R. *Meditationes de prima philosophia*, (Intro. and notes by G. Rodis-Lewis), Paris, J. Vrin, 1963, 87 pp.

DONDEYNE, A. *Contemporary European Thought and Christian Faith*, (Translation of *Foi chrétienne et pensée contemporaine* by E. McMullin and J. Burnheim) Pittsburgh, Duquesne University, 1958, 208 pp.

— —. *Faith and the World*, (Translation of *Geloof en Wereld*), Pittsburgh, Duquesne University, 1963.

DUBRUEL, M. "Gallicanisme", in *Dictionnaire de Théologie Catholique*, T. VI, Paris, 1925, cols. 1096-1137.

FRIES, H. "Theological Reflections on the Problem of Pluralism", in *Theological Studies*, Woodstock, March, 1967, pp. 3-26.

GEREST, R. "La liberté religieuse dans la conscience de l'Église", in *Lumière et Vie*, Paris, juillet-octobre, 1964, pp. 5-35.

GOUHIER, H. *Les grandes avenues de la pensée philosophique en France depuis Descartes*, Louvain-Paris, Nauwelaerts, 1966, 94 pp.

HAMER, J. and CONGAR, Y. (Ed.) *La liberté religieuse: Déclaration "Dignitatis humanae personae"*, Éditions du Cerf. (Unam Sanctam 60), Paris, 1967, 283 pp.

HARTMANN, A. *Vraie et Fausse Tolérance*, (Translation of *Toleranz und Christlicher Glaube*), Paris, Éditions du Cerf, 1958, 289 pp.

BIBLIOGRAPHY

HAZARD, P.   The European Mind 1680-1715, (Translation of *La crise de la conscience européenne*), London, Pelican (Paperback), 1964, 512 pp.

JANSSENS, L.   *Liberté de conscience et liberté religieuse*, Paris, Desclée de Brouwer, 1964, 207 pp.

KANT, E.   *Vers la paix perpétuelle*, (Translation and Introduction by J. Darbellay) Paris, Presses Universitaires de France, 1958, 188 pp.

LACROIX, J.   *La sociologie d'Auguste Comte*, Paris, Presses Universitaires de France (Initiation Philosophique), 1961, 114 pp.

LASKI, H. J.   *Political Thought in England from Locke to Bentham*, London, (Tenth Printing) Oxford University Press, 1961, 214 pp.

— —.   *The Rise of European Liberalism*, London, Unwin Books (Paperback) 1962, 192 pp.

LECLER, J.   *Histoire de la Tolérance au siècle de la Réforme*, 2 Vols., Paris, Aubier, 1955, 403 pp.; 459 pp.

LECLERCQ, J.   *L'état ou la politique*, T. II of *Leçons de Droit naturel*, Louvain, Société d'Études Morales, Sociales et Juridiques, (4ième éd.) 1958, 432 pp.

— —.   *La liberté d'opinion et les catholiques*, Paris, Éditions du Cerf, 367 pp.

LOCKE, J.   *Locke Selections* (Selections and Introduction by S. P. Lamprecht), New York, Charles Scribner's Sons, 1922, 349 pp.

LUIJPEN, W.   *Existential Phenomenology*, Pittsburgh, Duquesne University, 1960, 362 pp.

MARITAIN, J.   *The Social and Political Philosophy of Jacques Maritain*, (ed. J. W. Evans and L. R. Ward), New York, Charles Scribner's Sons, 1955, 348 pp.

MICHEL, A.   "Tolérance", in *Dictionnaire de Théologie Catholique*, T. XV, 1ière Partie, Paris, 1946, cols. 1208-1223.

MONOD, A.   *De Pascal à Châteaubriand: les défenseurs français du christianisme de 1670 à 1802*, Paris, Alcan, 1916, 606 pp.

MOSSÉ-BASTIDE, R.   *La liberté*, Paris, Presses Universitaires de France (Initiation Philosophique), 1966, 120 pp.

MURRAY, J. C.   *We Hold These Truths, Catholic Reflections on the American Proposition*, New York, Sheed & Ward, 1960.

NEDONCELLE, M.   *Existe-t-il une philosophie chrétienne?*, Paris, Fayard, 1956, 117 pp.

PASCAL, B.   *Œuvres Complètes*, (Introduction by H. Gouhier), Paris, Éditions du Seuil, 1963, 677 pp.

RICHARD, P.   "Indifférence Religieuse", in *Dictionnaire de Théologie Catholique*, T. VII, 2ième Partie, Paris, 1923, COLS. 1580-1594.

RICOEUR, P.   *Histoire et Vérité*, Paris, Éditions du Seuil (2nd Ed.), 1955, 332 pp.

ROMMEN, H.   *The State in Catholic Thought: A Treatise in Political Philosophy*, St. Louis, B. Herder, 1955, 747 pp.

ROUSSEAU, J.   *Du Contrat Social ou Principes du droit politique* (Éd. Classiques Garnier), Paris, Garnier Frères, 1962, 506 pp.

— —.   *Émile ou de l'éducation* (Éd. Classiques Garnier) (Introduction, notes, bibliography and analytic index by F. and P. Richard) Paris, Garnier Frères, 1964, 666 pp.

P.-M. "Profession de foi du Vicaire *Savoyard*", (Critical edition by P.-H. Masson), Paris, Collectanea Friburgensia, 1914, 607 pp.

TALMON, J. *The Origins of Totalitarian Democracy*, London, Mercury (Paperback), 1961, 366 pp.

VOEGELIN, E. *The New Science of Politics*, Chicago, University of Chicago Press, 1952, 193 pp.

VOLTAIRE. *Dictionnaire Philosophique* (Introduction by R. Pomeau), Paris, Garnier-Flammarion, 1964, 380 pp.

WAHL, J. *Tableau de la philosophie française*, Paris, Gallimard (New Edition), 1962, 178 pp.

WEIL, E. *Philosophie Politique*, Paris, J. Vrin, 1956, 261 pp.

WESTOW, T. "The Argument about Pacifism: A Critical Survey of Studies in English", in *Concilium*, London, May 1966, pp. 56-63.

WILKS, M. *The Problem of Sovereignty in the Later Middle Ages*, Cambridge, Cambridge University Press, 1964, 619 pp.

V. OTHER REFERENCES

Diccionario de Filosofia, Ed. J. Ferrater Mora, Buenos Aires, Editorial Sudamericana, 2 Vols., 1965.

Vocabulaire Technique et Critique de la Philosophie, Ed. A. Lalande, Paris, (9th Ed.) Presses Universitaires de France, 1962.

INDEX OF PROPER NAMES

SUBJECT INDEX

266